THE FIRST INTERVIEW
WITH THE FAMILY

The First Interview with the Family

by

HELM STIERLIN,
INGEBORG RUCKER-EMBDEN,
NORBERT WETZEL and
MICHAEL WIRSCHING

Translated by Sarah Tooze

BRUNNER/MAZEL, *Publishers* • New York

Library of Congress Cataloging in Publication Data

Main entry under title:
The first interview with the family.
  Translation of Das erste Familiengespräch.
  Bibliography: p.
  Includes index.
  1. Family psychotherapy.   2. Interviewing in psychiatry.   I. Stierlin, Helm.
RC488.5.E7613   616.89'156   79-27830
ISBN 0-87630-225-8

German Edition: *Das erste Familiengespräch*
(ISBN 3-12-907470-8)

Copyright © Ernst Klett, Stuttgart, Bundesrepublik Deutschland, 1977

Copyright © 1980 by Brunner/Mazel, Inc.

Published by
Brunner/Mazel, Inc.
19 Union Square
New York, New York 10003

MANUFACTURED IN THE UNITED STATES OF AMERICA

Contents

Preface ix

PART I

1. WHY THE WHOLE FAMILY? 5

    We Are All Dependent 5
    Family Therapy as a New Paradigm 6
    The Circular versus the Linear Causality Model 6
    The New Paradigm Revolutionizes Psychotherapeutic
        Practice 7
    The Reality of Family Relationships 7
    Experience and Mastery of Conflict at Source 7
    Mobilizing Family Resources 8
    Individual Therapy within the Family Therapeutic
        Paradigm 9
    The Bedrock of Therapy: The Family Interview 9

2. THE MAIN ELEMENTS OF THE CONCEPT 12

    The Theory Determines the Observation 12
    The Sources of the Model 12
    Positive versus Negative Mutuality 13
    The Relationship of the Individual to the Overall System .. 14
    Vertical versus Horizontal Structures 14

The Weight of History versus the Potential for New
    Beginnings 15
The Relevant Dynamic Structures Are Often Hidden 15
The Ethical Dimension 15
The Five Main Perspectives 16
1. Related Individuation 16
2. The Transactional Modes of Binding and Expelling ... 20
3. Delegation 23
4. Multigenerational Legacy and Merit 26
5. The State of Mutuality 28
The Integration of the Five Perspectives in Clinical Practice 33

3. EMPATHY, INTERPRETATION AND STRUCTURE 35

Empathy 35
Cognitive Stability 37
Staying Open 37
The Interviewer's Dual Functions 37
Participation and Disengagement 38
Multidirectional Partiality 39
Looking on the Positive Side 40
The Active Role of the Therapist 40
Transference and Countertransference 41
Family Rules, Myths and Secrets 43
Parents of the Index Patient 43
The Index Patient 44
Recognizing Ambivalence and Concealed Sabotage 45
The Problem of Cotherapy 45
Indications for Cotherapy 45
Cotherapy in Training 46
The Meaning of Teamwork 46

4. BASIC CONSIDERATIONS 48

Diagnosis 48
Motivation 49
The Therapeutic Contact 50
Deciding on the Direction of Further Therapy 51

5. THE SPECIFICS 56

  Where Should Family Therapy Be Done? 56
  Toys 57
  Audiovisual Material and the One-Way Screen 57
  The Interview Begins with the First Contact 58
  When Should Children Be Present? 61
  External or Internal Motivation 64
  The Fee 64
  Problems of Parallel Treatment 64
  A Short Waiting Time 65
  Use of Experts 65

6. THE PHASES OF THE FIRST INTERVIEW 66

  The Initial Phase: The Greeting 66
  The Initial Phase: Starting the Interview 69
  The Middle Phase: Interaction in the Family 78
  The Final Phase: Leave Taking 81
  Evaluating the First Interview 83
  Report of the First Interview 83
  The First Interview with the Schultz Family 85

7. PROBLEM FAMILIES 91

  Families that Are Separating 91
  Acute versus Chronic Problems 93
  Families with Psychotic Members 94
  Families with Delinquent Adolescents 97
  Families with Parents Who Abuse Their Children 99
  Families with Members at Risk from Drug Abuse 100
  Families with Suicidal Potential 102
  Families with Mentally or Physically Handicapped Children 104
  Families with Psychosomatically Ill Members 105

PART II

8. THE BOLT FAMILY INTERVIEW 113

  Introduction 113
  The First Interview with Mrs. Bolt 114
  Annotated Transcript of the First Family Interview 117

9. CASE DISCUSSION OF THE BOLT FAMILY 172

  The Family History of Mrs. Bolt 172
  Events in the Family History 176
  The Present Situation of the Family 178
  Hypothesis Regarding the Central Family Dynamics 180

10. THE FAMILY TESTS: RORSCHACH AND TAT 186

  Theoretical Background 186
  Transcript of the Conjoint Rorschach Procedure with the
    Bolt Family 190
  Transcript of the Conjoint TAT with the Bolt Family 197
  Report on the Consensus Rorschach and TAT of the Bolt
    Family 204

11. THE THERAPEUTIC PROSPECT 214

  What Were the Main Conflicts in the Bolt Family? 214
  What Forces Maintained This Conflict? 216
  How Could These Conflicts be Resolved? 217

  Epilogue 221

  Bibliography 225

  Name Index 231

  Subject Index 233

Preface

Increasing numbers of members of helping professions—medical practitioners, psychotherapists, marriage counsellors, social workers, teachers, etc.—are becoming involved in family therapy and counselling and must sooner or later conduct an interview with the whole family. They often do this, indeed have to do so, without the necessary experience, instruction, and training, although such an interview confronts the therapist or counsellor with special demands.

Faced with enormously complex and emotionally loaded relationships and a confusing outpouring of information, the therapist must attempt to grasp the family dynamics, to develop a sympathetic understanding of the members of the family, construct a working basis of mutual trust, distinguish the important from the irrelevant, and set the course of future work. Not for just one, but for several people, this may mean an experience of success or failure, hope or despair. The therapist or counsellor may gain an experience of confidence and security from such an interview or turn from family therapy in dismay.

The first interview with the family represents, therefore, a special challenge and task of reconciliation. It is the aim of our book to help in this special situation by indicating and illustrating with clinical examples the important points in such interviews. At the same time, this volume provides an introduction to family therapy.

The initial chapters of Part I summarize the theoretical concept, first developed by the senior author, on which the family therapeutic work of our Heidelberg group of authors is based. This concept comprises five main perspectives: related individuation, interactional modes of binding and expelling, delegation, the multigenerational perspective of legacies and merits, and the state of mutuality. In subsequent chapters we show how the use of these perspectives can illuminate particularly important areas or problems of the first interview. Above all, this concerns the empathic contact that the family therapist must establish with all the members of the family, as well as the particular structural features which must be considered in the first interview. Finally, we discuss special problem families that provide a particular challenge in the first interview, including families with psychotic or delinquent members, families where the parents mishandle the children, and families with potentially suicidal or psychotically sick members.

Part II includes the exact transcript of and a commentary on a first interview with a family with a psychosomatically sick index patient—the mother. This interview makes it clear how the previously developed overall concept, the empathy demanded of the therapist, and his or her understanding of the structural features of the first interview decide not only the course of that interview, but also the further therapy. Part II also presents the analysis of a family Rorschach Test and TAT, which extend and deepen the insights provided by the interview. This part ends with a chapter that integrates clinical and test data and assesses their therapeutic relevance.

ACKNOWLEDGMENTS

We are very grateful to many friends and colleagues for their contributions of important ideas and for their support of our work in many different ways. In America they include above all Ivan Boszormenyi-Nagy, Lyman Wynne, Margaret Singer, Theodore Lidz, Norman Paul, and Don Bloch, Director of the Ackerman Institute in New York and Editor of the journal *Family Process*. In Europe, we thank, above all Horst-Eberhard Richter, who gave family therapy its initial vital impetus in the German-speaking world, Eckard

Sperling, Jürg Willi, Luc Kaufmann, Josef Duss-von Werdt, who is, together with Helm Stierlin, Editor of *Familiendynamik*, as well as the Milan team led by Mara Selvini-Palazzoli. We also thank Walter Bräutigam, through whose initiative a department of basic psycho-analytical research and family therapy came into existence in a German university.

We further thank our secretaries Ms. Monika Engewald, Ms. Ingeborg Rüdgisch-Ballas, and Ms. Ilse Wolf for their selfless work. In particular, we are grateful to our patients, particularly to the families who allowed us to conduct the first and following interviews on which this book is based. Finally, we wish to acknowledge with thanks the financial help of the Deutsche Forschungsgemeinschaft which supported the research project from which this book results and the Robert-Bosch-Stiftung that supported our work on psycho-somatic illness.

HELM STIERLIN
INGEBORG RÜCKER-EMBDEN
NORBERT WETZEL
MICHAEL WIRSCHING

THE FIRST INTERVIEW
WITH THE FAMILY

PART I

1

Why the Whole Family?

WE ARE ALL DEPENDENT

As Bernard Shaw said, "Independence is a middle-class prejudice, for we are all dependent on each other."

THIS INSIGHT HAS INCREASINGLY INFLUENCED Western thought in the last decades. It is mirrored in our awareness of the complementarity and interdependence of ecosystems. It has also added a new dimension to psychological understanding so that the family—its structure, function, and relational dynamic—now occupies a central position.

The family is the single most important human system: from experience within the family the individual builds his or her identity, values and goals, and learns, or fails to learn, to adapt socially. It is here more than in any other area of life that, as Hegel said, "das Tun des einen ist das Tun des anderen"—the actions of one determine those of others—and, in our opinion, it is here preeminently that opportunities lie for prevention and therapy of mental disorders.

Family Therapy as a New Paradigm

Family therapy is a new paradigm—a frame of reference that reveals and reorganizes so that significant new meanings emerge and new perspectives open up. According to the American science historian Thomas Kuhn, such a paradigm is both the result and the expression of a scientific revolution. The individual-centered movement of dynamic psychotherapy which developed at the end of the 19th century is based on such a paradigm; family therapy, which requires a systems approach, presents another.

The Circular versus the Linear Causality Model

This paradigm compels us to break with trusted models and habits of thought. In particular, because it is systems oriented, it makes the concept of individuality increasingly problematic. It is now many decades since H. S. Sullivan first spoke of the illusion of personal individuality and the family psychotherapist is daily made aware of its chimeric character.

Members of a family are now seen as elements in an interacting group in which the behavior of one member inevitably influences all the others. Therefore, a particular individual behavior can no longer be seen one-dimensionally as cause of the behavior of others; every member influences the others and is in turn influenced by them.

This systems approach is indebted to cybernetics and communications theory. It can be described as a circular model and can be contrasted with the linear monocausal model which still underlies countless psychological concepts. In the light of this circular model, many of the usual categories, behavior patterns, and cause and effect models prove to be the result and expression of arbitrary distinctions (punctuations), grammatical constraints, verbal conventions, in short, of a familial, cultural and contemporary epistemology. In their attempt to introduce a "circular epistemology," family researchers and therapists face the problem of expressing these new principles in a language already grown centuries old in the conventions and communications based on linear principles. This book, also, must reflect the difficulties of such a task.

THE NEW PARADIGM REVOLUTIONIZES
PSYCHOTHERAPEUTIC PRACTICE

The new paradigm not only changes our concept of interpersonal causality, it also leads to a new understanding of pathology and revolutionizes psychotherapeutic practice. This was perhaps best expressed by the American family therapists Jay Haley and Lynn Hoffmann (1968). "One cannot call family therapy simply a new method of treatment; it is a new way of conceptualizing the cause and cure of psychiatric problems. Family therapists are distinct as a group largely because of a common assumption: if the individual is to change, the context in which he lives must change. The unit of treatment is no longer the person, even if only a single person is interviewed, it is the set of relationships in which the person is embedded" (p. v).

THE REALITY OF FAMILY RELATIONSHIPS

This basic therapeutic concept is consistent with certain aspects of the psychoanalytical paradigm. In common with psychoanalysis, it emphasizes the importance of deep-rooted conflict and the therapeutic aims of individuation, structural change (rather than removal of symptoms), achievement of mental maturity, capacity for work and love and readiness to bear responsibility. There are important differences, however, between psychoanalysis and family therapy; these primarily concern the greater significance attributed to the actual, currently operating relationship factors—such as long-lasting mutual estrangement, mystification, neglect, exploitation, unfulfilled needs for acceptance, denial of rights and betrayal of trust—compared with intrapsychic factors. We speak of the reality of family relationships, an existential dimension, that is now becoming increasingly central to therapy. This different theoretical emphasis engenders a different therapeutic practice.

EXPERIENCE AND MASTERY OF CONFLICT AT SOURCE

According to psychoanalytic theory, the curative process depends principally on the establishment of a one-to-one transference and countertransference and the mobilization and recognition of intrapsychic conflict. The patient must be able to turn to his analyst as a model in the long overdue process of positive identification and learning. In contrast, our form of family therapy emphasizes *the work of restructuring existing relationships*. There are many ways of achieving this. Very often *the conflict must be experienced and mastered at source*. This requires readiness for intrafamilial confrontation—and, whenever possible, a final, family-wide reconciliation. Thus, we would like to compare the well-known basic psychoanalytical rule, "Say everything that may come into your mind, including the unpleasant and apparently irrelevant," with the basic rule of family psychotherapy, as first formulated by Ivan Boszormenyi-Nagy, "Try, as much as possible, to talk about those matters you were so far unable to discuss," for example, family secrets, disappointed expectations and feelings of injustice. To realize such a family-wide conflict solution and reconciliation, the therapist must mobilize the family resources and at the same time be fair to each member of the family; she or he must be multipartial.

MOBILIZING FAMILY RESOURCES

A comparison with psychoanalytic therapy can illuminate the meaning of these factors in family therapy. In psychoanalysis two main effective resources operate: the analyst's competence in recognizing and dealing with specific conflict and transference dynamics, and the patient's readiness for self-confrontation, as triggered and sustained by personal suffering. In our form of family therapy this competence of the therapist is less important than the ability to recognize and mobilize the wasted or mis-applied resources of an entire family—above all, the members' capacity for initiative, self-sacrifice, confrontation and mourning and their ability to face reality and to "balance accounts." The concept of "ethical resources" is important here, although it is scarcely compatible with a strictly scientific approach. (The ethical dimension of our family therapeutic concept is discussed in the following chapter.)

Typically, a therapist finds resources of this kind exactly where they might be least expected: in an initially apparently uninvolved sibling, in a small child or, perhaps most often, in the so-called index patient, the symptom bearer, often a delinquent, psychotic or underachieving adolescent. To mobilize these resources requires much imagination and a carefully prepared and conducted therapeutic intervention that often has paradoxical features (Stierlin, 1979).

INDIVIDUAL THERAPY WITHIN THE FAMILY THERAPEUTIC PARADIGM

Therapeutic intervention may begin with the whole family or with one of its subsystems, for example, with the husband and wife, the mother and her parents, the father and his parents, or with the children. It often makes sense to work with one or more of these subsystems at different points in the therapy. Individuals are elements or subsystems of the whole family and individual therapy, consequently, has a place within family therapy. Quite often treatment of a family can or must begin with individuals. This is particularly true for certain families with schizophrenic adolescents. In some circumstances an initial individual therapy with the index patient may be the only way in which to help the whole family (Stierlin, 1976a).

It is clear, therefore, that many methods that are currently advocated by the most disparate individual and group-oriented psychotherapeutic schools find a place within the paradigm of family therapy, since they are all aiming, in one way or another or at one time or another, to solve conflicts, problems and defects which ultimately originate in disturbed family relationships.

Hence our central thesis: Family therapy is not yet another form of therapy to add to the many already existing and continually multiplying modes of individual, couple or group psychotherapy, e.g., behavior therapy, Gestalt therapy, primal scream therapy, communication therapy, sex therapy; it is something different and also something more—a paradigm, a basic therapeutic concept.

THE BEDROCK OF THERAPY: THE FAMILY INTERVIEW

Despite the scope we accord the various psychotherapeutic modalities, the interview with the entire family remains the core of family therapy. Our goal is the accomplishment or initiation of the intrafamilial work of confrontation, mourning, reconciliation, and peace-making within the family interview. For this reason the first interview is crucial; it is, indeed, the bedrock of family therapy.

When Is an Interview with the Whole Family Especially Indicated?

Although there are a great many grounds for therapy involving the whole family, there are several situations in which active work with the whole family is especially indicated. This is the case:

- When strong binding and exploitative familial relationships exist. Since most children and adolescents are necessarily more dependent on their families than are adults, psychiatric work with children and adolescents is the special domain of family therapy. (Within the German-speaking world, most psychiatric services for these age groups are, however, individual-centered; work with the parents and the family is seen as merely supportive—as an adjunct rather than as a primary therapy.)

- When because of strong, invisible loyalties a trusting commitment to a therapist, friend or lover is automatically experienced as betrayal of loyalty to the family. Attempts to separate from the family may produce massive "break-away guilt." Without simultaneous work on and with the family, such guilt leads to unconscious self-sabotage. The client relapses, or "founders on success."

- When the danger exists that a marriage or family, especially children and parents, may be "therapied apart" by individual treatment. Here too, the client's self-realization and separation from the family achieved by individual therapy can engender strong guilt which is often projected on others. The client transforms this guilt into righteous indignation, which allows him or her to attack, devalue or abandon the marriage partner or parents—at the price, however, of mutual alienation, conflict avoidance and still greater, though possibly unconscious, guilt.

- When the most effective deployment of therapeutic resources is essential. This applies particularly to a number of disorders, some of them potentially fatal, for which until now individual therapy has seemed indicated, but with which it has seldom had a satisfactory outcome. They include anorexia nervosa, the "starvation disease" of young adolescent girls (Selvini-Palazzoli, 1974), and certain cases of schizophrenic disturbance.

- When the healing of deep isolation and rejection is at issue. We meet this particularly often with many sick, old and dying. Thus, children and young people are not the sole domain of family therapy; its scope includes geriatric psychiatry as well.

These indications for the interview with the whole family will become clearer in the following chapters.

2

The Main Elements of the Concept

The Theory Determines the Observation

IT WAS EINSTEIN WHO SAID that our theory determines our observation. We can apply this insight to the conduct of family interviews. Within a family interview so much occurs, so much may be observed, and so much might be done, that we urgently need a theoretical orientation to lead us through the complexities, to distinguish the relevant from the irrelevant and to guide our interventions. In the following, we outline a theoretical framework that we have found useful, although it is still being developed. It summarizes material most of which has been more fully discussed by Stierlin elsewhere (1972a, 1972b, 1974, 1975a, 1976b, 1979).

The Sources of the Model

Cybernetics

We have already mentioned the significance we attach to modern cybernetics, the science of regulative or feedback systems. Gregory Bateson, one of the creators of the "double-bind" concept and of the family therapeutic paradigm, has called the cybernetic breakthrough "the biggest bite out of the fruit of the Tree of Knowledge that mankind has taken in the last two thousand years," adding that "most of such bites out of the apple have proved to be rather indigestible—usually for cybernetic reasons" (Bateson, 1972, p. 452). Subsequently, authors of the "Palo Alto group"—D. Jackson, J. Haley, P. Watzlawick, J. Weakland—and many others have used the insights and models of modern cybernetics and information theory in the development of family-dynamic concepts.

Dialectics

However, most of the commonly accepted cybernetic ideas are too narrow to comprehend the dynamics relevant to our purpose. A dialectical approach similar to that inherent in Hegelian thinking is also necessary. In *Conflict and Reconciliation* (1969) and *Das Tun des einen ist das Tun des anderen* (1971), to take only two examples, Stierlin attempted to show the relevance of such a dialectical approach to the understanding of complex psycho dynamics and interpersonal processes.

The main characteristic of this dialectical approach is that it forces us constantly to redirect our thinking and refocus our perception so that we question established concepts and distinctions such as conscious-unconscious, mental-physical, individual-interactional, sick-well, real-unreal. It makes, in Hegel's words, "den Begriff flüssig" (the concept fluid). In particular, entrenched characteristics, roles or power positions are thus challenged. It alerts us to the fact that a martyr-like peacefulness may hide extreme aggression (because it stirs massive guilt), that power may masquerade as weakness, and egotism as self-sacrificing altruism.

POSITIVE VERSUS NEGATIVE MUTUALITY

Such a dialectical approach reveals typical movements within relationships. They may take the form of either a positive or a negative mutuality (Stierlin, 1971). Positive mutuality reflects and fosters an expanding dialogue: the partners confirm and accept one another on ever more complex and existentially meaningful levels.

This permits true confrontation. In negative mutuality the dialogue is distorted and restricted. Detraction replaces acceptance and possibilities for true confrontation are absent or greatly diminished.

THE RELATIONSHIP OF THE INDIVIDUAL TO THE OVERALL SYSTEM

Such a dialectical approach also provides a view of the system's internal hierarchy as well as of the interplay between systems and subsystems. The individual, with all his or her characteristics, motives, transactions and expectations, is seen as a system in its own right as well as an element of other systems. Therefore, it would be untrue to suggest that the individual does not exist as such and that individuality is mere illusion. The problem is more complex: we are dealing with systems and their elements whose equilibrium is constantly undergoing some change. Accordingly, there is engendered an ebb and flow of tension, open or covert conflict, reconciliation or alienation. The relationship of the individual to the superordinate familial or societal systems may be best expressed by the Hegelian concept of "Aufheben," meaning "to conserve, to lift up, and to cancel." Thus one can say the individual is conserved and also lifted up, that is, is recognized and affirmed in his own individuality and significance. At the same time, his individuality is canceled insofar as it disappears in the wider web of supraordinate, as well as subordinate, systems.

VERTICAL VERSUS HORIZONTAL STRUCTURES

Our model distinguishes between vertical, i.e., intergenerational, systems of relationships involving several generations, and horizontal systems involving a single generation only, e.g., married couples, siblings, or peer groups. It aims to cover relationships within these types of systems and the relationships between systems: we ask, for example, how continuous involvement with parents affects an individual's relations with a marital partner. Vertical systems are no less relevant dynamically than horizontal ones. For this reason it is, in our view, not possible to conduct a couple therapy without consideration of the partners' vertical family dynamics.

The Weight of History versus the Potential for New Beginnings

The distinction between vertical and horizontal structures could suggest that what has occurred in the past makes future change impossible: our deepest motivations and attitudes result from, as well as express, events spanning many generations of family life. Such a view might perceive everything as being predetermined and might, thus, lead to therapeutic resignation. However, paradoxically, a historical awareness may facilitate rather than hinder a fresh start and highlight the importance of the here-and-now.

The Relevant Dynamic Structures Are Often Hidden

Although they may be readily recognizable to a participant observer, the family is often unaware or only partly aware of the dynamic structures, processes and patterns of conflict that we hold to be relevant. Yet while family therapy and psychoanalysis agree in emphasizing the importance of wholly or partly unconscious structures or processes, they disagree about their nature. Whereas in psychoanalysis these structures and processes are largely intrapsychic and inferable, in family therapy they are mostly interactional and observable.

The Ethical Dimension

Our dialectical model includes an ethical dimension which is outside the scope of purely scientific thinking and, hence, foreign to most psychological models. Concepts such as exploitation, fairness, legacy, obligation, integrity, willingness for self-sacrifice, justice, loyalty, trust and corruption indicate elements or forces that control the relational and motivational dynamics within families over generations. The family members become the transmitters, as well as victims and executors, of the vertical, intergenerational structures and processes. These forces shape at once the present and future.

Such ethical dimensions affect our basic therapeutic attitude. While this entails no license for moralizing, it nevertheless compels us to take seriously and possibly also influence forces which therapists operating merely within the framework of natural science can neither perceive nor articulate.

THE FIVE MAIN PERSPECTIVES

Our approach employs five main perspectives or points of view, that act like five basic settings of a telescope. Each perspective reveals different, though often overlapping, aspects of human reality. They can be compared to the well-known metapsychological perspectives of psychoanalysis, such as the dynamic, economic, genetic, developmental, topographic and adaptive points of view. The increasing complexity of psychoanalytical theory follows from, as well as reflects, these orientating perspectives.

Within our dialectical approach we are able to describe individual positions or contributions as well as forces operating within relationship systems. We are able to detect both actual conflict constellations and also possibilities for solution or reconciliation. Each of the five main points of view allows us to recognize destructive and healing forces and alerts us to possible therapeutic interventions. They are: 1) related individuation, 2) the transactional modes of binding and expelling, 3) delegation, 4) the multigenerational perspective of legacy and merit, and 5) the state of mutuality.

1. RELATED INDIVIDUATION

The Main Principle

Basically, individuation denotes the formation of individual characteristics and psychological boundaries. The evolution of life over millions of years towards ever more highly individuated species has been beset by two opposing dangers: over- and under-individuation.

Overindividuation sets too rigid and impenetrable boundaries: independence turns into isolation and separateness into bleak solitude; communication with others fails.

Underindividuation, however, means the boundaries are ineffective—too soft, porous, penetrable, and brittle. Diminished individuation may lead to fusion and absorption into other, stronger organisms.

Progress in individuation demands, therefore, ever new levels of communication and reconciliation. At certain times and in certain ways the otherwise firm and protective boundaries must open up so separateness can be reconciled with togetherness, individuality with solidarity, autonomy with interdependence. In animal and human development such reconciliation requires ever more complex relational structures and processes. Hence, our use of the term *related individuation*. It expresses the general principle that a higher level of individuation both requires and allows a higher level of relatedness. Also, it entails a task of reconciliation which must be performed by all higher forms of life and especially by the human species. It further counteracts the widespread tendency to regard and extoll individuation and self-realization without regard for interdependence and solidarity.

The Capacity for Self-Differentiation and Self-Demarcation

Related individuation comprises both self-differentiation and self-demarcation. Self-differentiation includes the differentiation of conscious and unconscious spheres of the inner world, the clear articulation of feelings, needs, expectations, and of inner and outer perceptions. Self-demarcation denotes the delimitation of such a differentiated inner world from the outer world, in particular from the ideas, needs, expectations and demands of others. Stierlin described this concept of individuation accomplished through differentiation and demarcation in his book *Conflict and Reconciliation* (1969).

Related individuation, therefore, allows the experience of being separate and discrete, but at the same time related, in the most diverse interpersonal contexts. Related individuation is crucial, but it is most seriously tested in personal relationships characterized by emotional closeness and empathy. This applies, for example, to sexual intercourse insofar as it forms part of an intimate relationship. Here, the regressive fusion experienced in the orgasm can have a regenerative effect only if their related individuation enables the partners to reestablish their separateness.

Disturbances of Related Individuation in Schizophrenic Patients

Schizophrenic patients especially show deficient or disturbed self-differentiation or self-demarcation in loaded interpersonal situations. They experience perceptions which arise from their own inner world as coming from without, i.e., they hallucinate, or they are unable to delimit their own world of feelings and ideas from that of other people. In clinical practice we see three important types of unsuccessful or deficient individuation to which the above distinctions between under- and overindividuation apply:

- symbiotic fusion, where personal experiences, feelings of self and personal gender, age and professional role are merged with those of another person;

- rigid autistic isolation, which often indicates a paranoid mistrust;

- ambivalent oscillation between these two extremes (Stierlin, (1975b).

Disturbances of Related Individuation as Systems Features

The concept of related individuation illuminates not only the characteristics and behavior of the individual but also the relational systems to which he belongs. From an individual-centered viewpoint, for example, schizophrenia can be seen as a disturbance in the related individuation of an individual; if, however, we consider the whole relationship system, the disorder may appropriately be seen as an intrinsic characteristic of that system.

Signs of Deficient Related Individuation in Families

Where related individuation is deficient in a family, the individual members are unable to distinguish personal wishes, expectations, feelings, ideas or motivations—particularly in situations demanding emotional closeness and empathy. The consequence is that feelings are not expressed and conflicts neither defined nor settled. But neither can they be settled when overindividuation prevails, i.e., when the members entrench themselves in rigid isolation.

Isolation versus Fusion

In the literature on families we find deficient individuation characterized in various ways. Until now most attention has been paid to the phenomenon of underindividuation. Murray Bowen (1960) speaks of an "undifferentiated family ego mass," Lyman Wynne and Margaret Singer (1963) of "collective cognitive chaos," David Reiss (1971) of "consensus sensitivity," and Ivan Boszormenyi-Nagy (1965) of "intersubjective fusion." Mark Karpel (1976) has described distorted forms of related individuation in marital relationships.

Ivan Boszormenyi-Nagy emphasizes fusion, the intersubjective merging of present feelings, sense of values, expectations and positions as the central form of disturbed individuation within the family. Because the members are unable, or unwilling, to be differentiated from one another by limits and definitions, they are unable to take responsibility for their own feelings and wishes. Instead, all is in a state of undifferentiated flux so nobody can call anyone to account nor be called to account. This has a decisive influence on the ethical dynamics we mentioned earlier.

The other extreme, overindividuation, involves withdrawal to rigid, defensive, isolated positions with a breakdown of communication and relatedness and is scarcely less frequent. Such a shield often serves as a desperate defense as every concession and attempted contact now holds the threat of fusion. Some families oscillate between fusion and withdrawal. It is clear, therefore, that we are concerned with two sides of the same coin: antithetical disturbances of related individuation.

Therapeutic Opportunities in Tendencies for Individuation

Even in families suffering from massive disturbances of related individuation, it is usually possible to find a therapeutic starting point. An inarticulate and apparently withdrawn father can have enough self-definition and hold on reality to act as a catalyst and model for the other members in their struggle for individuation. Sometimes a child can take this role. To promote individuation the family therapist, like the gestalt therapist, insists from the beginning on the importance of each member of the family or client speaking for him- or herself and so encourages an unambiguous communication and a sense of individual responsibility. Bandler and Grinder (1975; Grinder and Bandler, 1976) showed what this involves. Mere efforts towards improving the clarity and structure of communication are, however, often not very effective. This is because the disturbances of related individuation and communication, in our experience, usually reflect deep-rooted frustrations and divisions which cannot be resolved by intervention at the verbal level alone. Here, the disturbances of communication serve primarily to sweep massive and long drawn-out conflict under the carpet, to deny its existence, and to keep confrontation at bay. To grasp, and act effectively in, these deep-lying conflict constellations we need a new setting of our investigative telescope. This is provided by the concept of transactional modes of binding and expelling outlined in the following section.

2. THE TRANSACTIONAL MODES OF BINDING AND EXPELLING

Transactional modes are relational structures that act over long periods of time. They form a relational framework within which the separation of parents and children with its complexities and difficulties is attempted or not attempted, and within which it succeeds or fails. Stierlin, who introduced the concept of transactional modes in 1972, today refers only to two such modes: binding and expelling. Delegation, which he formerly referred to as a third transactional mode, he now considers as a third main perspective; we shall come to this later.

The concepts of binding and expelling reflect the action of centripetal and centrifugal forces in the intergenerational separation dynamics. In general, where the binding mode operates, the child remains imprisoned in the family, and a drawn-out separation from the parents results. Where the expelling mode dominates, separation from the parents is accelerated and an often precocious autonomy results. Binding and expelling comprise a dialectical moment aimed at a balance of forces: A child or a marriage partner, patient, etc. tries to break out of a binding relationship, but usually remains the prisoner of a deep-rooted, persistently active, binding structure. Similarly, expelling produces a desire for binding. This need for binding, however, is usually frustrated by the powers of the persistent, deep expelling-mode structures.

The Three Main Levels of Binding

Binding can operate on three levels, corresponding to well-known psychoanalytic concepts:

1) Id-binding is on an affective level, where, in particular, a child's dependency needs are manipulated and exploited;

2) Ego-binding is mainly on a cognitive level, where the binding parent(s) impose(s) their own distorted ego;

3) Superego-binding is on an ethical level, where the children's need for loyalty is both nurtured and exploited.

Binding on the id-level amounts frequently to massive regressive gratification. The child easily becomes passively dependent, or the symbiotic tendency may even reflect or promote disturbances of related individuation.

Binding on the ego-level usually takes the form of mystification (Laing, 1965): Parents present dependent children with contradictory messages, so that finally they are unable to read their own inner signals. The psychoanalyst Hilde Bruch (1962) has described how such mystification of the small child can contribute to childhood obesity. Here, the parents mystify the child about his or her own feelings of satiety and hunger; they convince the child that they, the parents, know best whether the child has eaten enough. The child's personal knowledge is devaluated. Such parents continue to feed their children when they already have had more than enough, so obesity results.

Finally, massive binding can be expressed on the superego-level. The child remains prisoner of an intense loyalty and develops a strong sense of obligation. The belief that the psychological survival of the parents depends on the child alone produces intense breakaway guilt when any separation or escape is attempted, if only in thought.

Further Aspects of Binding

Where the binding mode prevails, the members of a family are highly important for each other and for the whole system. Thus, we find that the origins of disturbances of related individuation lie in certain long-lasting patterns of relationships. Further, we find that certain, long-fused conflicts remain dormant for periods of time before they finally explode. Typical of such long dormant, and then suddenly exploding conflicts are those between parents and their regressively indulged (i.e., Id-bound) children during adolescence. These children who had been infantilized, that is regressively spoilt, become, as teenagers, pitiless tyrants paralysing their fear- and guilt-tortured parents with escalating demands.

Strong unresolved binding to parents can result in massive clinging (anaclitic) transference reactions. Such clinging can be seen as a counterphobic rush into a new relationship, designed to break away from the existing binding. Similarly, many hasty marriages (often doomed to failure) can be viewed as attempts to break away from overstrong binding. The unaccomplished work of unbinding must then be made good in a later marriage, or family therapy.

A victim of binding is deprived; abilities for self-assertion, for an autonomous conduct of life, remain underdeveloped.

Characteristics of the Expelling Mode

Massive deprivation, though mainly of a different kind, is also involved in the expelling mode. The expelling mode contrasts with the binding mode: here the child is rejected, neglected, and expelled. From parents or their substitutes the child experiences coldness, rejection and neglect above all. The central experience of such a child is emotional emptiness in relation to other people; by not being taken seriously, the child feels rejected—human surplus.

People who have experienced such expulsion typically have an immense need to recoup the warmth and security they have missed. This means that many of them constantly search for partners or substitute parents who can fill this need. But because they have never experienced a close trusting relationship and do not know how to take a constructive part in one, they quickly withdraw in fear or provoke a further rejection. They lack that minimum of related individuation that would allow them to exist within an intensive and changing field of needs, closeness and distance.

The quality of the experiences and relationships observed in the expelling mode contrasts with those observed in the binding mode. Some expelled individuals allow themselves to drift aimlessly through life. Since, from the beginning, they have never felt themselves to be important to anyone, nothing in later life seems important to them. In contrast, others search in overcompensating and narcissistic ways for affirmation, attempting to achieve a feeling of their own importance. In one way or another these expelled individuals try to capitalize on their precocious autonomy. Their relative incapacity for loyalty to and care for others facilitates an exploitative attitude.

The emphasis in the first interview with the family is different according to whether binding or expelling modes predominate. The interviewer must work from the beginning either to loosen a too narrow binding, to promote unbinding, or to facilitate a lasting binding where it is lacking.

3. DELEGATION

Delegation, the third of our main perspectives, involves the interplay of both centripetal and centrifugal forces. Both meanings of the Latin verb "delegare" are appropriate: "to send out" and "to entrust with a mission." The keystone of delegation is the loyalty bond that binds the delegate to the delegating individual. This bond is created in the intimacy of the early child-parent relationship, and in particular in the mother-child relationship. The missions that the parents delegate to their children may grow out of many different sources and may involve different motivational levels. Clinical examples of such missions are given in Stierlin's *Separating Parents and Adolescents* (1974).

Delegation is not necessarily pathologic. More often it is the expression of a necessary and legitimate process of relationship. Delegation gives our lives direction and significance; it is the sheet anchor of obligations reaching down through the generations. As delegates of our parents, we have the possibility of proving our loyalty and integrity and of fulfilling missions reaching beyond purely personal levels.

Derailments of the Delegation Process

There are, however, three main ways in which the delegation process can derail:

1) Where the mission is in conflict with the talents, reserves and particular age requirements of the delegate, the demands on the child may be too great. In this case the psychosocial development of the delegate becomes unbalanced or distorted —always a sign of psychological exploitation. Things can go wrong in this way, for example, where a child of average talents is expected to become a superstar of the artistic, academic, business or sport world, something which the delegating parent was unable to achieve.

2) Where the missions are incompatible. For example, the delegate may be given missions by one or more people which are inconsistent, point in different directions. Thus, a girl may be expected to be at once virtuous and domesticated and at the same time live out her mother's secret longing for sexual excitement and depravity.

3) Where there are conflicts of loyalty. In such cases the delegate is beset by massive guilt feelings towards the parent betrayed at the instigation of the other. Hamlet is the classic example. He has either to abnegate his loyalty to his father or destroy his mother.

In examining the ways in which the delegation process can derail, we notice intrapsychic and interpersonal conflicts that have formed and hardened over a long period. Such conflicts can be further differentiated according to transactional modes; we can distinguish bound and expelled delegates.

Bound versus Expelled Delegates

Bound delegates have missions to fulfill that keep them imprisoned within the family's emotional orbit. A frequently encountered mission, for example, is that of replacing a dead sibling. The expectations and ideals held for the dead sibling must be fulfilled; in this way the parents are saved from the vitally necessary work of mourning and impossible demands are made of the delegate.

The demands made of the expelled delegate are different but no less over-exacting. After the early experience of parental coldness and aloofness, the delegate believes that here at last he can achieve a modicum of parental approbation; he often carries out his mission with perfectionism and despairing self-sacrifice. To satisfy the limited bourgeois Ego-ideals of the parents, such delegates often become nonprotesting, conformist "success" seekers.

Therapeutic Implications of the Delegation Model

Even from the first interview with the family, it is often possible to lay down a therapeutic strategy using this delegation model.

The index patient is often an exploited delegate, on the one hand trying conscientiously to carry out overdemanding and often irreconcilable missions, and on the other rebelling and trying to bring home to the parents the effects of their demands.

As delegate of the parents the child then takes on the role of victim, procuring for the parents, through the fulfillment of this mission, a vital satisfaction, indeed often securing their psychological survival. The delegate relieves the parents of their fear, shame and guilt, since she or he, and not they, the parents, is the patient, the failure. It is often the index patient, also, who is the only member of the family, who actually personally embodies the problems and conflicts that the others must conceal, and acts, therefore, as the initiator and catalyst for family therapy, from which all benefit.

However, it is exactly in the performance of this service to the family, by acting as a victim, that the delegate is able to scare the parents and other family members and load them with shame and guilt. The mere fact of the symptoms, of illness, of failure, is living proof of the failure and wickedness of the parents. Now armed with the ability to arouse guilt by being "sick," "disturbed," and "underachieving," the "victim" wreaks a terrible and obstinate revenge on his or her true or imagined parental exploiters.

Here the therapist must first of all show understanding for the parents. This understanding is based on a certain distinct perspective: family therapists must assume that basically all parents wish to be good and loving. Parents are, however, always the children of their own parents and often bear a heavy burden of disappointment, of withheld love and rights, of failure, of undeserved trauma and privation—all of which they must *nolens volens* in some way or other pass on to their children. Thus, they make the children the delegates of impossible missions and try to obtain from them the satisfactions and confirmations which they so painfully missed in their own childhoods. In order to do justice to the parents in their role as victims, we must consider a further main perspective—that of legacy and merit.

4. MULTIGENERATIONAL LEGACY AND MERIT

Legacy

This perspective, developed mainly in the work of Ivan Boszormenyi-Nagy, may in part be understood as the transgenerational extension of the delegation principle. The Latin "delegate" stems from "lex," meaning law, and also from "ligare," to bind. The concept of delegation can, therefore, be very appropriately used to express a binding over several generations, an obligation or a need to settle accounts. In the light of such a multigenerational perspective, many of the unrealistic demands and conflicting missions described above are seen to be transgenerationally determined.

A young woman can, for example, be expected to fulfill the legacy of working for women's rights. She can only achieve this if she pursues an emancipated career, is politically active and particularly successful. If, at the same time, she tries to fulfill another family legacy by becoming a giving, serving mother of many children and a self-sacrificing housewife, the two missions will inevitably conflict. Not only will this conflict burden the woman herself, but her children will suffer. She will be both overdemanding and neglectful of them and may indeed pass on the legacy she has not been able to fulfill.

Such legacies are loaded with loyalty conflicts and needs for reconciliation in which not merely a few generations, but entire strife-ridden family clans may be involved. Ivan Boszormenyi-Nagy (1975) discusses this concept of "the legacy of split loyalty" in the context of Romeo and Juliet. Our clinical experience is that schizophrenic disorders are often the expressions as well as the result of such legacies. Other legacies may aim, for example, to remove some source of shame in the family history, by redressing humble origins or taking revenge for some injustice. In his book on Hitler (1977a), Stierlin described how political and historical actions may be determined by legacies and conflicts arising within the family.

Merit

The second component of the multigenerational perspective is the concept of merit. Ivan Boszormenyi-Nagy (1972) maintains that the dynamics of important family relationships are determined by a "ledger of merits." To merit or the consciousness of merit he ascribes a motivating force similar to the drive or need of individual-centered psychodynamic theory. The fulfillment of or failure to fulfill legacies affects the "ledger of merits" of each family member; it is the source of a sense of just or unjust treatment and a feeling of personal integrity and a meaningful life.

The concept of the ledger of merits allows us to envisage how the need to render account and to demand settlement can act over generations. Unsettled accounts hold the threat that individual members of the family may be exploited and the whole system corrupted; at the same time, the dialogue of the relationship may cease to expand, with positive mutuality being replaced by a state of negative mutuality in which stagnation and isolation prevail.

The perspectives we have described above involve reality, existential reality and real relational structures and events. However, these structures and events may be intrapsychically transmuted in various ways so as to reemerge, in the consciousness of the members of a family, in frequently broken, cryptic and distorted forms, and possibly as family myths (Stierlin, 1973).

The multigenerational perspective opens a dimension of human relationships where, over generations, legacies are handed down, ledgers of merit are opened and closed, obligations are fulfilled or abnegated and invisible loyalties proved or betrayed. The therapeutic goal is to define these legacies and ledgers of merit, to bring them into the therapeutic transaction and so redress the balance and settle the accounts to make a final reconciliation possible. This aim should, we believe, be kept in mind in the conduct of the first interview with the family.

5. THE STATE OF MUTUALITY

The four main points of view discussed above are implicit in the "state of mutuality," but there emerges a new gestalt (concept) and with that a fifth perspective. Whereas the other perspectives revealed primarily historical, vertical relational dimensions, this fifth perspective focuses on the here-and-now, the present condition of the system, the relationship constellation of the moment. One might term this the actual systems perspective, though that would, in fact, imply too narrow a definition of the word system.

Gregory Bateson was probably the first to apply this perspective. In 1949 he described competitive relational structures or contexts which "inevitably reduce the complex gamut of values to very simple and even linear and monotonous terms" (1972, p. 96). Put simply, all relationships are here drawn into a power struggle. Such a power struggle which Bateson calls "symmetrical escalation" is indeed like the arms race—the contender who falls behind strives to overtake his opponent who then in turn struggles to regain his former position, and so on ad infinitum. Subsequently, many authors including J. Haley (1963), P. Watzlawick et al. (1974), and in particular M. Selvini-Palazzoli (1978a) have investigated the conduct and results of such arms races and power struggles in marital and family relationships.

The Malign Stalemate

The concept of negative mutuality that we discussed above enables us to sharpen this fifth perspective. At its worst, this type of power struggle degenerates into an extreme form of negative mutuality, which we call "malign stalemate." The whole system rigidifies totally and, despite some seemingly dramatic outbursts, actually remains static; the partners are like boxers in a clinch. As every power struggle and conflict in turn fails, the system ossifies still more. (An ossification also occurs when the relationship is not escalating and symmetrical but rigidly complementary: This too may be considered a form of negative mutuality.) Malign stalemate may involve either deadlocked or fluctuating alliances (or, according to M. Bowen (1960) deadlocked or fluctuating triangulations).

The Clinch

To understand the forces contributing to a malign stalemate, we must further explore the concept of the "clinch." The deadlocked opponents in such a clinch are belligerent and often attack each other wildly, without, however, shifting the balance of the fight. Neither can loosen the clinch or resolve the fight. And further, the various strategies and tactics, reflecting the individual preconceptions, aims, experience and life history of the opponents, seem to be neutralized in the clinch. What remains are two fulminating, undifferentiated partners locked in battle.

It is often harder to recognize the clinch character of struggles in relationships than in the boxing ring. Using a traditional, individual-centered view that focuses on only one contender at a time, for example, an anorexic or schizophrenic patient, the rest of the family falls into the background. Even so, elements of escalating and of deadlocked power struggles reappear with monotonous regularity, though there is variety in the weapons. Such weapons include masochistic behavior (and other symptoms that render the opponent helpless and load her or him with guilt), mutual mystification, exposure to double-binds, unwillingness to define one's relationship, the evasion of leadership and personal responsibility, and the whole arsenal of often subtle power tactics as described by G. Bateson, J. Haley and M. Selvini-Palazzoli.

It is above all in families with schizophrenic members that one finds such clinch relationship. A closer look shows its presence in many other syndromes and relational constellations. Many sexual disorders are the result and expression of a power struggle in which sexuality, far from giving the partners a joy through which they can relax and deepen and confirm their relationship, provides a weaponry which they use to injure one another, for example, by abusing each other as failures, cowards and weaklings, by punishing each other and depriving each other sexually. Such a power struggle often intensifies by turns of the sadomasochistic screw. Eventually, it hardens into a clinch and reaches a malign stalemate in which, in the long run, there can be only losers.

Therapeutic Considerations of Malign Stalemate

No less than the first four perspectives this one has therapeutic consequences. In the boxing ring it is the referee who usually ends the clinch. To separate the opponents' deadlock he must often intervene actively and energetically; indeed, he must sometimes quite literally throw in his weight. By such a heavy, active intervention he sets the deadlocked fight in motion again and creates the space necessary for the interplay of the different individualities, strategies, motivations, etc., which were absent as long as the clinch held.

The family or marital therapist must, we believe, intervene in just such an active way in cases of malign stalemate, interposing the weight of personality and authority to break the deadlock and create the free space in which the contenders can unfold their individual differentiated values and motives. Of course, the therapeutic situation is incomparably more complex than the boxing ring and the therapist has a commensurately greater repertoire of possibilities for intervention.

The weight and authority of the therapist can be best expressed as "the stronger person's reality" (Stierlin, 1959). Originally the concept described the relationship between the schizophrenic and his or her mother. However, it is significant not only in the relationships of the particularly vulnerable and easily mystified schizophrenic, but also in other relationships which develop extreme dependencies and consequent accompanying hopes and expectations. Dependence on, and hopes and expectations of the family therapist or family doctor increase as the relationship between the patient and his family becomes deadlocked and irresolvable. Frequently, the nearer the patient and his family come to being at the end of their tether, the more likely it is that the therapist will seem to be a potential savior. However, the therapist is not only a potential savior, but also a potential judge—someone with the power to deepen the fear and insecurity of patients already burdened with fear, insecurity, shame and guilt.

The art of the therapist lies in his ability in what M. Selvini-Palazzoli (1974) has called positive connotation, the giving of positive meaning. It is exactly in this beginning phase of the therapeutic relationship that the therapist must avoid any tendency to censure, frighten or arouse guilt, however subtle or well concealed; instead he must show as much approval as possible. Together, the active interpolation of the "stronger reality" of the therapist and the total avoidance of fear and guilt arousal create the optimal basis for breaking the malign stalemate, clinch and power struggle.

It is then possible to initiate an unlocking strategy, for example, the strategy known as "paradoxical intervention" or "prescription." As part of such an intervention the therapist approves the behavior of the symptom bearer, despite its causing crises and suffering, and thereby paradoxically mobilizes the wills of both the symptom bearer and of the other members of the family to end such behavior (for example, the hunger strike of an anoretic girl). We do not have space here to discuss how and why this happens, but refer those interested to the relevant literature (Weeks and L'Abate, 1978). The assertion must suffice that such an unlocking of the power struggle gives all the participants the chance to make a new start in their mutual individuation and separation, to begin a true dialogue in which they can own up to their own ambivalences while seeing others as persons in their own right.

Paradoxical intervention is not the only means of breaking a malign stalemate. The more experience, flexibility and initiative a therapist possesses, the more options are available. For example, by using what could be called an existential appeal, the therapist can arouse the clinch-locked parents of a critically anoretic girl finally to co-operate; together, they now bring their daughter to eat, thereby showing that they care and do not want to let her die (S. Minuchin et al., 1978). However, as soon as the child eats, she is allowed to select her own food. Thus, this struggle ends not in humiliation of one by another, but in the affirmation of the right of each to assert his or her (relative) autonomy. Further, and here Minuchin sets an example too, the therapist can ally first with one and then with another family member and so break down rigid alliances and relational structures.

Norman Paul (1975) is the principal proponent of a further method for breaking the malign stalemate: confronting the partners with a tape-recording or videotape of the therapeutic session. This is often the first time in their lives that they see the malign stalemate as outsiders, and this "objective" self-perception may lead to a turning point. Alternatively, the therapist can bring the family rapidly and directly to a confrontation with the "root issue" out of which the malign stalemate developed. This is often a massive and tragic, but unmourned, loss: the members of the family colluded to stave off the pain, for example, by mutual reproach that then led to a power struggle. Here the therapist can often facilitate a solution by initiating the long-overdue work of mourning.

However diverse the unclinching methods may be, their common factors are the active engagement of the therapist and the rapid establishment of a positive and fair relationship to all participants. In particular, such fairness must exist even when, from time to time, the therapist sides with particular members of the family against the others in order to break down rigid alliances.

Once the malign stalemate is broken, a positive mutuality often develops spontaneously; the forces released give every participant the chance of new growth, change, and development. In many cases, however, the chance alone is not enough: mere unclinching cannot lastingly change negative to positive mutuality. Intensive work is needed on each of the relational structures discussed under the other four perspectives. Here, one can say the main work of therapy begins after the initial unclinching; its aims are strengthening of related individuation, unbinding, the clarification and, where possible, correction of overtaxing missions, confrontation and balancing of accounts, and, finally, reunion and reconciliation.

THE INTEGRATION OF THE FIVE PERSPECTIVES IN CLINICAL PRACTICE

The relational dynamics of anorexia nervosa, the starvation disease of adolescent girls, exemplifies the applicability and integration of the five perspectives in clinical practice and, once again, reveals the distinctive features of malign stalemate. Here we build on our own experiences and the observations and reports of M. Selvini-Palazzoli (1974), H. Bruch (1978), S. Minuchin et al. (1978) and others.

Investigation of these girls and their families shows that anorexia nervosa regularly involves a disturbance of related individuation. The girl's perceptions are undifferentiated, at least in so far as they concern other members of the family and her relationship with them. Her thinking is often concrete; she is unable to accept or tolerate ambivalence, cannot get on the same wavelength as the other members of the family, and so is unable to establish a true dialogue. Such a disturbance of related individuation seems to inhere in the long-term relational structures of the family, but—and here our fifth perspective is important—as the power struggle approaches a climax, the clinch hardens and the disturbance of individuation grows worse so as to signal an almost qualitative change.

This also applies to the transactional perspective. Our own observations and those of others show that these girls have usually been deeply bound up with their parents, above all on the super-ego level. Such a binding now tightens as a result of the sharpening power struggle and changes its quality, becoming a malign stalemate.

Further, anoretic girls regularly seem to have been made the delegates of over-exacting parental expectations and ideals that often embody both massive overdemands and the deepest mission and loyalty conflicts. These conflicts mould the ongoing family relationship and contribute feelings of hurt, frustration, revengefulness and defiance. The more the power struggle intensifies, the less the participants are able to recognize or discuss such destructive delegation processes or mission and loyalty conflicts. The malign clinch extinguishes both the inclination and ability for such discussion.

The same is true for the legacies and ledger of merits discussed above as the fourth perspective. Neglected legacies and unbalanced accounts produce feelings of unjust treatment and exploitation leading to frustration, revenge taking and power struggles. Here too, as long as the malign clinch holds, there is little chance of initiating a dialogue, clarifying issues, restoring balance, and finally reaching reconciliation.

In summary, although disorders at the four levels discussed above —related individuation, transactional modes of binding and expelling, delegation, and the multigenerational perspective of legacy and merit—contribute to the ongoing system of the anoretic family, the fifth form of relationship, our so-called "malign stalemate," is pivotal. Therefore, an unclinching strategy must, if at all possible, be adopted from the first interview with the family. At the same time, we must initiate or prepare the ground for work on the long-standing relational structures revealed by the first four perspectives.

3

Empathy, Interpretation and Structure

MERELY TO UNDERSTAND A CONCEPT is not enough, one must know how to apply it. To this end we now look at the attitudes, abilities and specific problems of the therapist in the first interview with the family.

Stage fright, anxiety and fear are not confined to beginners who have worked with only one patient. Any therapist may feel like an actor called on short notice to play a role in an unfamiliar drama. It is necessary to cope with masses of diverse information. The therapist may feel threatened by the family's engulfing power or hurt by their imagined or real rejection; may notice how the family or individual members try to involve her or him as judge, parental figure, or savior; may find her- or himself enshrined as an expert to whom the family demonstrates their powerlessness; or may find her- or himself unwelcome, an intruder, isolated and ejected by the family.

EMPATHY

Many of the abilities and attitudes that the therapist must adopt are conveyed in the concept of empathy. Empathy, which also plays an important role in psychoanalysis, denotes the refined ability to tune oneself to the experiences and state of mind of others. Sensibility, comprehensive understanding and intuition are related concepts. Correspondingly, in both psychoanalysis and family therapy, empathy is an integrative achievement. In the dyadic psychoanalytic relationship the analyst uses his empathic understanding to gain an impression of the patient which holds at least for that moment and that interview. The therapist in the family interview works in a similar way, but in contrast the information and impressions available to the family interviewer multiply by leaps and bounds with each additional person. Therefore, an integrative empathic perception must be focused not only on the processes within individuals (the intrapsychic level) and their relationships to the therapist, but also on the interaction between the family members.

Further, the therapist must be aware of the intrapsychic aspects of these interactions and, therefore, of the forces within the systems as revealed by the five perspectives discussed previously. Finally, the therapist must be conscious of the relationship of the whole family to her- or himself.

The Systems Forces

The success of such empathic integration depends basically on the interviewer's ability to adopt a comprehensive outlook and to acquire and maintain a systems view. Here many therapists accustomed to work in a one-to-one situation have failed, finding the demands of the change too great. The central question now is not primarily what is going on inside these people, but rather, how these people affect each other. The following leading questions, or viewpoints can help in the detection of the systems forces: Do disorders and conflicts of the individual members depend on one another? Does, for example, the frigidity of the wife secure and compensate for the impotence of her husband, the delinquent behavior of the children for the narrow-minded respectability of the parents, or one's dependence for the other's overgenerosity? Which feedback processes maintain the various behaviors so that the pathological cycle of negative mutuality spirals onwards? How much is the family like a prison from which there is no escape? How strongly and over what length of time (it may be years) has the equilibrium of mutual needs, expectations and defensive postures existed?

Where the therapist is unable in the first interview to understand the family as more than a mere collection of individuals, not only is information lost, but, even in the first interview, the therapeutic effect is negative. The neglected relational dynamic sets a negative cycle in action. The disordered relational pattern escalates further; the interview breaks down and frequently cannot be repeated.

Nevertheless a systems view does not imply neglect of the individual. On the contrary, she or he must be addressed and respected as an individual and be understood as an individual system.

COGNITIVE STABILITY

To remain in charge of the situation, the interviewer not only must collect and order information, but must structure the interview. As soon as some relevant information is gleaned, a recurring relational pattern is recognized, the therapist must change the focus of the interview and invite the family's cooperation. By imposing an unequivocal, ordered conduct of the interview on the family's confused communicational style, the therapist represents reality and combats mystification.

STAYING OPEN

Although the therapist must strive for clarity and structure, this should not be at the expense of frankness and flexibility. The therapist must be able to enter promptly into any situation that arises and include it in the interview. For example, when a child cries, a parent suddenly ends a discussion or the nonverbal and verbal communication are discrepant. It is helpful to be surprised by unexpected feelings and attitudes and be able to react in a normal human way.

THE INTERVIEWER'S DUAL FUNCTIONS

The dynamic process of the first interview with the family is like a drama in which the therapist plays two interweaving roles: producer and participant observer. The producer directs the dramatic process, giving momentum when the drama threatens to stagnate. As the interview reaches increasingly relevant sensitive levels, participants must be protected from the destructive potential of the feelings they express. The expression of thoughts and feelings which have been taboo must be encouraged, but simultaneously, the family must be hindered from merely repeating well-worn patterns in their aggressive outbursts. While so directing its course, the therapist takes part in the family dynamic as a participant observer, listening attentively and noting the often contradictory tendencies, forces, and feelings within the family. The data gained in this way as observer can then be used promptly as producer.

PARTICIPATION AND DISENGAGEMENT

The therapist's dual functions lead us to the problems arising from deep involvement with and subsequent disengagement from the family system.

Involvement with the system can entail a variety of experiences. Frequently the interviewer is heavily encumbered by the experience, feeling confused and helpless and losing perspective. Sometimes this submergence in the family is pleasant: the therapist feels at one with them and experiences a deep harmony and security, perhaps something like euphoria.

Should the therapist avoid becoming so deeply involved in the family system? In our view this process is unavoidable and even desirable. In this way the therapist finds out what the whole family feels like from the inside, what it feels like to be a member of the system. If the therapist consciously and energetically avoids such involvement from the start, by maintaining detachment, distance and a rigid structure in the interview, it will be hard to recognize any of the hidden structures within the family or to achieve an emotional, trusting contact with them. The therapist remains an outsider.

Only after the interviewer has been spontaneously included by the family within their relational system can she or he decide when and where to draw personal boundaries. The first step is to realize that the interviewer is involved and in what way. This is the easier if such involvement is expected.

There are many ways in which the therapist can disengage and regain a therapeutic stance. One method is to change the pattern of relationship. For example, in a poorly delimited family in which each speaks for the other and each "knows" what the other thinks, the therapist can draw attention to this and press for change. ("Do you really think exactly what your wife said?" "Why not ask your husband what he thinks?" "Did you hear what your wife said?") If the interactional pattern in the family changes, the therapist is "released." In other situations the therapist may detach by adopting a more structured and exploratory attitude. Or, the therapist might break off discussion and call for a recess during which discussion of the next steps in the therapy can occur with the cotherapist (or perhaps with the observers) behind the one-way screen.

MULTIDIRECTIONAL PARTIALITY

The concept of multidirectional partiality was first introduced by I. Boszormenyi-Nagy. We can view it as an extension of the concept of empathy. It refers to the ability of the therapist empathically to adopt the positions of all members, present and absent, in the total, often multigenerational, drama of conflicts, guilt and merit ledgers. Far from being a neutral, evenhanded judge of all parties, the therapist must actually, in the course of the therapy, at some point side with each individual member of the family; at the same time he must constantly be guided by a sense of the balance of justice.

Multidirectional partiality does not mean that the therapist gives every member of the family the same amount of attention and time —even in the first interview. Rather, the therapist must convey to each the feeling that she or he is a worthwhile person, somebody who counts and whose position the therapist is trying to understand and respect. In some way each member of the family must be made to feel liked.

This many-sided partiality enables the therapist to influence the members of the family in important ways. By siding with the grandmother, for example, the therapist helps the others to sympathize with her in her roles of mother and child of her own family. The family becomes much more perceptive of interpersonal justice and this promotes the wish for family fairness and reconciliation, the balancing of accounts and mutual forgiveness.

The more the age, interests, jobs and experiences of a particular member of the family differ from those of the therapist, the more difficult it tends to be for the therapist to take sides with this individual. An empathic ability must help the therapist to bridge the gap. Success depends then on how far the therapist has come to terms with his or her own negative transference (see below) and in particular on, as Boszormenyi-Nagy (1975, pp. 129) said, "his ability to tune himself to the suffering in the past of his own parents."

Looking on the Positive Side

The multipartial and overall view reveals that even grave disorders of individual family members may have a surprisingly meaningful function: The aggressive provocative behavior of an adolescent appears as a self-destructive self-victimization designed to distract the parents from their own conflicts and/or aimed to alert them to the critical state of the family; the adolescent is delegated to provide the family with worry, excitement or problems. In general, positive forces, resources and potentials for growth should be sought where they seem most lacking: in the index patient; in destructive behavior; in a young, quiet but alertly observant child; in the absent member of the family; or even in the family's symbiotic clinch.

It is easy for an inexperienced therapist to spot and discuss disorders, conflicts and pathology, while the resources of the family remain unnoticed, neglected and unused. While searching for conflicts and weaknesses, we must also ask where the strengths of the family lie. Who or what could help? What attempts has the family itself made to overcome its difficulties?

Such a constructive systems view is particularly important because dysfunctional patterns usually emerge much more readily in interviews with the whole family than in individual therapy. When an inexperienced therapist is concerned with only the disturbed patterns, the family's feeling that they are hopelessly sick is strengthened.

The Active Role of the Therapist

More than in most other forms of individual or group therapy, family therapy demands an active role by the therapist. When the session is allowed to run an undirected course, the destructive relational patterns usually escalate or rigidify to a malign clinch (Stierlin, 1979). The established defensive maneuvers reinforce the system under the stress of the interview situation, and the "pathology" is aggravated. Disturbed communication and interaction flourish in the hothouse atmosphere, causing the family to leave the interview with the feeling that everything is even worse than before.

It is essential to find the right point at which to interrupt a repetitive dysfunctional interaction by a short structuring or corrective intervention. The nature and rigidity of malign stalemate are both relevant here. Here, the therapist must frequently bring the whole weight of authority and the strength of a positive trusting relationship to bear in order to break a destructive cycle. Various important points which are relevant have been developed by S. Minuchin (1974a, b), J. Haley (1963), R. Bandler and J. Grinder (1975, 1976) and summarized by H. Stierlin (1979). The active role of the therapist does not imply talking a great deal, organizing or manipulating, but rather a readiness to take responsibility, to become involved. As Minuchin et al. (1967) have shown, chaotic families, usually from underprivileged social classes, may require a particular structuring effort on the part of the therapist.

It is an important aspect of the therapist's activity to convey hope and faith. However, it is important, of course, that this not be based on illusion so it will not give rise to later disappointment.

TRANSFERENCE AND COUNTERTRANSFERENCE

The concepts of transference and countertransference go back to Freud's observations on analytic dyadic relationships. The psychoanalytic transference concept widens and changes in the context of family relationships (Stierlin, 1977b). Here it is important to distinguish between transfamilial and intrafamilial transference.

Transfamilial transference, that is transference beyond the family, means that attitudes, expectations, perceptions, etc. (the so-called "givens" of the transference) which originated within one's family of origin (in particular within the parent-child relationship) are inappropriately transferred to an outsider, someone not belonging to the family of origin, such as the analyst or therapist. This is often the only form of transference discussed as therapeutically relevant.

Intrafamilial transference, on the contrary, means that such givens are inappropriately transferred within the family. Usually at least two generations are involved, thus one can call this "transgenerational transference."

Two axes of intrafamilial transference can be distinguished in family therapy. First, one sees transference from parents to child. The parents unload on the child fantasies, attributes, and perceptions which are often so overwhelming that "a false self" is imposed on the child, causing the child to be "parentified." Second, the transference may be from child to parents, so that even as an adult the child transfers to the parents attitudes, perceptions, conflict patterns, etc. which are no longer appropriate. This adult child still experiences his or her parents as fantasy objects, whether as wicked persecutors or as preambivalently idealized heroes. In other words, the grown-up child sees the living parents with the eyes of childhood and is unable to differentiate between a fantasy image of the parents and the real parents.

In family therapy the interviewer is concerned with both transfamilial and intrafamilial transference. In general, intrafamilial transference is more significant than transfamilial transference. This means that, in contrast to the analytic dyadic relationship, the family therapist works less on the unfolding of the complex transference and countertransference dynamics in relation to her- or himself and more on the development and harnessing of the intrafamilial relational dynamic. Through multi-directed partiality and empathy the therapist will, however, try to minimize such transfamilial transference and to give it a positive form where it occurs.

The relational framework we have sketched lends a wider, and in part new, meaning to the concept of countertransference in family therapy. As in psychoanalysis it implies that the therapist has "blind spots"—that attitudes and perceptions might in some way make it difficult or impossible to achieve a fair empathic stance towards all family members.

Typically, such countertransference problems have their origins in the experiences and unresolved problems within the therapist's own family background. Because of its significance, some form of work with one's own family is increasingly included in the training of family therapists.

FAMILY RULES, MYTHS AND SECRETS

Family rules act over generations to mould the roles, missions and legacies of the individual members, who for the most part are unaware that the rules exist. Such a rule, for example, might be that "in our family one must either look after others or be looked after." Over generations this may lead to a rigid distinction between sick and healthy members of the family.

Family myths (Ferreira, 1963; Stierlin 1973) mean mind-blunting formulas or clichés used by the whole family to conceal conflicts, problems and tensions. Examples are myths of unalloyed harmony, general stoically accepted misfortune, persecution by outsiders, etc. Family myths are often interwoven with *family secrets*. Suicide attempts or revenge-seeking disinheritance do not square with myths of family harmony and must be made taboo. At the same time the secret remains hidden away in the sump of the family memory.

In the first interview with the family such rules, myths and secrets frequently come to light and their often enormously stabilizing (homeostatic) force can be recognized. However, as a rule the therapist should not attempt any abrupt disclosure here but should create the right atmosphere for the family themselves eventually to initiate the discussion.

PARENTS OF THE INDEX PATIENT

A book on the first family interview must strive to be just to the parents of the symptom-bearing child, the index patient. Such parents resist, often massively, every open or concealed suggestion of their own patient status. Heavily afflicted with fear, shame, and guilt, they feel themselves on trial as bad "failed" parents and tend, therefore, to divert and project their own weakness and disturbances onto their children and outsiders. For such parents to be compelled, in their children's presence, to turn for help to someone more competent seems to complete their sense of defeat and powerlessness. Their willingness to cooperate becomes minimal.

Nevertheless the therapist must win their constructive cooperation. To this end it is necessary to be able to recognize and acknowledge the positive side of the parents' so far ineffective efforts and
to establish a bond with them. The chances of success are greater
if the therapist is able to understand the parents as the children of
their own families. They have had no option but to pass on to their
children the wounds and reproaches they received and to exact from
their own children the justice their own parents did not accord
them.

If a trustful relationship is not established between the therapist
and the parents, the family therapy cannot succeed. Without trust
the therapist's attempts to act against parents who are massively ex-
ploiting their children for their own needs and interest, will plunge
the children into a conflict of loyalties. Furthermore, the therapist
should not compete with the parents, purporting to be a better father
or better mother. Only after gaining the parents' trust may the therapist take the children's side and criticize the parents from the children's point of view.

THE INDEX PATIENT

The index patient or symptom bearer is in a position dialectically
contrary to the parents. In contrast to the apparently healthy parents
(and other members of the family), the index patient is weak, is sick,
needs help, is loaded with problems, and is often made the family
scapegoat. A closer look, however, often shows that this apparent
weakness represents strength: the others can shift all their insecurity,
weaknesses, and difficulties onto her or him, freeing themselves at
his or her expense and, in contrast, remaining strong, healthy and
supportive. It is often only through the index patient that the others
are able "safely" to embark on therapy; she or he bears their burdens
—indeed, sacrifices her- or himself for them. However, through this
martyr role the index patient also has the power to face the others
with their own guilt. One aim of the first interview is to recognize
and where possible discuss the achievements, strengths and power of
the index patient.

Recognizing Ambivalence and Concealed Sabotage

Resistance of many kinds frequently causes the first interview to fail even before it has begun. The family may not appear for the appointment agreed on by telephone. They call the appointment off at the last minute. Some of the family are ready to come, but others are frightened or strongly object. The interview is thwarted. Or, compelling reasons are found for putting it off: there is an important meeting at the time of the appointment, a child has essential school work, it is the grandmother's birthday, etc.—all of which may be true but still reveals a conscious or unconscious defense, resistance or ambivalence. There is usually some specific ground for this ambivalence. It may be that the referring person—the family doctor, child psychiatrist, or the acting analytic psychotherapist—has inner reservations about family therapy. In a concealed form these reservations may be conveyed to the clients, who may in turn express them in ambivalent sabotage. One important job of the first interview is to recognize and work on such initial ambivalence.

The Problem of Cotherapy

Treatment of a family by two cotherapists makes the interview more open and increases the complexity of the empathic process. Not only must both therapists develop a sympathetic understanding of the family and each of its members, they must maintain awareness of each other. They must have trust and confidence in each other, and above all, they must have enough respect for each other to avoid wrecking their cooperative work by entering into even a surreptitious rivalry. The personalities of the therapists should not be too alike, as this makes it difficult to recognize problems of countertransference; in fact their personalities, relational styles, and family backgrounds should, as far as possible, be complementary. However, it is particularly important that their theoretical orientations agree.

Indications for Cotherapy

Although cotherapy is frequently practiced in family therapy, our experience is that it is difficult and even burdensome for inexperienced therapists. We confine its use to certain specific situations. In

our institute, cotherapy, with male and female therapists, is confined
to the problem of families where there is long-standing conflict between the marital couple. In these cases the relations and behavior
of the cotherapists can provide an important model. It has proved
most successful for one therapist to take the main responsibility
during the interview, while the other supports and extends interventions and, where possible, supplements them with further points.
Differences in approach between the two therapists do no harm if
they are noticed and taken into account; they may in fact be discussed during the interview with the family. In any case there should
be a discussion by the therapists after the interview in which any
such conflict that has arisen between them can be resolved.

COTHERAPY IN TRAINING

We cannot recommend cotherapy as a means of training. Above
all in the first interview the effect on the empathic process is dele-
terious if two as yet inexperienced family therapists rely on each
other's help to compensate for their insecurity and anxiety. It is all
too easy for them to become dependent on each other. If one of the
cotherapists already has experience with family therapy, the other
seldom dares to take the responsibility of acting independently. In
our view it is better for a supervisor, colleague or group of colleagues to watch the interview from behind a one-way screen and
to discuss the interview subsequently with the trainee therapist. In
this way the trainee learns more quickly how to conduct the interview with the family, to maintain empathic ability, and to correct
mistakes in subsequent interviews.

THE MEANING OF TEAMWORK

From years of experience the importance of teamwork in family
therapy and especially in the first interview has become continually
clearer to us. It usually requires the resources of a whole team to
master the huge amounts of information that become so rapidly
available to the interviewer and, at the same time, to combine them
into a comprehensive dynamic hypothesis, to avoid time-wasting
and profitless confusion, and to plan innovative interventions.

In our experience the formation of an efficient team requires years of joint work and study. The following format has proved valuable in our work in Heidelberg. Members of the team take turns working in pairs in the therapy room, while the others watch from behind the one-way screen. Usually one therapist directs the interview actively, while the other steps in when needed. The family knows from the beginning that a whole team is involved in the therapy—not only an individual therapist or the interviewing couple, but also those behind the one-way screen. There is a free flow of information between therapists and observers according to the needs and problems of the situation. Either the therapists seek advice from the observers, or the observers interrupt the interview by knocking on the door and asking the therapist to come out for a short consultation. A recess in the interview is routinely made after 50 to 60 minutes; therapists and observers exchange impressions and ideas, and a joint strategy is decided on which further therapy is based. This strategy is then applied in the final five to ten minutes of the sitting. The main points on which we base our choice of strategy are the subject of the next chapter.

4

Basic Considerations

THE MOST IMPORTANT ASPECTS of the first interview with the family derive from its principal aims, which are: diagnosis, motivation for work on the common problem, drawing up the therapeutic contract and deciding the direction of further therapy.

DIAGNOSIS

The concepts of diagnosis normally used in organic medicine are not applicable in family therapy. Possible exceptions might be when working in conjunction with some referring agency (such as the social services, health department or family doctor), or when the interviewer has a narrowly defined diagnostic or advisory job (for example, to consider grounds for abortion, financial or legal aid or special schooling). In these cases it would be hardly possible to distinguish between diagnosis and therapy or counseling.

Wherever more extensive therapy is considered, there are two main aspects of diagnosis: an assessment of systems forces as revealed through the five perspectives and an evaluation of the family's motivation.

In assessing the systems forces, possibly through collaborative teamwork, we aim at a hypothesis which covers the family's crucial

48

relational dynamics. This hypothesis, although it remains open to revision, should be formulated by the end of the first interview as the basis for a clearly thought out therapeutic plan. Where essential information is not available (because, for example, an important member of the family is absent), making it impossible to arrive at such a hypothesis in the first session, we usually ask for a second interview to follow as soon as possible. We may invite a third generation (the grandparents) to this second interview.

The information on which this hypothesis is based comes from two main sources: exploration of the central, "existential" family "facts" revealed by the five perspectives (for example, strong binding; expulsion; massively exploitative delegations; deep, unmourned bereavement; long-standing feelings of illness; enduring antipathy; very demanding or rigid attitudes; etc.) and observation of typical and in part self-activating transactional patterns in the family. As a rule, we act to stop all potentially destructive patterns (for example, symmetrically escalating recriminations or mutual withdrawal into taciturnity) as soon as they are clearly recognizable. In our experience much "existential" information about the family is obtained most quickly and safely by asking one member to talk about some particular aspect of another member of the family who has already been under discussion (for example, his or her behavior or apparent feelings in crisis situations, or his or her relationship to the parental family).

MOTIVATION

The second diagnostic task—assessing the motivation of the family—requires awareness of possible ambivalence and concealed sabotage (cf. Chapter 3). The family members who initiate the interview do not always intend personally to work on the problems they themselves have raised. Sometimes the request will be made by a member of the family for the therapy of another member—the "patient." Or the family produces a "problem child," often an adolescent, who is unaware of having any "problem." In these and similar situations the interviewer must decide what motivates *each* member of the family, as there is no external pressure to work on a common problem. A judgment must be made about whether absent, uncooperative or apparently bored members of the family are being delegated to express the resistance of the whole family. Finally, the therapist must assess how far the system is rigid and how far it has potential for change: how strong are the morphostatic forces, tending to maintain the ongoing system, compared with the morphogenetic forces, tending to produce change?

Capacity for Being Motivated

In assessing the family we must consider whether, and to what extent, it is possible during the first interview to motivate the family for further joint work. Such potential for being motivated is a function both of the above-described familial factors and of the therapeutic factors which play a role in the first interview. These include the ability of the therapist to reduce shame, guilt and fear, to awaken hope and trust, to free emotions through discussion of what was previously taboo, and to strengthen feelings of personal worth by positive connotation. If the therapist is able to bring such skills to bear on the first interview, a relationship of cooperation and trust can rapidly be built. On the other hand, clumsy and unempathic conduct can prove as swiftly destructive.

THE THERAPEUTIC CONTRACT

In the first interview the therapist and the family must come to at least a minimal agreement on further steps that are necessary. This must reflect not only the expectations and aims of the therapist, but also those of the family. The entire family must go home aware that they have a common problem that affects them all. A family therapeutic contract must be set up that lays down the scope and conditions for further interviews. (The exceptions to this rule are discussed below.)

Frequently, the members of the family are initially unaware of certain motivational sources of their aims and expectations; they only become conscious of these later as a result of the therapeutic process. As these sources progressively emerge, new aims and expectations appear that compel change, reformulation and extension of the contract between therapist and family. Therapy that originally revolved around a child's school problems, for example, can unmask a conflict between the parents. The aims and expectations of the contracting parties must, therefore, periodically be assessed and readjusted.

Disordered communication often hinders the achievement of a family consensus (cf., Chapter 6). Such families cannot agree because they are in a state of open or concealed strife, with the members pulling in different directions. Without a consensus the therapist cannot make a contract. The only recourse is to note the divergence of motivational interest and to achieve at least an agreement that no agreement is possible. Whether there is any point in extensive family therapy under these conditions must be decided at a later interview.

DECIDING ON THE DIRECTION OF FURTHER THERAPY

This question is central to the first interview. To illuminate the problem we go back to the interviewer's "producer" role (Chapter 3). We said that as producer the therapist must intervene actively to steer the family drama in a specific direction. A good guide is a therapeutic model that lays down a specific strategy or program for this situation or moment. The more experienced and flexible the therapist, the more models and strategies can be employed. At the same time, it is important to question the potentialities and limits of the various models and strategies and to ask whether, and how far, they exclude or complement each other.

The therapeutic models discussed here may be classified according to various principles. The classification that has proved most valuable for our work in Heidelberg is outlined below. It employs "ideal types"—constructs which, according to the sociologist Max Weber, embody what is typical but do not always mirror real-life situations.

The classification ranges between two therapeutic poles: these we call "healing through encounter" and "healing through systemic change."*

---

* In the original: "Heilung durch Begegnung" and "Heilung durch Systemänderung." The German adjective "heil" means not only healthy but also "undamaged, safe, complete, intact." "Heilung" therefore not only means healing in the narrow sense of getting well, but refers to such central phenomena as integration, cleansing, reconciliation and, indeed, preservation or salvation.

Healing through Encounter

We borrow the term "healing through encounter" from the title of a book by the German psychotherapist Hans Trüb (1971) that deals with the encounter between therapist and individual patient. In family therapy the therapist initiates and leads encounters between the various members and generations of a family according to the basic family therapeutic rule: "Try, as much as possible, to talk about those matters you were so far unable to discusss"—for example, family secrets, disappointed hopes, feelings of injustice. As we mentioned above, it was Ivan Boszormenyi-Nagy who first developed and distinguished this from the basic rule of psychoanalysis. The aim of the family-wide encounter is a dialogue that covers increasingly significant levels and leads to final reconciliation (Stierlin, 1969) and reunion (Boszormenyi-Nagy and Spark, 1973).

In their recent book *The Family Crucible* (1978), Napier and Whitaker describe a typical example of healing through encounter.* We see here how, as a result of the therapist's empathic engagement, the encounter between the members of the family who up to this point have been deeply estranged and alienated reaches increasingly important levels. This allows for the articulation of long-concealed conflicts and finally leads to a reconciliation and reunification including the grandparents.

Healing through Systemic Change

In contrast to "healing through encounter," in the process of "healing through systemic change" the therapist works on the assumption that the members of the family are trapped in a malign clinch. Therefore, for the time being they are unable either to come together or to part; the system has undergone a decisive change. The therapist's central strategy, at least during the initial stage of therapy, is to aim for systemic change by bringing his or her own stronger reality to bear on the family (described in Chapter 2). Exemplary work of this kind has been done by the Milanese team under Mara

---

* We assume that an experienced family therapist would from time to time use all the models described here or elements of them, though eventually tending to prefer a specific model, so her or his work could, therefore, be taken as representative of that particular model.

Selvini-Palazzoli (1978a) . The main reagent of systemic change is the paradoxical prescription (Chapter 2) which acts on the entire system and, at best, actually "dissolves" the clinch. Other therapeutic orientations within this basic model that effect systemic change have been described by P. Steinglass (1978) and C. E. Sluzki (1978) .

Healing through Active Restructuring

Between "healing through encounter" and "healing through systemic change" we set a third model that we call "healing through active restructuring." As we have already shown in Chapter 3, a family therapist must usually structure an interview more actively than a psychoanalyst. In comparison with the other models, the family therapist has a particularly active and frequently even managing role in this third model.

Although this includes elements of both previously described models, it is quite distinct from them. As S. Minuchin (1974a) describes it, in the course of a structural family therapy the therapist attempts actively to change ongoing relational patterns and alliances within the family. To this end the therapist may side with one member against another and force a crisis in the family that makes fresh experiences possible; may set tasks that confuse and so lead to rethinking; or may organize a "family lunch," etc. Even Norman Paul (1975) , although he seems more psychoanalytically orientated than Minuchin, employs active restructuring, as when he confronts the members of the family with a videotape of previous sessions or prompts them to search for long neglected relations, to visit the grave of a member of the family, or to mourn together.

Working within or outside the Family Session

To complete this discussion we must mention one further principle for the classification of therapeutic models that has become increasingly important for our own work in Heidelberg. This principle establishes whether the essential systemic or restructuring work must be done within or outside the conjoint family session.

In applying this classificatory principle we find that the basic model of "healing through encounter" implies that the significant therapeutic work is done in relatively frequent (most often weekly) sessions over an extended time period. It resembles the psychoanalytical model where the decisive work of restructuring the intrapsychic system is also done in the course of regular, relatively frequent appointments. Here, the patient (analysand) should avoid discussing what occurs during the therapeutic session with anyone else; otherwise the emotional tension necessary for structural change is lowered or, in other words, the energy that propels the analytical work is dissipated. Many family therapists, working within the model of healing through encounter (including Napier and Whitaker, 1978) advise their families similarly to bring all emotionally loaded and potentially destructive material to the therapeutic session and as far as possible to avoid its discussion outside the session.

The model of healing through systemic change reflects the reverse situation: here the family session merely provides an initial impetus —it lays a fuse to effects that only become apparent over longer periods of time. The family sessions must, therefore, be relatively infrequent and spaced at longer intervals. During the interval the system is given time to change. For example, in a family where massive binding has so far prevented the age-appropriate individuation and separation of the teenage daughter, the daughter can now experience the storms and disappointments of this stage of life, while the parents can learn to cope with their concomitant fears and mourning and, at the same time, adjust their own marital relationship.

Our third model, healing through active restructuring, occupies a middle position. One important part of the restructuring work occurs within and another outside the therapeutic session. The "work of reunion and mourning" prescribed for his patients by Norman Paul (1975), for example, is done both within the therapeutic session and outside by the performance of joint therapeutic tasks.

All these models find a place in our Heidelberg family dynamic concept. We are aware that the three models cannot be casually employed. Complex considerations are necessary to decide how and when specific models, or elements of models, exclude one another or can augment one another within the frame of a well-thought-out and flexible therapeutic plan.

Such considerations show, for example, that an active restructuring approach, like that of Minuchin (1974a, b) involving a temporary) partiality towards one member of the family, reduces the chances of achieving a paradoxical prescription encompassing the entire family by the end of the interview. Similarly, when the therapist promotes arguments and confrontations in the early phases of the first session, she or he hinders a paradoxical conclusion at its end. Premature and too frequent interpreting (as distinct from eliciting information) also has a similar "anti-paradoxical" effect. However, we consider it both useful and legitimate, in certain circumstances, after the first therapeutic phase that is molded by a paradoxical prescription, to adopt a model centered on healing through encounter, which then necessitates active confrontation and exposure to conflict, possibly including other generations.

Summary

To summarize these aspects of the conduct of the first interview with the family: The more experienced the therapist the more options are available for deciding the direction of further therapy. These options (or strategies) reflect different therapeutic models. One option or model can permanently exclude another, or may be appropriate only for a certain phase or limited goal; it may then be replaced by another option or model adapted to a different phase or goal. Many of the therapeutic requirements and abilities detailed in the foregoing chapters as associated with the first interview apply to all three of the ideal-typical models sketched here. The main points discussed in this chapter emphasize that the indications for a particular therapeutic approach should be continually reviewed, the priorities constantly re-evaluated, and new decisions reached based on reconsideration of the aims, entire situation and phase of the therapy.

5

The Specifics

BECAUSE EVERY FAMILY is a unique and complex organism, the therapist faces a new and unique situation with every interview. It is impossible, therefore, to standardize the procedure a therapist might adopt in the first interview. There must be room for flexibility, spontaneity and establishment of empathic understanding. At the same time we find that there are specific aspects common to every family interview and that these are independent of whatever intentions there may be for further work. The therapist should be aware of these and apply this knowledge for his or her own and the family's benefit. They relate both to the external conditions under which the first contact is made and to the various phases of the interview.

WHERE SHOULD FAMILY THERAPY BE DONE?

Some family therapists prefer to visit families in their everyday surroundings—at home or wherever the difficulties occur, such as at school or at work. Usually, however, family and therapist meet in conditions familiar to the therapist, in the rooms of his or her practice. This room should be big enough so that each member of a large family can find a seat as close to or as distant from the others as feels comfortable. When a family is confined in a room which is too small, the undue proximity can increase tension and make the therapy more difficult. The lighting should enable the therapist to observe each individual present. Subdued living-room style lighting might create a fear-reducing cosiness, but this would be at the cost of the working atmosphere necessary for every therapy.

Toys

We consider it important that sufficient suitable toys for children of all ages be available in the therapy room. There should not be too many, however. A few model cars, dolls and an accessible supply of drawing materials are usually enough. The Sceno-box (a set of figures used for test purposes) can also be useful. Games such as playing cards or board games that are so absorbing that they effectively remove one or more children from the interview with the family are obviously not suitable. The toys and drawing materials should be invitingly accessible, not hidden in a cupboard.

Audiovisual Material and the One-Way Screen

Audiovisual material—tape and videotape recorders—and one-way screens are widely used today in family and group therapy, often even from the first interview. This is for three main reasons:

1) They help the therapist to check his or her own work. Such supervision is above all important when the therapist is faced with a flow of complex transactions and information, as is typical of family and group therapy situations.

2) They can be used therapeutically. The therapist may suggest that the family watch the playback of some section of the tape in order to reflect on and correct their own behavior. The potential therapeutic gain must be assessed against the potential danger. The confrontation with their own errors and weakness may be so deeply wounding that the individual (s) concerned withdraw into themselves.

3) They are aids to training and research. Although the use of audiovisual material can generally be justified on the above grounds, it can sometimes hinder the development of trust

between therapist and client and also, therefore, the therapy itself. Discretion must be exercised, as it would with individual therapy. Even so, a number of patients fear observation and feel that they are being "checked-up on" and harassed. The therapist also may be made anxious by being watched and "exposed." It often helps to cover the one-way screen with a curtain. But in any case the family and therapist most often rapidly forget that they are being observed.

All the so-called aids have advantages and disadvantages. The one-way screen is perhaps the best means of observing all that happens in the session. It should be big enough to provide a view of the entire therapy room. Videotapes, although they allow playback, distort and filter the true atmosphere through the necessarily limited picture, lack of color and often inadequate sound quality.

Tape recordings convey an even more highly filtered and remote version of the interview, but for supervision purposes are preferable to a verbal report.

THE INTERVIEW BEGINS WITH THE FIRST CONTACT

From the external conditions of the therapy we now turn to the interview itself. Our first question is: What are the steps between initial contact with the family and the entrance of the whole family together into the therapy room?

The initial contact is frequently a telephone call, usually from the mother, less often from the father or an adolescent, to the institution or therapist asking for an appointment. Even this first telephone contact is important and should not be dealt with on a routinely administrative level as is normal in other apparently similar situations such as a visit to a medical practitioner. Even at this stage there are considerations that are important for the conduct of the first interview with the family and perhaps for further therapy (cf. Chapter 4). We do not, therefore, leave it to a secretary to set up the appointment and to note date, name, year of birth and reason for the call. In our opinion, this normal administrative procedure would confirm the family in their view that the symptom of a member of the family (usually a child) is in fact the actual or only problem. Rather, the caller is immediately put through to the therapist who is at that moment on telephone duty.

The Therapist on Telephone Duty

Even at the first telephone contact this therapist has a task that far exceeds the mere taking of details and making of appointments. First the reason for the call must be determined and the formation of an initial picture of the family attempted.

Second, even during this first contact, the therapist must be ready to establish an emotional relationship with the client. The questions and attitude determine whether the caller feels understood, whether a feeling of trust is gained, and indeed whether the almost inevitable shame of having made the call can be overcome.

Third, the therapist's questions can change the attitude to the problems. By asking about other members of the family who are in some way affected by the problem presented, the therapist makes clear an interest in a fair allocation of responsibility. She or he can show the caller that an individual member of the family will not be considered solely responsible or to blame for the symptom of another member of the family, or for that matter, for the deterioration of a marital relationship. Finally, the resolve the caller has shown in deciding to act as representative of the whole family by contacting the therapist or institution can be acknowledged. By in this way making clear that responsibility cannot lie with a single individual alone, the therapist may, even at this stage, initiate a loosening of deep-lying problems.

Fourth, the therapist makes the appointment for the first interview with the family in which all the members can take part.

Other Aspects of the First Telephone Contact

The first telephone contact should not be allowed to develop into an "individual" interview with the caller. A therapist on the line with an over-excited, gushing mother who is complaining about the various symptoms of her children should try as soon as possible to interrupt the flow by asking about another member of the family whom she has not yet mentioned, for example, the husband. If the caller is taciturn or speaks anxiously or hesitantly, the therapist should ask precise questions, for example, what the names of the children are, how they are doing at school, about the relationship with the husband (or wife), whether he (or she) is also concerned about the children, whether he (or she) knows about the telephone call, etc.

Family therapy is something relatively new. So, despite the increasing spread of information through television and popular books and articles, one cannot assume that the caller is familiar with the paradigm of family therapy. The therapist must be prepared for the suggestion that the entire family attend the interview to be met with astonishment and be ready to give a persuasive explanation. The way in which this explanation is received may be significant for the planned interview. It can also provide a first indication of resistance. The therapist may be told "my husband won't be able to come" because "he can't take the time off work," that the children have to be in school at that time or that the children will not be able to come because one of the children "shouldn't be told anything about the other child's difficulties or the parents' problems," or because "she copes best with her husband and the children." The therapist must try to weigh the strength of this fear and resistance and assess how far they are shared by the other members of the family. She or he can ignore all the apparent ambivalence and set up an appointment, or suggest that the family think over the situation and call back.

To be persuasive, the therapist must be convinced of the correctness of the paradigm of family therapy as described in the earlier chapters. His or her attitude must convince without being authoritarian. An unbending stance expressed in stern rules such as, "if you don't all come, we can't accept you," only serves to provoke rejection and increase the family's apprehensions. The first interview can all too easily flounder before it has begun. While still upholding the importance of the interview, the therapist should not insist on all members of the family being present and should respect legitimate reasons for some members' absence such as school or working hours. Indeed, it is best if she or he can be flexible in setting up the appointment, for example, by fitting in with the family's working hours.

WHEN SHOULD CHILDREN BE PRESENT?

From the first contact, it is important to decide whether the children should take part in the first interview with the family. It is very often children's symptoms that bring families to us. Does this mean that *all* the other children, including preschool children, toddlers and babies, should be present at the interview? Should adolescents, who are in the process of separating from the parental home, be interviewed individually? Should any child be present at an interview concerned with a marital conflict due to sexual disturbance? What have they to do with the parents' sexual problems? Such justifiable questions can underlie the resistance to the whole family taking part in this first interview. We want, therefore, to discuss these points before going on to specific questions about the conduct of the interview.

Here we must refer back to the circular and dialectical model discussed in the initial chapters of this book: every member of a family influences the behavior of the other members and is in turn influenced by them. This is true for the symptom bearer as much as for a newborn sibling, for the grandmother (if living in the home) as for the father and mother. It must follow from our theory that the children should be present. In other words, we consider it desirable that all members of the family should be present together at the first interview.

The Sacrifices Children Make

As we have shown in the previous chapters, the symptoms of a child often represent sacrifices for the benefit of the parents— whether the child remains bound to the parents at the cost of his own individuality or whether he is delegated to take on, or to live out, personality traits the parents themselves reject, or to fulfill their wishes or expectations. Even in the first interview the various functions of each child for the parents and for each other may become clear.

The following example shows how a family can delegate and exploit even a baby as a means of avoiding conflict. The Müller family came to us because of the school problems of their 10-year-old eldest son. The 8-year-old second son, who also came to the interview did not attract particular attention. The 6-month-old daughter was also present. Initially attention was centered on the very prettily dressed little girl, who seemed to be fully aware of her importance. Having sat on every participant's lap in turn, she began to cry. Finally, in an attempt to quiet her, she was laid on a pink blanket on the floor. The boys played with her, but she started to cry again. Despite the mother's efforts she continued to scream. After 20 minutes of unbroken howling that effectively stopped all discussion, the therapist noticed that every time the child began to quiet down some one tried to attract her attention, teased her, poked her or tickled her, until she began to cry again. The therapist told the family of this observation and added that the child seemed to be helping them all to avoid discussing their mutual problems. In that instant the mother's face broke into a smile. "It's just the same at home," she said thoughtfully. From that moment the baby was left in peace and during the second half of the session, while the parents and her two older brothers had a constructive discussion, she lay on the floor crowing with delight.

Can Children Be Harmed by Taking Part in a General Interview?

This question is often asked and to answer it we must go beyond the considerations of the preceding sections. It expresses a justifiable concern on the part of parents and therapists that children should be kept away from the general interview to prevent their being unnecessarily burdened with the problems of marital dissent. However, the problems are already part of these children's existence. They live as part of the family and consciously or unconsciously are aware of their parents' or siblings' difficulties. Strife is part of their daily lives; so are the arguments they hear at night through closed doors. Precisely because the problems are never discussed in a way that can lead to a truly clarifying solution and reconciliation, they tend to nourish unhealthy fantasies or feelings of unexpressed insecurity. Therefore, the first interview with the whole family offers a good chance of relief for the child. Here at last the long-concealed doubts, anger and differences can be openly discussed and the children's fears that they are the cause of their parents' difficulties can be stilled.

A therapist who feels very anxious that the children will be burdened by the first interview should consider whether this anxiety hides a personal fear of being embarrassed by the children. Perhaps the therapist does not feel secure handling young children, is easily irritated by crying babies, or has difficulties with wild, rejecting adolescents.

The Child as the Therapist's Accomplice

Children often represent the whole family's main resources (cf. Chapters 1 and 2). They can be a crucial help to the therapist in his efforts to establish contact with the family. Younger children, especially, who are relatively untouched by convention and inhibitions can become the therapist's most cooperative accomplices. While the fear- and guilt-laden parents often find it hard to be open about their quarrels and culpability, their little children are often very quick to come to the central problem. For example, a family with two boys of five and six came to us because their younger son had various physical symptoms, was underdeveloped and uncontrollably hyperkinetic. As the parents were complaining about their child's intolerable activity, the child suddenly broke into a pause in the interview with, "But you are always fighting." Indeed, the marital conflict became the central theme of the subsequent therapeutic sessions, and from this point on was dealt with constructively. The child's hyperactivity decreased as the parents communicated better.

Family Secrets and Privacy

The preceding considerations also apply to the therapeutic treatment of family secrets. An important task of the therapist is to destroy the anathematizing power of those secrets that underlie divisions, misunderstandings and conflicts in the family. This is only possible when all those involved are present. Nevertheless, the therapist must not discount legitimate wishes for privacy, for example, when parents want to discuss their sexual problems. It may then be appropriate to send the children to a playroom. Some explanation should be offered, though. Children usually accept that adults may want to discuss adult matters among themselves, just as adults should accept their exclusion from what concerns the children only. Thus, the wish for an individual interview, such as one requested by an adolescent, can be legitimate as long as it will not tend to promote either division or stagnation in the family relationship.

External or Internal Motivation

Although increasing numbers of families approach the institution or the therapist on their own initiative, many are referred by the family doctor, youth agencies, teachers or sometimes by the courts of law. Some of these families concur in the referral, but others come to us against their own will. It is then often very difficult to set up the first appointment, particularly when a family has been referred by the law courts, youth agencies or social services and sees the family interview as a punishment. The caller's misgivings may well be apparent over the telephone, and the therapist must make suitable allowances for this attitude.

The Fee

Not every caller will ask about fees. Those that ask should be given the clearest possible answer. In some cases insurance will cover the treatment, in others religious charities; otherwise, a private agreement is made between the patient (family) and the therapist, all details of which should be settled before the therapy begins.

Problems of Parallel Treatment

If the caller indicates that one or more of the family is already undergoing some form of treatment—for example, group therapy, analysis, or play therapy—the therapist should tell the caller that the other doctor or therapist concerned must agree to the family interview. Close cooperation is recommended. To this end we invite the doctor or social worker who made the referral or who is involved in treating the family to attend the family interview as observer and to take part in the planning of further therapy. In this way misunderstandings, manipulation of the family members, and in particular the danger that one institution or therapist may be played off against the other can be minimized or controlled from the beginning.

A SHORT WAITING TIME

As we shall show in the next chapter, every crisis has therapeutic potential. To exploit this potential, a family should not be asked to wait more than two weeks for the first interview. It is our experience that many conflicts can be quickly resolved by rapid initial intervention or that some procedure can be found to bridge the gap before the beginning of a more extensive therapy. Long waiting lists can be shortened in this way, and treatment has a more rapid and effective beginning.

USE OF EXPERTS

Because the first interview with the family both makes great demands on the experience and empathic facilities of the therapist and also lays the foundation for further work, it should not be left to the inexperienced. (The use of audiovisual aids allows inexperienced participants to be integrated into the observation team.) This frequently implies a new distribution of assignments in counseling centers that have previously worked with individual clients. The tasks of conducting the first interview and collecting anamnestic data should be handled by experts and not by students or beginners.

6

The Phases of the First Interview

IN A FIRST INTERVIEW WITH A FAMILY there are several phases. Following the telephone contact described above, these are:

1) Initial phase: (a) greeting and (b) starting the interview;
2) Middle phase;
3) End phase and leave-taking.

THE INITIAL PHASE: THE GREETING

We generally ask the family to come half an hour to an hour before the actual beginning of the interview. In this time a secretary takes down particulars of each member of the family and may ask them to complete a questionnaire. Occasionally, for research purposes, we may ask them to perform some test. Even in this prelude to the first interview there may be particular phenomena that require special attention.

Who Is Late?

As a rule all the members of the family come to the institute together. However, occasionally one or more may be late, in which case we usually wait for them before beginning the interview. It

66

would be premature to regard one person being late as an expression of intrafamilial tension. However, if individual members are regularly late for subsequent sessions, we discuss this with the family.

When to Begin?

Sometimes the therapist finds only part of the family in the waiting room and it is obvious that one or more members are not going to attend. This may be an expression of ambivalence or concealed sabotage by individual members or all the members of the family and has negative implications for the therapy. The first interview should nevertheless go ahead. The therapist should immediately broach the subject that individual family members are missing and try to find out whether any of those present are either openly or in some surreptious way a party to the absence. Very often it becomes clear that those present have reasons, though often well-concealed ones, for keeping one or more members of the family away from the interview in order to impede effective therapy.

The Mood in the Waiting Room

The therapist should assess and adapt to the mood in which the family comes to him. It may be sad or angry. The family may behave in an apparently cheerful and uninhibited way to play down their agitation and apprehension. Certain members of the family, usually the problem child, may see the visit to the therapist as punishment for malicious or thoughtless behavior. Some parents, too—particularly when they have been sent for treatment against their will—may feel that the whole process is a penalty inflicted on them. Feelings of fear and shame are almost always involved.

Entering the Treatment Room

Important aspects of the parent-child relationship are often already apparent in the way the family enters the treatment room. Some parents warn their children strictly not to run, not to push forward, to let the therapist go first, while others seem not to notice their children and forge straight ahead into the room. The children may appear nervous and fearful or open, inquisitive and disciplined.

The parents show how they discipline or do not discipline their children and in general how they get on with their children. However, if for example it were part of the parents' way of bringing up their children to box them on the ears, this style of relationship might well be modified by the therapist's presence so that the initial observations do not truly reflect the family's daily life at home.

Seating

We recommend that every member of the family be allowed to choose his own seat and that the therapist sit down last. Even the way in which the family seat themselves can reflect coalitions and alienation, closeness and distance within the family, indeed the entire matrix of relationships. Which child wants to sit by which parent? Who sits on whose lap? Who does not want to meet the eyes of the person sitting opposite? Who chooses the greatest possible distance from the others and from the therapist? The technicalities of videotaping can, of course, restrict the scope and applicability of these observations.

Initial Reactions

After introducing her- or himself, the therapist should greet each member of the family and ask each child his or her name. (This first greeting may, of course, happen in the waiting room.) Each participant should be individually addressed so that she or he has the feeling of being personally important and accepted. If one member of the family interrupts these greetings by presenting a specific problem, the therapist should, if possible, insist on getting to know each member of the family before starting on individual difficulties. Through such behavior the therapist sets up a standard establishing that each individual member of the family has a right to acknowledgment and in this way begins to deploy multidirected partiality.

After the greeting and introduction, the therapist shows the family the set-up in the treatment room. It is essential to make it clear why the room is fitted with microphone, tape recorder and video camera. When pointing out the one-way screen, the therapist should say openly that one or more observers are behind it. As we have already said, most families (and therapists) forget the microphone and one-way screen within minutes. When anxieties and queries remain despite the introductory explanation, the observation situation should be explained in detail. In particular, we take younger children who are either fascinated or worried by the mirror, into the observation room, introduce them to the observers, and let them look through the screen into the treatment room. If one or all members of the family do not want to be observed or filmed, we, of course, do not insist.

Questions of Discretion

Audiovisual material may so easily be misused that we cannot overemphasize the importance of discretion. All participants and, of course, the therapeutic team must continually bear in mind that they are bound by the Hippocratic oath. The family must give their written consent to the use of tape or videotape recordings for research or training purposes. Under no circumstances may data obtained by the use of audiovisual aids be used for any purpose other than one that has been approved by the family. Discretion is particularly important where an observer is privately acquainted with one or more of the family. The observer should either withdraw from the team or obtain express permission from the family. Although we do not generally introduce the observers to the family personally, we respect their right to meet them if they wish.

THE INITIAL PHASE: STARTING THE INTERVIEW

The process of greeting, introduction, and making acquaintance does not differ from normal social observances. However, the subsequent part of the interview should be orientated to its therapeutic purpose. This is a new and unusual situation for all participants and there are no ready-made rules for the therapeutic interview. Neither are there clear indications as to how the therapist or the clients should behave. The therapist normally takes the lead at this crucial point by asking the family why they have come. This question may be put in several ways—all of which have advantages and disadvantages—depending on how and to whom the therapist puts his question.

The Therapist Begins

Often, despite the explanatory telephone conversation, the family does not understand why they should all be present. Some members of the family may still think the matter is none of their concern, but has to do only with a parent or a certain child. They may, therefore, seem surprised and perplexed, if not downright uncooperative. As we have already explained, this surprise is legitimate.

The therapist should explain what she or he already knows about the family and its individual members, particularly because the initial telephone contact was with one member only. The therapist should also explain once again why the whole family has been invited to the interview; this explanation usually makes it easier for the family to begin to talk themselves. A good beginning might be: "Mrs. M., you have already explained to me over the telephone what it is all about. But I invited you *all* to come today because I wanted to know what each of you thinks about your family." Or, another possibility, "I wanted you all to come to the interview today so that I could hear what each of you thinks about what is happening in your family." In these or similar ways the therapist can ask each individual member of the family for his opinion. The therapist's explanation should be adapted to the educational level of the family so they can all understand what is meant. Even if the family seems particularly secretive—so that, for example, the children have no idea why they are there—the therapist should still not hesitate to repeat exactly whatever information was received on the telephone.

Opening Questions

The conduct of the interview will be characterized by the way in which the therapist questions the family: how and to whom questions are put, whether to individuals or to the whole family. The therapist could ask the whole family, "What is your problem?" or better "What do you think the difficulty is?" These questions make clear the therapist's concern with problems and disturbances within the family. Usually, the person most affected by the disturbance, often the mother, has expected this question and is the first to anwer.

She then will report how the disturbance began and developed and how things now stand, for example, as regards the "problem child."

The therapist can make questions more personal, by referring to her- or himself: "How can I help you?" However, this restricts the potential answers, because the family members have to think not only about their problems, but also about what the therapist can do. This question may, in fact, relax the atmosphere, although perhaps more than some therapists find congenial.

Instead of referring to problems and disturbances, the therapist could ask: "What do you want to change?" This leads directly to the aim of the therapy, the achievement of change. Where there is a "problem child" the parents must be alerted to the possibility of change. The parents cannot remain entrenched in their view that the child is the cause of all the trouble and they are, therefore, exonerated. When the child's pathological behavior comes into discussion later, the therapist can then always refer back to the possibility of change.

Another possible approach is: "Why have you come to us?" The therapist presents the family with the choice of speaking about disturbances or about the possibility of change. The parents may answer "Because of Peter" or "We want to be able to do something about Peter's bedwetting." As a rule, the more general the therapist's question, the more freedom of expression the family has in explaining the situation.

Questions to Individual Members of the Family

Whether a question such as, "Why have you come to me?" is put to a particular member of the family depends to a great extent on the therapist's personal focus. Some therapists feel a particular bond with children as the victims of their parents. They tend, therefore, to address themselves to the "problem child" whom they consider to have suffered most and to feel misunderstood by its parents. A therapist who gets along better with men than women will tend to approach the father rather than the mother. An older therapist who finds it more difficult to develop an understanding with children might turn to the parents or even the grandparents first if they are present. The presence, of several people of different sexes and ages compels an initial choice. In the further course of the interview, she or he must succeed in developing a multidirected partiality toward each individual of the family.

Questions to an "Outsider"

When the therapist has the impression that a certain member of the family—for example, the father—is not participating or holds himself aloof from the others, she or he can speak to him first, in order to draw him back into the family circle. At the same time the therapist can judge whether and how far the father takes responsibility for the family, the index patient or the family's difficulties.

Questions to the Index Patient

If the index patient is a child, it is often not desirable immediately to begin a direct discussion of his or her disturbance, as this can exacerbate any possible feelings of being trapped or the victim of or cause of a punitive exercise. It is often better for this child to be the last to speak. If such a child seems to feel particularly anxious or disturbed or wanting to withdraw fearfully into her- or himself without answering, the therapist should next explain his or her own view of the situation. This might be as follows: "I can guess how it feels if you think you're being made to talk. I don't think I'd want to talk if I were really bothered." This facilitates an approach to the child whose behavior is represented neither as malicious nor as insane, but rather as simply fearful and needing sympathy.

Questions to the Whole Family

If the therapist puts a general question, such as "Perhaps someone could tell me what your problem is?" without looking at anyone—i.e., gazing at the floor or the ceiling—the family "spokesman" will feel called on to answer. The parents often disagree about this role or try to push the responsibility onto each other so that the other will speak first. This reveals the family hierarchy, which the therapist must notice and respect. However, it is not always the first to answer who has the actual authority in the family. The parents are often rendered powerless by their child's symptoms and have lost their hold. In this way even the therapist's first question can lay the basis for (re)affirmation and constructive development of the parental authority.

In certain cases it may be superfluous for the therapist to inquire why the family have come because she or he is immediately confronted with the family drama. It is then equally meaningless to ask about the index patient.

Avoiding Trivialities

There are some families who from the first moments of the interview immerse the therapist in trivial chat. There is a danger that both the therapist and the family may confuse this exchange of trivialities with an interview directed to a therapeutic goal. It is often impossible to distinguish whether the session is therapeutic or merely sociable. In such cases if the therapist neglects to ask the family exactly why they have come to him, they are left with the impression that their problem is too serious, monstrously indescribable or too burdensome for the therapist.

Acknowledging the Family

For most families their appearance at the first session is in itself already a considerable achievement that necessitated coming to terms with feelings of fear and guilt. This should be acknowledged, quite apart from the fact that the family is itself asking for our help. We do not, therefore, take the family's presence for granted, but say unequivocally that we recognize the effort the members of the family have made to be open and to cope with their guilt feelings and anxieties. We say, for example: "It is really amazing and you should be congratulated for having all managed to be here, despite all these difficulties." Or, "It certainly can't have been easy for you to come to us when you have all these difficulties." Or we express our own feelings by saying "We're really glad that you've all managed to come today, so that we have the chance to talk about how everything has happened and where we should go from here." This expresses our wish to help the family and also that we depend on their cooperation.

If the family is irritated by having had to wait unexpectedly long or having been involved with some form of test, we must be understanding and, at the same time, expressly acknowledge their actually having come at all. For example: The M. family had unexpectedly to wait an hour for their session and had complained bitterly to the secretary. Mrs. M. had been particularly vociferous. The therapist began the interview by saying: "I'm afraid you've all had a very long and provoking wait—as if it hadn't already been difficult enough for you all to come here today." Mrs. M. met this with a smile, her irritation evaporated; feeling herself understood, she no longer needed to stay on the defensive. The therapist had recognized Mrs. M.'s quite justifiable anger and established a bond with the family by mentioning the difficulties the members had had to overcome to be punctual for the interview.

Facilitating the Discussion

Fear and distrust of the situation may block the family's ability to talk freely or may result in a flood of inconclusive words. The therapist can counteract both tendencies by speaking calmly and decisively. She or he can make things easier by cracking a joke at the beginning of the session or perhaps introducing her or himself with some diffidence, thus expressing some personal feeling. When someone has special difficulty in talking, the therapist should be encouraging, but not overly pressing.

Everyone Should Have the Chance to Speak

The therapist's ability to ensure that each member of the family gets the chance to speak, if possible even in the first interview, is an important proof of his multidirected partiality. After asking why the family has come, the therapist can, for example, turn directly to each in turn and ask for his or her opinion. If one parent always wants to butt in or interrupts the others, the therapist should in a calm and friendly way insist that each should have a chance to speak and should be allowed to finish what she or he has to say.

The Therapist as Leader

Family therapy demands the therapist's active participation (cf. Chapter 3). This has nothing to do with how much or how loudly she or he talks. Some family therapists talk a lot, others talk very little but listen very carefully. Whatever their style, all are both able and ready to shoulder the main responsibility for the family interview. In other words, the family members are responsible for what they say, the therapist for how it is said. This can mean that the therapist interrupts the garrulous and encourages the taciturn to take part in the discussion, reassures the fearful and holds back the overly self-assertive, supports the weak and keeps the boaster within bounds.

Inviting the Children to Play or Draw

During the first minutes of the interview, the children usually sit quiet, alert, and well-behaved in their places. But after a few minutes the younger ones frequently neither can nor will sit still any longer. Some get up and independently begin to occupy themselves in some other way without being asked, others fidget about without daring to leave their seats. Under these conditions the therapist should wait a few minutes to give the parents the chance to react to their children. He should then show the play-things provided and specifically allow the children to move about and play. By making his position clear in this way, he puts the participants at their ease, especially the parents, who may worry that their children will not behave themselves in these strange surroundings, or that they may be too loud or start quarrelling.

Children who are actively playing are not necessarily outside the discussion. On the contrary, we often find that even little children who seem to be playing absorbed and self-forgetful in a corner may actually be taking an active part in the session. One small boy, for example, played with a toy ambulance and formed a man on a stretcher out of playdough while the adults were discussing the possibility of the father being hospitalized. Children's noise level seems to be an accurate barometer of the significance of the session: the more important the theme the adults are discussing the quieter, tenser and more attentive the children become.

Children between 6 and 12 Like Drawing

During the first ten minutes of the general interview we often ask the children to draw their family as a family of animals. At the end of the session we all look at the picture together. We avoid deep psychological interpretation, but almost every time we find that the parents are deeply astonished or even shocked by the spontaneity and sometimes startling frankness with which the children are able to represent complex roles and feelings.

For example, during the first interview with a family with sons 10 and 12 years old, the younger drew himself as an all-devouring monster. This led the mother to consider how much this boy suffered in the role he had been given as hyperkinetic underachiever.

Observation in the First Minutes

It is not only from what the family say, but also from what they do that the therapist gains important information. Who replies to the generally addressed question as to why they have come? Is it the mother who speaks first at length and uninterruptedly while the father and children sit staring unconcernedly in front of them? Do the parents argue about who should speak first? Is the mother's tone of voice whining and the father's harsh? Is the parents' speech intellectual? Does it reflect a particular class? Is it slovenly and colloquial? Do they tell the children to be quiet or surreptitiously encourage noisiness? Do the children call the parents' attention to their difficulties? What is the expression on the face of the index patient while the father complains about him? Do mother and son suddenly both smile at some particular point without anything being said? Does the mother or a certain child suddenly begin to cry? In the latter cases the therapist should interrupt the interview and turn to the crying or smiling member of the family. Although he must be careful to steer clear of premature interpretation of nonverbal behavior, he should at this point inquire how the family themselves see such behavior.

Differences of Opinion

It will already be apparent at the beginning of the session whether the family agree why they have come or have different views of the problem. An adolescent, for example, probably sees his problems in school as far less important than his problems in getting on with his peers. His parents, however, are probably far more concerned with school performance and regard his inhibitions about the other sex with a concealed satisfaction that their son is still a firmly attached member of the family clan.

The Relational Gestalt

The concealed relational conflict within the family can be seen as a "gestalt" (cf. Chapter 3). From the start of the first interview, an experienced therapist will try to gain an impression of this gestalt in the form of a hypothesis about the function fulfilled by the symptom(s) within the entire relational configuration. However, it is not yet the proper time at which to test this hypothesis by an interpretation of the behavior of individual family members. In the first interview, the therapist's role is confined to accepting what the family says and asking appropriately aimed questions. The answer to questions seeking advice could be: "I cannot say yet; I would like to know you all better first."

Summary

The first phase of the first interview with the family includes the greeting, the start of the interview, the introduction to the new surroundings, and the invitation to speak. It is centered on the question of why the family have come. The therapist observes normal courtesy, introduces her or himself, helps the family get to know the therapy room, pays due acknowledgment to the fact that they have come, and tries to adapt to the family's speech and style so that the family members feel at ease and are ready to entrust her or him with the leadership of the interview. The main point of this initial phase is to understand why the family come to us.

THE MIDDLE PHASE: INTERACTION IN THE FAMILY

It is true of this phase even more than of the initial phase that rigid adherence to a particular scheme can obscure the complexity of the situation. Nevertheless it seems desirable to set up some simplified guidelines for the therapist who is new to this work. These guidelines are derived from the five main perspectives described in Chapter 2. They will help the therapist to find an orientation within the complex transactional process.

Recognizing Related Individuation

The concept of related individuation leads us to ask: How far is each member able to demarcate his own feelings, expectations, needs, ideas, etc., from those of the rest of the family? Does she or he say *I* did, *I* expect, *I* feel this or that, or instead avoid responsibilities by frequent use of generalities introduced by "one," "you," or "we." Further, if the emotional "temperature" or level of tension in the family rises, do the members appear to lose individuation, sinking into an "undifferentiated family ego mass"?

The example we give here illustrates not only aspects of related individuation, but also the transactional modes of binding and expelling.

Eleven-year-old Peter was brought to us by his parents because of massive reading and writing problems. He has a brother two years younger who appears to have no such problems and an illegitimate half-sister 10 years older who had grown up with Peter's mother's parents. Peter represents the mother's attempt to "make good" her earlier "mistake" (her child born out of wedlock). Still today a deep relationship binds him to his mother, who not only spends up to four hours a day helping with schoolwork, spreads his bread, ties his shoelaces, washes him and, until recently, helped him clean himself after he had been to the toilet. Peter has not yet succeeded in having any personal wishes or demarcating them from his mother's expectations. This was made clear in the interview: Peter is unable to answer any question on his own; the mother immediately butts in and speaks for him. In the first interview, the therapist does not yet interpret this behavior but encourages the boy to answer for himself.

Recognizing Binding and Expulsion

The example described above shows how hard the strong emotional proximity makes it for mother and son to achieve self-demarcation. This relationship also reflects a disturbance of transactional modes, a massive binding at the Id level. The mother indulges the son to a massive degree, she removes every difficulty in his path, thereby keeping him in a state of symbiotic, childish dependence. The therapist can initiate the first steps towards "unbinding" and individuation by carefully showing how this behavior fulfills a mutual need, by comparing the parents' attitudes with those of the child and emphasizing differences, and by counteracting the mother's mystification of the child (cf. Chapter 1).

To help recognize other disturbances of transactional modes, the therapist can ask: To what extent do the members of the family depend on each other emotionally? How important are they for each other and for the entire system? Is there an intergenerational collusion to hinder age-appropriate separation between children and parents? Are the hate and frustration shown by both sides primarily an expression of extensive emotional binding, or do they indicate alienation, neglect or even possibly expulsion?

Recognizing Delegation

By the concept of delegation we mean the assignment of missions that give significance and direction and are based on strong, though often invisible loyalties (Chapter 2). Excessive demands and mission and loyalty conflicts reveal derailments of the delegation process. The therapist may begin to assess the extent of such derailments in the first interview by asking questions such as: Are the parental expectations consonant with the child's talents and age-appropriate needs? Is one child expected to fill the place of a tragically deceased but unmourned sibling (cf. Chapter 7)? Does the observed behavior of individual family members indicate central mission or loyalty conflicts? Do the children seem to be primarily bound or expelled delegates? (Cf. Stierlin 1972b, 1974, 1975a, 1976b, 1978a on the various phenomena of delegation.)

Studying the Multigenerational Perspective

Many parents quite spontaneously compare their children's situation with their own childhood. This provides the therapist with an easy means of finding out more about the grandparental families. When both parents avoid talking about their own families the therapist can put pointed questions. In the example above, the therapist asked the mother whether her parents had helped her with schoolwork. Alternatively, the therapist can take up some parental side remark such as when a father complaining about his adolescent son's disobedience says, "Things were different when I was young." The therapist can respond: "What was it like when you were your son's age?" By such pointed questions the therapist makes it possible for the family to begin to understand how legacies and obligations act over generations. We often find that questions about the parents' childhood lead to the grandparents appearing at further sessions.

Defining the State of Mutuality

To judge whether the family is in a state of malign stalemate or clinch (as described in Chapter 2), the interviewer should consider how far the family is still willing to establish a dialogue. That is, are they willing and able to maintain an articulate and coherent discussion of the problems revealed? How far are they caught up in a "game" or power struggle no one can win? To what degree is the whole system in stagnation? The therapist frequently gets an accurate feeling of such a family clinch. Has the therapist become drawn into the system and so deprived of the role of participant observer? To what extent does this render the therapist powerless, and require the exertion of his or her "stronger reality" against the family's engulfing power? Communication with the observation team behind the one-way screen can help in answering the last questions.

Team Discussion

Indications for and possibilities and disadvantages of further treatment emerge in discussion with the therapeutic team (see Chapter 3). At this point practical questions come first: Does the institution have the capacity required? Is it possible to accept another family for treatment in the immediate future? Which therapist would be involved? Would it be possible to refer the family to another colleague? What possibilities are there for supervision? As regards the family we ask ourselves: What are its strengths and assets? How strongly is the family motivated for a more extensive therapy? How good is the prognosis? Independently of these questions, the therapeutic team can—provided the model "healing through systemic change" applies—work out a paradoxical task which then becomes, as it were, the family's homework (Chapter 4).

Paradoxical Tasks and Interventions

Paradoxical tasks and interventions have been developed and described by well-known family therapists such as Mara Selvini-Palazzoli (1978a), Paul Watzlawick, et al. (1967, 1974), and Jay Haley (1976). In our view, they can be a potent therapeutic instrument. However, they require special skill and a firm grasp of circular causality in family relations (cf. Chapter 2). Also, they are not without risk. For example, the use of a therapeutic paradox involves the risk that should a paradoxical prescription not "succeed" the possibilities for later—paradoxical or nonparadoxical—intervention are drastically reduced. It is not within the scope of this book to do justice to this problem and we can only refer the reader to the bibliography which includes a selection from the extensive literature on the subject.

THE FINAL PHASE: LEAVE TAKING

At the end of the first interview the therapist should consider whether she or he has succeeded in reaching the goals described in Chapter 4, namely:

1) To formulate a hypothesis about the family's relational dynamics and to assess their motivational situation;

2) To motivate the family for therapy;

3) To arrive at a family therapeutic contract;

4) To set the direction for further therapy.

When further preparation for therapy is determined by the basic models of "healing through encounter" or "healing through active restructuring," the therapist should next summarize the information obtained during the interview. In doing this, emphasis should be on the positive forces in the family, including positive forces concealed by what is apparently negative. It is essential that the therapist make it clear to the family that the symptoms of the index patient are the result and expression of their common problem. The necessity for further interviews almost inevitably is apparent in the mutually shared definition of the remaining problem. For example it might be evident that certain questions remain unclear or that important members of the family are absent who should also become involved. In view of the family's revealed difficulties, there is usually general agreement that there should be further therapy for the whole family.

As we have seen, the therapist can invite the grandparents to the following sessions and in this way open up a further relational field. It would usually be better to wait, however, until all those concerned have overcome their surprise, until there is more willingness for cooperation, and until the emotional relationship to the therapist has strengthened.

After all the considerations outlined above, if the therapist suggests that there should be a family therapy, it is necessary to decide whether a time limit for the therapy should be set.

A time limit is particularly advisable when there is a clearly defined familial problem—for example, with a child's achievement in school—or when a family is particularly anxious about the close relationship with the therapist or the prospect of an endless series of family quarrels and conflicts. However, the therapist should not lose sight of the possibility that in such cases the therapy could be prolonged as these anxieties prove groundless, and the clients want the therapy extended. Finally, together with the family the therapist must redefine and reinforce the therapeutic goals. There must be a consensus on the aims and scope of the prospective joint effort.

This consensus is the foundation of the therapeutic contract. It requires the members of the family to agree to abide by the "rules of the game" established in the first interview. This implies they accept external working parameters, namely, that they should appear at whatever times and places and in whatever groups (i.e., with the whole family or in subgroups) are agreed upon with the therapist, that they should let the therapist know in good time when they are unable to attend, that the therapist should receive a certain fee, etc.

EVALUATING THE FIRST INTERVIEW

After the family has departed, the therapist and observers should discuss details of the interview, such as family dynamics, therapeutic interventions and the observers' impressions. The data and constructive criticisms offered by the observers can help the therapist to understand better his or her own reactions to, or difficulties with, individual members and the whole family as these arise from personal attitudes and experiences. From the contributions of all participants a hypothesis concerning the relational dynamics of the family is formulated and the necessary therapeutic steps made clearer. At the same time important gaps in the information may become apparent. From this general discussion a summarizing report is written, which should be clear, precise and short, but also comprehensive and vivid enough to provide another therapist, who does not know the family but might take over the therapy, with the most exact picture possible. We give below an outline for the preparation of such a report on the first interview. It is not intended to be comprehensive and may be added to as necessary.

REPORT OF THE FIRST INTERVIEW

Referral

Who referred the family and why?

Description of the Family

How is the family made up? (Name, age, job, school class, etc. of each member)

Who came to the first interview?
How did the individual members of the family appear and behave?

The Course of the Interview

Initial Phase

Why has the family come to the interview?
What problems were discussed?
Is there a general family problem?
How did the difficulties begin? How were they solved? How great were they? What course did the interview take at this point?
What outside help has the family enlisted?
What attempts to solve their problems have failed? Why?

Middle Phase:

How is the family organized as a system?

Transactions observed in the interview:

1. Related Individuation
   Which forms of individuation predominates: over- or underindividuation or related individuation?
   What are the boundaries between generations?
   To what degree do the marital couple appear to be symbiotically fused?

2. Binding and Expelling

   Which of these transactional modes is observable?

3. Delegation

   What missions have the parents given their children?
   What indications are there of excessive demands, or mission and loyalty conflicts?

4. Multigenerational Perspective

   What is the parents' family background?
   What relational legacies have they inherited?
   What family myths are there?

5. Ascertaining the State of Mutuality

Is there a state of malign stalemate?

Are all the participants in a state of deadlock?

Are they ready to establish a dialogue?

How fast is the therapist drawn into a family clinch and rendered powerless? How forcefully must the therapist maintain a stronger reality against the family's engulfing power?

Final Phase:

Therapeutic plans:

What are the family's strengths and weaknesses?

What motivation towards, or resistance to, change does the whole family show?

What are the family's resources?

What are the family's expectations of the therapist?

What short- or long-term goals can be set up?

What further diagnostic measures, for example, IQ tests, EEG, etc., seem indicated? Why?

What other institutions should be contacted (for example, school, youth agency, etc.)?

Disposition

What recommendations were made? What paradoxical tasks were set? What agreements were reached?

To what persons or institutions have reports been made?

THE FIRST INTERVIEW WITH THE SCHULZ FAMILY

The following is an example of an interview report.

Referral

The Schulz family was referred to us by the city's educational advisory center. A course of play therapy and individual interviews with the mother had failed to produce any improvement in the symptoms shown by the index patient (11-year-old Peter).

The educational advisory center asked us:

1. Was there a family problem?
2. If so, was family therapy indicated?

3. What was the prognosis?
4. Where could family therapy be carried out?

Description of the Family

The Schulz family consists of:

Mr. S. 37 years old, salesman
Mrs. S. 35 years old, housewife, formerly a bookkeeper
Peter S., 11 years old, 4th grade in elementary school
Hans S., 9 years old, 3rd grade in elementary school
Ute, 16 years old, training as a salesgirl
An illegitimate daughter of Mrs. S. living with her mother's parents in the same neighborhood.

The parents and the two sons come to the first interview. All are in their Sunday best. Mr. S., underaverage height, strongly built, red-cheeked, with neat blond hair, has an impressively deep voice and rugged appearance. Mrs. S. with her fashionable high hairdo, elegant clothes, pale face, somewhat tired, sad eyes, and downturned mouth seems more emotional and prematurely aged.

Peter's soft face resembles his mother's, although in his powerful build and hair color he is like his father. He watches his mother very carefully during the interview and reacts nervously. The twitching of his eyes and the corners of his mouth is almost like a tic.

Hans has the normal physical development for his age and a cheerful face. Although brunette and fine-limbed like his mother, he has his father's vigorous appearance. In the waiting room he carries on a lively discussion with his father about a magazine, while Peter and his mother sit quietly, tense with anxiety, side-by-side on their chairs.

The Course of the Interview

Initial Phase. The question about why they have come for an interview, which is addressed to the family as a whole, produces general hesitation and is finally answered by Mrs. S. It concerns Peter's difficulties. For years she has been practicing with him daily up to four hours so that at home he can write a perfect dictation. The next day at school, however, he breaks down completely producing an average of 50 or 60 mistakes.* The school has diagnosed dyslexia. Peter has already repeated one year of school and is now expected to repeat another. She cannot understand what is happening and is at the end of her tether.

Peter's difficulties began at the end of the second school year when there was a change of teachers. He did not like the new teacher. Mrs. S. can understand why—she also did not like her. He now has a very nice man, who would perhaps like to try and pull him through, but *she*, Mrs. S., cannot go on. She gets so upset about the marks it ruins her whole day, spoils her digestion, and she cannot even sleep at night. Mrs. S. is now in tears; Peter gazes sheepishly at the floor, Mr. S. appears impassive and unconcerned; and Hans is amusing himself with a mirror.

In reply to our questions, it emerges that Mr. S. is not able to give Peter much attention because his work has, for the last two years, involved travelling, so he is usually at home only on weekends. He does not then want to scold his sons about their misdemeanors in the previous week. He prefers to go hunting and enjoys taking the two boys with him. However, Hans is more interested in wild-life than Peter, who is often too frightened. He cannot explain Peter's learning problems. After all, they have tried everything. The mother has given intensive help with the homework and there has even been play therapy. He thinks that Peter will grow out of it. According to him, his wife takes everything too seriously, gets upset too easily, and is always near the end of her tether.

Middle Phase. As, in a sad and tearful voice, Mrs. S. speaks about her troubles, her guilt feelings and her feelings of anger towards her husband, Peter becomes clearly disturbed. He relaxes as his mother describes how pleased she is when he occasionally achieves a slightly better grade. Throughout the interview he is unable to answer a single question without first glancing at his mother, as if for permission to speak. Most often Mrs. S. speaks for him. It is clear that mother and son exist in an almost symbiotic unity. Mr. S. and Hans

---

* The German school system is different from the usual American and English system in that classes are limited to morning hours and afternoons reserved for homework. Often such homework requires the parents' active assistance and supervision.

remain uninvolved outsiders, whose only bonds even with each other seem to be their shared hobbies.

Generational boundaries between the mother and Peter seem to have vanished. Peter apparently has to fulfill the greater part of Mrs. S.'s emotional needs, because she feels abandoned by her husband. During the week he sleeps in his father's bed and allows himself to be indulged like an infant, thereby confirming his mother's feeling of being a "good mother."

The family clinch is indicated by the covert accusation that Mr. S. does not pay enough attention to Mrs. S. as a woman as well as mother of their children. The parents are now almost incapable of establishing a dialogue about their mutual needs and complaints.

The parents do not yet leave the boys alone in the house for fear of some catastrophe. In fact, the children do not seem to have reached an appropriate level of self-reliance for their ages. The parents' expectations for their children are over-ambitious: Peter is supposed to become an engineer—his father's former dream—while Hans is "made to be a scientist."

Mr. S.'s high expectations can be explained from his own scholastic and career disappointment. He describes how, when his father died when he was five years old, he had to support his mother, to care for two younger sisters and to act as father to them. For family financial reasons he had to leave school early and get a job. He was not as successful as his father, who had been a senior high school teacher, and he had, therefore, to bear his mother's reproaches on the subject. Nevertheless, he is still very attached to his mother.

Mrs. S. came from a solid family of craftsmen. An only child, she was strictly brought up, always had good marks in school, was overprotected as a young girl and was then involved in massive conflict with her parents when, at eighteen, she became pregnant by a young artist who abandoned her shortly afterwards. The father would have turned her out of the house, but the mother had kept her daughter at home and herself brought up the child. This girl still lived with the grandmother, and the mother cannot even now lay claim to her. The grandparents have accepted the present husband and are almost warmer towards him than towards their daughter. She was still intensely bound to her parents, visiting them nearly every day and also frequently telephoning her mother. Finally, the mother has always taken the daughter's part.

Final Phase. We formulated the following summary of the general family problem. At the same time, we thereby answered the question from the educational advisory center.

Peter's reading and writing problems date from the time when Mr. S. began to work as a traveling salesman and, therefore, had to spend longer periods of time away from home. Her loneliness and the increased burden of responsibility for the children's education bound Mrs. S. more strongly to her own family (hence the daily visits). At the same time, her anxiety for her elder son increased; his ever more dependent behavior and massive sensibility provoked increasing concern. (Up to four hours daily were spent together on school work.) This relationship still seems to be characterized by strong feelings of obligation and guilt. Both for his mother and for her parents the boy has special significance: he is her attempt to "make good" her "mistake" (the birth of the illegitimate daughter representing her breakaway from parental conventions), but this seems actually to have made a true separation from the parents and subsequent satisfactory bond with the husband even harder.

Family therapy seems indicated. The following therapeutic goals must be paramount:

1) Work on the separation and guilt problematic in the relationship of Mrs. S. with her parents (if possible with their participation);

2) Work on the marital relationship, in particular with redefinition of mutual needs and expectations (possibly also with interviews with the marital couple alone);

3) Integrated with (2), work on the possible redistribution of responsibility in the family, above all including the stronger involvement of Mr. S. in the children's upbringing;

4) Early contact should be made with Peter's school to explore possibilities for having the homework supervised outside the family.

The members of the family seem to be strongly bound to one another. The symbiotic, disturbed relationship between Peter and his mother is the result and expression of this binding. Even within this binding, positive forces—responsiveness and readiness for self-sacrifice—can be recognized, which are valuable for therapy and allow a positive prognosis. Another positive prognostic indication is the obvious willingness on the part of the members of the family, including the husband and the two boys, to risk confrontation and to react constructively to the therapist's interventions.

Disposition

a) It was agreed that there should be a family therapy lasting six months, with weekly sessions, which will begin in four weeks.

b) It was promised and generally accepted that the parents of Mrs. S. and her daughter Ute should attend the latter part of the therapy.

c) With the parents' agreement the therapist would make contact with the school as soon as possible.

7

Problem Families

SO FAR WE HAVE DISCUSSED general aspects of the first interview with the family without dealing directly with specific problem families. Some family constellations are especially typical and frequent. These, to the extent that they are relevant to the first interview, form the subject of this chapter.

FAMILIES THAT ARE SEPARATING

Families that are breaking down or with parents considering separating present a special problem. It can be very helpful for a family in this situation to come to a family session.

The first interview is often also the family's last as the basic conditions and motivation for further meetings are lacking. These families often come not of their own volition, but because they have been advised or compelled to do so by courts of law or some other social institution. Frequently the parents communicate only through their lawyers.

At such an interview the therapist or counselor should consider the following questions: Does any significant negative, positive or ambivalent bond remain between the parents? If so, in what way are they bound up with each other? How far does even a hate bond reflect positive forces with therapeutic potential that could be exploited for the benefit of all participants? Is the litigation and communication through lawyers the continuation of a hate-loaded relationship with the partner? Is it, in fact, the result and expression of deeper invisible loyalties to parents? (cf. Chapter 2.) Does such a vertical loyalty bond require that the marriage partner be degraded and destroyed?

Further: How far do the parents recruit the children as allies? How far does each delegate the children to combat and destroy the other partner, thus imposing insoluble missions and loyalty conflicts? Are certain children, because their existence inhibits the parents' new relationships or abilities to start a new family, threatened with neglect and expulsion? Are they, thereby, fated to become inadequate, insignificant human "surplus"?

To be able to answer such questions and to set up guidelines for therapeutic practice, the therapist must have a great capacity for multipartiality. Above all, she or he must take into account the positions and rights of those who cannot (or cannot yet) speak for themselves and whose future is most at stake: the children, whether they are now bound, expelled or delegated in some overdemanding way. In our view the children's interests are still too often neglected in most discussion of separation and divorce.

At the same time the therapist should make a strong bid to mobilize the children's resources—their sensitivity, their loyalty and their willingness for action—to help the parents to be better parents, even when they have decided on separation. It is in the most fundamental interests of the children to help the parents in this way: they experience a feeling of having grown up and of having shown integrity and moral strength.

On the other hand, these parents will, by and large, be better parents to the extent that the separation from the partner—if it is unavoidable—leads to maturer forms of related individuation and a greater capacity for understanding and willingness for reconciliation. This willingness for reconciliation creates the necessary basis from which, despite—or maybe because of—their separation, the parents can work together for their children. In this sense we can refer to a "constructive separation" of partners, perhaps through "divorce therapy." The reverse is also true: Parental activity and cooperation are not only for the good of the children, but also beneficial the parents. Their chances of being loved and respected by the children are increased and their personal integrity and freedom from guilt are strengthened.

ACUTE VERSUS CHRONIC PROBLEMS

In the first interview acute and chronic problems provide different grounds for decisions about interventions and preparations for further therapy. It is of lesser importance whether the problems are labeled as psychiatric or medical. Theodore Lidz et al. (1965), in their exemplary classical investigations of families with schizophrenic members, demonstrated the systemic aspect of chronic psychosis. It is almost possible to refer to an "institutionalization of irrationality" in these families. The chronic psychotic symptoms or behavior patterns of the index patient are interlocked at every conceivable level with the needs, expectations and defensive attitudes of the rest of the family. Many neurotics are similarly placed. So, for example, the obsessive, compulsive symptoms and structures of an index patient may be both matched and reinforced by the members of his family. Where an index patient shows a chronic psychosomatic disorder, we can be sure that an unbalanced psychophysiological development and inhibited individuation are not confined to her or him alone.

Chronic symptoms and difficulties will have an important function for the members of the patient's relational system. Rheumatic arthritis in a young woman that restricts her sexual life can, for example, not only have the function of legitimizing and "cementing" her frigidity, but may also serve to "protect" her husband from the burdens and fear associated with his own impotence. Further, her arthritic condition may allow her to fulfill her mission as delegate of an oversolicitous mother and so remain within her mother's sphere of influence. She gives her mother's life point and purpose —the care of a chronically sick daughter—and at the same time she is freed from breakaway guilt.

This has many consequences for the interviewer at the first session. While guarding against premature action in the precarious homeostasis of such relational systems, the therapist must be able to see and therapeutically exploit for the benefit of all members the growth-promoting possibilities inherent in every crisis. It is important to identify and pay special attention to tendencies for improvement and healing that may be present even though the members of the family are themselves able to see only sickness, disorder, relapse or difficulty. Also, the therapist must sometimes precipitate a real crisis in order to help effectively the symptom bearer and the family.

Whenever a family comes to us on its own initiative, we can assume that some crisis in the system is in progress and that homeostatic (or morphostatic) tendencies are in conflict with (morphogenetic) tendencies toward change. The more acute the crisis, the stronger grounds the therapist has for hoping that it is moving to a solution and the initiation of a positive mutuality (Stierlin 1971, cf. Chapter 2). It is often the dynamic of separation and reconciliation in adolescence that causes the crisis to become acute (Stierlin 1974). It is crucially important that the therapist be able empathically to understand this crisis and adequately intervene during the first interview. In the following sections we discuss various problem families in which crises can arise that demand rapid therapeutic intervention.

FAMILIES WITH PSYCHOTIC MEMBERS

A family with one or more members suffering from a psychotic disturbance presents the therapist with a special challenge. This is especially true of a schizophrenic disturbance. In such cases typical problems arise in reaching consensus and agreeing on a therapeutic contract since clear unequivocal communication and the establishment of a common focus of attention are necessary. Over the last decades family research has shown (in particular, Wynne et al., 1977) that many families with schizophrenic members are neither able nor willing to communicate in this way. On the contrary, in many, if not all, such families a style of communication has developed over the years that confuses any outsider and causes even the therapist to feel that she or he is sinking in quicksand. This may be called the schizophrenic or schizophrenogenic style of relationship and communication. The members of the family "talk past" each other, they seem even to "talk each other crazy" by, in a subtle way, disqualifying what has just been said. In Luc Kaufmann's words (1975a), they give each other "false receipts," insidiously changing the subject, and answering each other on different wavelengths.

The characteristics of such schizophrenic or schizophrenogenic family communication and systems have a diverse terminology. Wynne and Singer (1963) speak of "collective cognitive chaos," Lidz et al. (1965) of "distorted or absent age and gender boundaries," Bowen (1960) of the "undifferentiated family ego mass," Laing (1965) of "mystification," Reiss (1971) of "consensus sensitivity," and Stierlin (1972a) of "cognitive binding." Although communication disturbances of this kind hinder the setting up of a therapeutic contract, it is especially for these families that family therapy seems indicated. It is the task of the first interviewer to lay the basic foundation for the contractual and working bond; that is, to create the conditions under which definite structures, precise expectations and firm orientation points can be set up.

In this task, the therapist may assume that these so-called communication and relational disturbances reflect and maintain deeply-lying interpersonal and intrapsychic conflicts. The family therapeutic concept we have outlined helps us to interpret these conflicts, which are deeply rooted in the family history, and also to distinguish similarities to and differences from other conflict structures. Many schizophrenic index patients are bound (triangulated) delegates, who are typically subject to over-demands and so forced into an unbalanced psychological development. They are, so to speak, "specialists in symbiotic survival." They often have the unfulfillable mission to act as go-between for their profoundly strife-ridden parents and, by presenting problems of their own, to divert their parents from their explosive difficulties.

Further, they must often corroborate their parents' self-estimations and self-justification by acting as "containers" for the parental weaknesses and "craziness" that the parents themselves deny (Stierlin 1974). Or, they must in some particularly oppressive way live out the existence of a tragically deceased, but unmourned sibling. These mission and loyalty conflicts cannot be discussed and account rendered while the family play the game of disqualifications and mystification that destroy the sense and meaning of their behavior and cement the state of malign clinch.

From the first interview on, the therapist must, in our opinion, make clear an unwillingness to join this game, even if she or he then, within specific limits, appears to be participating in the communication and relational system. This stance must be combined with a hopeful, active engagement (such as we described in Chapter 3) as an element of the requisite empathic behavior. In this way the therapist mitigates the family's resignation and foreboding that the "illness" must follow a severe, genetically determined course— a mistaken view that has often been fostered by doctors and therapists working according to organic models and that is supported by popular opinion.

The therapist should from the start plan realistically and take fully into account the results of long periods of institutionalization, inappropriate treatment and possible loyalty bonds to doctors or institutions involved in previous or parallel treatment. Practical considerations alone prevent premature dissolution of these bonds, as the index patient is frequently under medication and may have to return to the hospital. The first interviewer must therefore find out what kinds of treatment have been tried or begun, what the expectations of family therapy are, and what relationships there are to doctors or the members of other supportive professions or institutions. Only through active cooperative work with any other therapist or institution involved in the family's referral, in setting their expectations, or in any further treatment has family therapy real hope of success.

If further family therapy is indicated and agreed on, it often makes sense to apply the basic model of "healing through systemic change" and close the first session with a paradoxical prescription that embraces the entire system. According to Selvini-Palazzoli et al. (1978a), it is often desirable to introduce the family therapy in a paradoxical fashion—i.e. to plan therapy without referring to it directly as therapy. To many members of such families the term "therapy" implies that a patient status is being imposed on them, against which they must erect a concealed or open defense. Hence the strategy in the first interview would be to question the family's ability to endure the strains of the therapy but to invite them notwithstanding to a further session in which the feasibility of family therapy can be discussed.

This procedure is an exception to the rule outlined in Chapter 4, since it may not be possible to draw up any meaningful contract by the end of the first interview. However, a decision must be reached in the first interview on whether to use the model "healing through encounter" or "healing through active restructuring." It may also be better to work with some subsystem, perhaps the index patient, rather than with the whole family (see Stierlin 1976a). Also, with families with psychotic members, the relationship with the grandparental generation seems from the start to be particularly important.

Families with Delinquent Adolescents

Many families do not come to us of their own accord, but because they have been sent by law courts, welfare departments, teachers, etc. The family therapist is then seen not as somebody who can help and with whom one can come to an agreement, but as the extended arm of the referring institution. These families, and in particular the parents, are in the greatest difficulties. The delinquent adolescent is drastic proof of their failure as parents capable of maintaining values and boundaries. The delinquency exposes them, publicizes their shame, and quite rightly fills them with misgivings about the future. At the same time, such an adolescent reveals his or her parents' real or apparent powerlessness.

With such families the therapist must, from the very first contact, strive to relieve the parents of their guilt and to increase their efficiency as parents. Both aims—relief of guilt and increase of efficiency—are at risk if the therapist tactlessly and clumsily pushes into the foreground as a strong substitute parent, thereby devaluing the parents in their own eyes and in those of their children. Nevertheless, during the interview the therapist must have the situation firmly in hand.

Paradoxically, the therapist can help the parents to become stronger and more efficient by helping them to accept and to admit their own weaknesses in front of the children. This reduces to nonsense the power struggle (Bateson, 1972, called it the "symmetrical escalation") between delinquent adolescents and parents. The hate-filled conflict gives way to a "loving fight"—a dialogue with trust and respect on both sides in which differences are clearly articulated, conflicts understood and defined, and accounts negotiated and settled (Stierlin, 1974).

If an adolescent—often with an unconscious self-victimizing intent—provokes aggression, recrimination and contempt, it is particularly important to be fair, and to grant some degree of approbation, if possible, so as to win his or her cooperation. As a rule this should not prove difficult if one concedes that it is typically the delinquent who achieves what is important for the family. Often the delinquent is the only one who is able to mobilize the limit-setting, therapeutic resources of the community that the whole family needs. The parents have often in a concealed way delegated her or him to become delinquent: that is, to steal, vandalize, play truant, drop-out, etc. (see Stierlin 1974). By recognizing the achievement and self-sacrifice for the parents' benefit that are concealed in the delinquent behavior, rather than joining the chorus of moralistic recrimination, the therapist makes it possible for the delinquent to give up some of his or her power (of terrorizing the parents) and so face up to the possibility of reconciliation and understanding.

Often the therapist is faced with a situation that precludes both dialogue and final reconciliation. When an adolescent runs away, no family dialogue is possible, and the parents' feeling of impotence increases. Sometimes the running away is sustained by parental collusion. The adolescent runaway "helps" his or her parents by hindering an open debate and the exposure of the family problem. The therapist has often no recourse but to wait until the runaway comes back (which in most cases happens sooner or later). In the meanwhile some constructive work with the parents and other relations can often be accomplished.

FAMILIES WITH PARENTS WHO ABUSE THEIR CHILDREN

Families in which children are battered come less often to the therapist or counselor on their own initiative than do those of juvenile delinquents. The predominant question from the start is whether parents who batter or terrorize their children may or can keep them in their care. Such parents' feelings of fear, shame and guilt are often, therefore, extreme. These feelings will increase if the parents notice that the counselor or therapist's thoughts and endeavors are—for understandable humane reasons—concerned with the best way to save the mistreated child from its monstrous parents. The first interview has a special meaning in these cases, since very often there is no second.

In this extreme situation it is better for the therapist not to express a wish to save the children. Like other research groups, we find that, despite the apparently particularly poor initial situation, family therapy is often the most humane and sensible form of aid for such families, because, as one so often sees, even grossly mistreated children are often deeply loyal to their parents and very willing to help them. These resources can contribute to a successful therapy that helps the parents and, hence, the children also.

Parents who abuse their children frequently exhibit characteristic disturbances of related individuation. They are not able to see the young child as a being with needs, feelings and rights that are basically different from their own. A mother, for example, who comes home exhausted in the evening, may feel hurt and irritated if her 11-month-old baby fails to smile at her spontaneously. She hits it out of anger at its inadequate response. Such disturbance of individuation is often accompanied by a strong binding between mother and child. Contrary to popular belief many of these parents have a strong emotional investment in their children. However, there are also expelling parents who grossly neglect their children, kicking them out of their path like so many stray dogs.

Battered children are often delegated to take over parental functions; they are supposed to provide their parents with the tenderness, love and attention their childhood lacked. Or sometimes the children serve their parents as "psychological trashcans": The parents "dispose of" all the badness and meanness that they must resist and isolate in their own characters onto the children, and then punish and mistreat the children as bearers of these alienated characteristics.

Finally, a specific multigenerational perspective is almost always definitive. Time and again one finds that parents who abuse their children were themselves maltreated and are only passing on what they themselves experienced. For these families empathy and multipartiality, directed also towards earlier generations, are of essential therapeutic importance.

FAMILIES WITH MEMBERS AT RISK FROM DRUG ABUSE

Drug abuse has, besides biophysiological and psychological aspects, political, sociological and legal implications which influence our approach and therapeutic method. We cannot cover all these here, and we must also remember that the emotionally fraught words "drug abuse" label a heterogeneous concept. The drugs used have diverse biopsychological effects and are not all equally dangerous. The spectrum ranges from LSD, heroin, and marijuana (pot) through barbiturates and amphetamines to alcohol, the most misused drug of our culture. Drug abuse includes both casual adolescent experimentation and hopeless addiction.

Family relationships often play an important role in drug addiction and the most effective possible therapeutic intervention therefore often needs to include the family. Drug addicts typically show disturbances of related individuation in two areas: 1) They are unable or unwilling to own up to and come to terms with certain unpleasant feelings—above all, lasting rage, loneliness, and boredom—and 2) they lack the self-control and concern for the future necessary for responsible action. In our experience these disturbances of individuation are almost always accompanied by parallel disturbances in the family system.

The transactional modes may be characterized by extreme binding or expelling. Stierlin (1974) recalls the case of an American "ghetto" family in which the mother bound the growing children to her by regressive gratification, and even from time to time arranged the supply of heroin. Other drug-addicted adolescents are, in contrast, early and massively expelled. No one gave them the experience of feeling needed and important. Such expelled adolescents turn to drugs in their search for "injections of warm nourishing milk," as it were, for some of the warmth and security denied them in their families of origin. They tend to parentify their peers, which the peers find overdemanding, and massive conflict typically results. The therapeutic strategy depends on whether binding or expelling modes predominate. It may involve work with the family to achieve an "unbinding" or group work with peers, for example, on the Synanon model.

From the aspect of delegation, many drug-abusing adolescents are the recipients and victims of missions and loyalty conflicts that are massively over-demanding but which they make heroic efforts to fulfill. A 16-year-old high school girl, the daughter of a solid middle-class family, suddenly "flipped out" and submerged in the drug scene. Even at the first interview it became clear that this girl embodied the whole of her mother's existence and ensured her mother's psychological and physical survival. The mother had been chronically depressed and from time to time suicidal since the tragic death of a sibling in a traffic accident. Both the depression and the suicidal tendencies increased as the daughter approached her school-leaving exam and the mother's fear of separation grew. The daughter's behavior whipped the mother out of her depressive lethargy. The constant agitation and worry the daughter caused galvanized the mother so that she could neither rest nor forget the future.

Finally, the multigenerational perspective of legacies and merits reveals that many drug addicts have inherited a legacy of self-destruction that has accumulated over several generations and now assumes extreme forms. In one family, who came to us for therapy, the youngest sons had become alcoholic for three generations. The son we saw was both the victim of a tragic "repetition compulsion" that acted over generations and the prisoner of legacies that decreed that the youngest should live parasitically on the achievements of the elder brothers and, conversely, that his behavior should show their "achievements" in the best possible light. Such a multigenerational perspective points inevitably to a multigenerational therapy.

A view of the multigenerational dynamic makes it clearer that in many families with members at risk from drug abuse a family clinch blocks or distorts necessary work of mourning. We agree with other authors (e.g., Reilly, 1975) that this is a key to the feelings of privation, emptiness and joylessness that characterize these families. We must, therefore, even in the first interview often begin to pave the way for this overdue work of mourning to start as quickly and effectively as possible.

FAMILIES WITH SUICIDAL POTENTIAL

Where there is danger that one or more members of the family may commit suicide, the therapist must, first of all, try to evaluate the seriousness of the risk. She or he must grasp the relational pattern(s) which drive one or more members into suicide, and must negotiate a therapeutic contract with the suicidal members and the whole family that, as far as possible, covers the measures taken to counteract the risk. The first interviewer must allow time to accomplish these tasks; sometimes several interviews are necessary.

If, in the first interview we receive any intimation of suicide risk or tendency, we take it seriously. How seriously depends primarily on two main points: 1) on the tendency for suicide attempts to be repeated and 2) on the family constellation.

The literature on suicide (Shneidman, 1967, 1969) and our own experience show unequivocally that with each repeated suicide attempt the risk of death increases. This is particularly true when each new suicide attempt is more serious than the previous one. We believe that where there is such escalating repetition, the situation is comparable to a malignant illness. How severe the malignity is depends, first of all, on the relational and, in particular, on the familial constellation of the potential suicide.

Where there is an acute danger of suicide, our experience shows that three factors are almost always present:

1. The member at risk feels increasingly exhausted, exploited and abandoned in his or her difficulties, yet very often cannot admit these feelings or share them with his or her family.

2. At the same time, she or he experiences strong feelings of loneliness, neglect, having no way out, hopelessness and helplessness. These, too, are kept back or not accepted by the other members of the family.

3. She or he thirsts for a rageful revenge on the other members of the family—in whom the suicide will arouse profoundest guilt feelings that could never be assuaged—and also against her- or himself.

A well conducted first interview not only may reveal these factors but may also influence them so that the suicide risk is substantially reduced. Even acknowledging that the member of the family at risk feels exhausted, neglected and exploited—and very often is so—can initiate a discussion of merit accounts (Chapter 2) that reduces the suicidal threat. At the same time, the first interview can provide a framework within which long-withheld, retroflective aggression may be directed towards the true or imagined culprit (the exploiter, liar, etc.). Where parents are suicidal these feelings are usually directed against their own parents who should, therefore, be brought into the family therapy as soon as possible. The further multigenerational therapy must create the space in which this aggression may be expressed and accounts balanced so that justice and true reconciliation between all participants on increasingly significant levels can be achieved.

The contract for further therapy must lay down that all members of the family bear responsibility with respect to the danger of suicide. As a rule, the potentially suicidal member, as well as the rest of the family, should bind themselves to inform the therapist immediately of any possible ominous developments and danger signals, so that steps can be taken to admit the patient to a hospital, if necessary. The therapist should make absolutely clear what she or he is ready and able to do in the event of such a danger of suicide, and what not. In this way the possibilities for (conscious or unconscious) blackmailing manoeuvers by which some such families tend to escalate the risk of suicide are restricted. At the same time, certain, albeit limited, assistance is guaranteed in the event of a crisis. In our experience this guarantee alone is often enough to keep a patient from suicide. Lastly, therapeutic work with the whole family is generally the most effective prophylaxis against suicide.

FAMILIES WITH MENTALLY OR PHYSICALLY HANDICAPPED CHILDREN

These families frequently bear exceptionally heavy burdens which are often further increased by a negative cycle of mutually reinforcing calamities in which they are trapped. The problems are often economic as well as social and emotional. They challenge the first interviewer to take a stand and as far as possible to provide fast and efficient help.

The therapist or counselor may often be able to reduce the economic problems by providing the family with information about social services, tax reductions, etc., and where necessary establishing the required contacts.

The social burdens are more difficult to relieve because families with handicapped children are often isolated in the community. Time and again they experience how other children stare at their child, how she or he is avoided and even teased, and how adults feel helpless towards the child and with a greater or lesser degree of guilt wish to turn away.

This withdrawal increases the emotional burdens of all members of the family. Cut off from the resources of the outside world, they feel themselves increasingly under pressure. Lasting exhaustion, irritation, depression, somatic disorders, alcoholism and drug abuse can result, which further exacerbate the loneliness, helplessness, shame and guilt in which the family is trapped.

Even in the first interview, such families can express massive mutual recrimination and depressive self-denigration through which they momentarily relieve individual feelings, but which increase the general dilemma in the long run. The burdens and merits of all must be acknowledged and, at the same time, the family must be brought to face the necessary confrontation with their particular situation and the needed work of mourning, which the self- and mutual recrimination have helped them avoid.

Families with Psychosomatically Ill Members

In this section, we will discuss the problems of families with psychosomatically ill members in greater detail than we have discussed other problem families. This will serve to introduce Part II which is an annotated transcript of the first interview with a psychosomatically burdened family.

Characteristics of Communication and Transactions

Family structures that promote the development of chronic physical illness have been described many times. Such families characteristically have reduced contact with the outside world and within themselves. Jackson (1966) spoke of the "restricted family." All forms of communication are qualitatively and quantitatively drastically reduced. In contrast to families with schizophrenic transaction, the little that is said is clear and meaningful, but has little emotional content and refers only scantly to the person being addressed (Hassan, 1974). A "rigid homeostasis" (Minuchin, et al., 1975) predominates, leaving little room for adjustment and restricting the capacity of the members of the family to solve conflicts. Each is fatefully enmeshed with the others. Each trespasses on the other's territory; the interpersonal demarcations are brittle, and generational boundaries in part nonexistent (Minuchin et al. (1975). The parents seem to be over-concerned about the children, and the children feel similarly about the parents. This concern is, however, not empathic and sympathetic, but is more often distorted through projections.

Relational Dynamics

In our experience the behavior patterns described above arise from relational structures which have been transmitted for generations and which, unless therapeutically influenced, will continue to be handed on (Stierlin 1978b, c; Stierlin et al., 1977).

On the level of related individuation there are disturbances of the fusion type, that is, the capacity for the flexible maintenance of boundaries is hardly developed. The functions of the inner objects that determine relations with others are disturbed or weakened

(Stierlin, 1970). The partner (the outer object) must therefore always be actually present because every real or imagined separation evokes massive fear of actual loss. The loss of someone with whom they have an important relationship amounts to a psychic catastrophe. The work of mourning that allows this object to be given up cannot be done. Years later they are as affected by the loss as they were on the first day.

Correspondingly, the predominant *transactional mode* is binding. We see again and again how strong binding forces are active on all three levels: in the form of regressive gratification on the Id level, on the Ego level through the mystifying attribution of weaknesses and illnesses (though this generally is less marked and in part qualitatively different from families with schizophrenic members), and on the Superego level in the form of massive breakaway guilt (Overbeck & Overbeck, 1978).

Care for the family is the main task of *delegation* in these families. Missions often involve serving as substitute for an object that has been lost, for example, a deceased, unmourned sibling. Equally characteristic, missions may require the delegate to prevent conflict in the family, for example, a child may have to act as arbitrator or buffer between parents. Such derailed delegation interferes with age-appropriate needs and often results in loyalty conflicts in the relationships with parents, "peers" and marital partners.

Finally, even in the first interview with the family a *stagnation in the balancing of obligation and merit* can be recognized. This becomes evident in the way significant, "existential" family events, for example, something the father did to the mother years before, are dealt with. All the participants have known about such an event for years, but it is either never talked about or is kept alive in constantly reiterated painful quarrels, and in any event never constructively solved. The result is that the relationship between the members of the family is fraught with a chronic unremitting tension that brings them ever closer to a malign clinch.

The Central Importance of the Illness

The physical illness of one or more members often provides these families with their only ground for referral to a family therapist.

Therefore, they see no reason for working on a solution of psychic problems in the family. Accordingly, the conditions for beginning therapy can be considered to be difficult—some may even think they are hopeless. The therapist's sole recourse at the beginning of the first interview with such a family is to accept and take seriously whatever the family "offers." For example, the mother or father might say, "Our problem is that our child has this illness." If the therapist interrupts the family's own introduction by insisting, for example, "But we're here to talk about your psychic conflicts and difficulties", the family will have been lost before any real contact has been made.

The family therapist therefore carefully and patiently notes the various accounts of physical problems which the individual members give. She or he also asks the healthy members of the family what they think about the father (partner, child, etc.) being ill, and in this way recognizes the significance of the sickness for the family. The therapist must accept that, at the beginning, his or her relationship with the family will correspond more to the classical doctor-patient format, and must adapt to a more passive, expectant, help-seeking attitude of the patients.

It is, further, a good idea to follow up on the development of the illness. This history-taking procedure is familiar to the family members and fits into the less intimidating conventional model of a doctor-patient relationship.

Leaving the Medical Level

However, the interview can often take a surprising turn when the family therapist expresses interest in the family's situation at the time when the illness began, asking, for example, "What was going on in the family at the time when this illness started?" The family will often show great emotional involvement in relating deeply affecting family events that quite obviously have not been worked through. Nevertheless, it would be quite wrong to interpret their connection with the start of the illness at this point in the interview. Instead the therapist should use the opportunity to shift the focus away from the illness to events that affected *all* members of the family. At the same time she or he should take advantage of the moment to involve members in the interview who have not so far taken part.

The restrictions and defensive reactions of these families reflect their attempts to cope with deep (existential) burdens and conflicts. Often it is some unmourned loss (for example, a death) that still comes frequently into the awareness and is then pushed away by "primitive" psychic mechanisms such as a stubborn denial: "Just don't think about it anymore."

In the open atmosphere of the family interview these brittle defenses easily break down and strong and painful feelings, for example, of grief, are released. Although talking about these feelings together can have a healing effect, the therapist must be aware that they also represent a dangerous threat. How can they be contained after they have been released? After all, the family has to go on living together after the interview.

Overcoming Feelings of Shame and Guilt

The therapist should at all costs avoid prematurely associating the physical illnesses with any conflicts that may have become apparent. The family can only accept the connection between such family conflicts and the physical illnesses once they have overcome some of the guilt and shame they feel about their emotional problems.

The referral to the psychotherapist alone often causes insecurity and mortification that brings out all sorts of negative associations. They range from "But we're not crazy" to "I'm not inventing the illness." It is even harder to accept the connection between the physical complaints and the conflicts within the family. Feelings of guilt are automatically involved: "Is it supposed to be my fault I'm sick?" or "Are they (the therapists) saying that our child is so ill because we fight?" To ease these feelings we allow the various problem levels—in this case the physical illness and the family conflict—to remain some time adjacent but unconnected. In the first interview with the family we take care not to pressure the family to notice the connection between these levels, even though the data may be unequivocal. It is almost always better to wait until the family can see the connection for themselves.

A Trusting Relationship

The precept of no therapeutic action without a trusting relationship with every family member applies even more to psychosomatic families than to family therapy in general. The therapist cannot be too aware of the fragility of the psychosomatic family system, if she or he wants to avoid interventions that, though intended to disclose and change the systemic forces, actually release an uncontrollable and destructive crisis.

A comparison can illustrate this point: We can easily understand that a family which has just suffered a severe loss (maybe through death) may appear to an outsider to be controlled and little affected. Their interests may seem reduced and their mood subdued or depressed. No one would think of confronting people in this condition with their own aggressiveness or try to stimulate them to get involved in outside activities, nor would anyone expect the family to make a radical change in its life style. Only after a long and trusting contact would an outsider perhaps be allowed to share the family's grief. Anyone can understand that the family mourning must for a long time overshadow everything else; that it is necessary; and that only after the mourning is over can life become normal again.

Families with psychosomatic illness are in a similar situation. The difference is that the mourning or the attempts to overcome the heavy emotional burden have completely stagnated. The therapist's task is, therefore, to achieve a relationship of trust with the family that will allow them to work with her or him to overcome this stagnation. Only on the basis of such a trusting alliance can changes in the family structure be affected that may prevent such stagnation developing in future.

The Fragile Block of Ice

The special characteristics involved in the handling of psychosomatically disturbed families can be summarized through the metaphor of a block of ice. Superficially such families are cold and smooth; they seem transparent. However, the image one sees below the surface is a reflection of oneself: the family adapts itself massively to the environment, which nevertheless, is cut off from the family's true inner life.

The ice is threatened by two dangers: A severe shock can shatter it into little pieces that separate from the smooth matrix. Or warmth can melt it, so that if the emotional temperature of the family is carelessly increased it loses it shape, loses its bearings, and is in danger of disintegration.

Even in the interview the family defends itself against both forms of disruption or existential threats. The price it pays is physical illness. The therapist's task is to free each member of the family from the ice and make his individual existence possible.

Do All Families with Psychosomatically Ill Members Have the Same Structures?

Working with a multifactorial model of physical illness, we assume a complex interplay of various factors. Biological elements (for example, a hereditary allergic disposition or harmful environmental stimuli) combine with psychosocial stresses (such as heavy strains, severe deprivation, conflict at the place of work, etc). The given family structure shapes the personality and finally determines what is experienced as strain or conflict and what possibilities there are for regeneration and liberation. Each of the above factors can have a different weight in making the illness manifest.

The family therapist is primarily concerned with cases where the "family structure" has greatest weight. Within this perspective the usual distinction between so-called psychosomatic and somatic illness disappears. Accordingly, not every asthma is "psychosomatic." But, on the other hand, family structural factors may have significance for many diseases which until now have been accepted as "purely physical" (for example, diabetes, and even cancer). If an illness is chronic and cannot be influenced by biological-medical therapeutic measures, it can generally be assumed that its origins are psychosomatic. An experienced family therapist does not judge such cases unfavorably merely in the light of the, so far, unsuccessful attempts at treatment, but asks how far characteristic, psychosomatic family structures are blocking the healing process and how far these structures can be influenced in a positive way.

PART II

8

The Bolt Family Interview

INTRODUCTION

IN PART I WE DESCRIBED details relevant to the conduct of the first interview with the family. Part II presents an actual clinical case. The verbatim transcript of a complete family interview* was given in the original German language edition of this book. In the translation we have tried to use words that an analogous American family might say under comparable emotional, psychological, and social circumstances. Much of the original was in a local dialect which often increased in strength with the emotional tension. The transcript has an interpolated commentary. Finally, in Chapter 9, there is a comprehensive discussion of the underlying family dynamics.

In Chapter 10 we give the results of two family tests—a consensus Rorschach and consensus TAT test—in the same form, of a transcript and discussion. In Chapter 11 we investigate how far the information from these two tests is either corroborative or contradictory and what conclusions relevant to the therapeutic process may be drawn.

---

* For discretionary reasons all names, dates, places and characteristic details have been changed.

Referral

The designated patient in the Bolt family was the mother. She was referred to the Psychosomatic Clinic, December 1975, with the diagnosis of Morbus Crohn, or ulcerative inflammation of the small intestine. In a first, psychoanalytically oriented interview she described a series of exclusively physical symptoms, in a monotonous, complaining voice: She suffered from diarrhea which occurred up to ten or twelve times a day and was usually mixed with blood and mucous. This had begun three years previously. At first the attacks occurred every six months, but now they were more frequent. One day before the start of the diarrhea she suffered joint pains in the knees and hips. At this time she felt weak, depressed, and enervated. She had been hospitalized three times with severe gastric bleeding. Each time the condition improved relatively quickly once she was in the hospital.

The medical reports the patient brought with her showed that the inflammation was initially localized in the small intestine, but had now spread to the entire intestinal area. Pseudopolyps and fistula were already present. It emerged that, in addition to the colitis, she had suffered a number of other illnesses and operations: at the age of fifteen rheumatism and tonsillectomy; in 1966, after the birth of her second daughter by Caesarean section, heavy bleeding necessitated a hysterectomy; since 1970, gallbladder trouble and gastric ulcers; since 1973, pains in the main joints which were treated over an extended period with injections of anti-inflammatory drugs (Butazolidin); and treatment of varicose veins. In August 1973 the inflammation of the small intestine was noticed during an operation for removal of the gallbladder and appendix. In August 1975, she began to have attacks of cramplike "tightness" in the heart.

Triggering Events

On her own initiative, during the preliminary individual interview, Mrs. Bolt began to talk about the possible trigger events of 1972/73. They started when she and her husband took over from

the parents-in-law the restaurant business which all four, together
with the husband's grandmother, had been running since Mr. and
Mrs. Bolt married. It was primarily due to her efforts in modernizing
and building up the business that the returns had risen by 200 percent. According to her description, she was the one that "kept the
business going." Immediately after the change in ownership, the
parents-in-law took the youngest daughter Annette to a health resort
as both granddaughter and grandfather suffered from asthma.

While Mr. and Mrs. Bolt were trying to adjust to their new responsibilities, Mr. Bolt got appendicitis, which he neglected for so
long that a perforation resulted in his hospitalization in a very grave
condition. Mrs. Bolt admitted that it was then that she first felt
alone, abandoned and overstressed. She had to gather all her strength,
to "stop herself breaking down." It was precisely at this point that
she was hit by a whole series of bereavements. First, in 1972 her
80-year-old father died. Asked how she felt, she said: "I was very
attached to him, but there wasn't really any time for mourning."
She had been very hurt that those around her had shown so little
understanding. Her brother-in-law, for example, had said, "Life's
got to go on."

As in previous years she spent Christmas of 1972 with her husband and children near her parents' home. There she visited her
78-year-old mother who had become bedridden in the months since
her husband's death. They had planned to take the grandmother
home with them for a rest, but she said goodbye to them very cheer-
fully and thanked her daughter for all that she had wanted to do
for her. An hour later she was dead. Mrs. Bolt felt as if she were
paralysed; she was unable to mourn and could not talk about the
death. She reproached herself bitterly: she had not understood her
mother properly; she had gone off too easily. But once again the
business had to go on. It was during the following days that the joint
pains first began.

Three months later an aunt (the mother's sister, Mrs. Bolt's godmother) to whom Mrs. Bolt was very attached also died. And then,
suddenly and unexpectedly, a good friend of the family who was
only 41 died. This accumulation of deaths caused great distress in
the home village, which was so small that no more than one death

a year was usually expected. At this time the patient felt completely lacking in energy, depressed and exhausted; everything was an effort. She felt alone and abandoned in the world, devoid of any hope. Her husband and mother-in-law showed no sympathy. The diarrhea and stomach pains began. After a bowel movement she always felt somewhat better.

In August 1973, the father-in-law died—the one person by whom she felt at all understood. The granddaughter Annette brought him his evening meal in his room and afterwards told how Grandad said she would not see him in the morning—he would perhaps already be dead. In fact he did suffer a severe asthma attack in the night. Before he died he called, "I can't go on." His son tried everything to revive him, but it was useless.

A few days later Mrs. Bolt was hospitalized and operated on for the removal of the gallbladder and the appendix; during the operation severe inflammation of the small intestine was diagnosed.

The interviewer asked Mrs. Bolt if she had got over all these deep bereavements. She began to cry and complain about her husband and mother-in-law, who were so lacking in understanding that they had even said that she had herself to blame for her illness, that the diarrhea was due to nerves, and that she should pull herself together. She knew, though, that the injections she had had for the joint pains had harmed the intestine.

It became clear that one important element hindered a clear psychological understanding of the illness at this point: connecting her illness with emotionally charged events, such as the loss of important relations and her husband's reaction, raised her guilt titer in relationship to her husband and his mother. Once she raised these connections, she was told she was herself to blame and she ought to pull herself together. Even in the first interview this mechanism blocked every further effort at clarification.

It was suggested to the patient that she should come to the second interview together with her husband and children. She spontaneously rejected this offer, saying that her husband would never take part as he had no understanding for psychological things. It was then suggested that she tell him that we had no intention of criticizing him, but that we needed him to help us understand his wife's illness better. We also offered to discuss these things with her husband on the telephone.

Without any further contact the entire family appeared punctually for the agreed appointment in February 1976. Rorschach and TAT tests were given to the whole family before the family interview (see Chapter 8).

ANNOTATED TRANSCRIPT OF THE FIRST FAMILY INTERVIEW

Mother = M. (39 years)	Brigitte = B. (12 years)
Father = F. (40 years)	Annette = A. (10 years)

Two therapists took part in the interview: one therapist (Th.) led the interview, the other (Th. 2) observed, then took part later.

First Contact with the Family

Th.: I'm afraid we've made you tired before you even got here, didn't we?

M.: Pardon?

Th.: Didn't the test make you tired?

M.: Oh well, maybe . . .

Th.: Well, did you understand it, some of it anyway?

M.: Yes, only, can you find out anything really definite with it . . . that's true. . . .

Th.: Eh, Eh. . . .

M.: One really can't imagine exactly what it can be.

Th.: Sometimes we ourselves can't either.

> *The therapist enters into the situation by acknowledging the extra stress caused by the preliminary test and, at the same time making it clear that this test is necessary. In this way he tries to prevent the negative feelings created by this situation from having an effect on the discussion that follows.*

Th.: Yes, we're glad that you have come so that we can have the interview.

> *The therapist acknowledges to the family that they have come to the interview and so helps them to overcome their feelings of shame and guilt.*

F.: Sure we've come, but I've told her already (*points to his wife*) I don't know what you. . . . You wanted something from her and I had to get the kids out of school.

> *Initially Mr. B.'s readiness to take part in the family interview seems minimal. As far as he is concerned, the problem lies primarily with his sick wife. It is possible that he is reacting to the way in which the referral was made.*

Th.: Yes.

F.: (*Speaking quickly and quietly*) I guess it's basically meant to be a family interview . . . but if it would sometimes be OK without me . . . I don't know if it would do.

Th.: It's hard for you to get away, isn't it?

F.: Well, we've got a restaurant, I guess you know. . . .

Th.: Hm, hm. . . .

F.: . . . and a bit of farm, and now it's the Olympic games.

Th.: As well!

F.: (*Nods*) As well (*everyone laughs*).

Th.: It's asking a lot of you.

F.: Oh well, we'll get home again, won't we?

> *Here in an enciphered form the father expresses his fear of the interview: the fear of being found "mad" and not allowed to go home.*

Th.: Yes, shall we just wait and see what comes out in the discussion? Let's say, we'll see what comes out in the discussion, and then we'll decide how to go on from there, what seems to make sense.

(*Pause*)

> *The therapist acknowledges the difficulty the family had to face in order to come to the discussion. He takes the family seriously and makes a first offer of open discussion. This creates an atmosphere in which it is possible to begin the interview proper.*

Taking the Illness Seriously

Th.: Yes. Who would like to start?

F.: Yes, what's going to be the basis of the discussion? Do you lead or do I have to ask you what you want?

The offer of an unstructured discussion makes Mr. Bolt increasingly unsure.

Th.: Yes, I, I've heard something about illnesses in the family. . . .

The therapist reacts to the family's feelings of fear by steering the discussion towards the physical illness. In this way he sustains, at least for the time being, the family's own definition of the problem, and so lays a basis of trust which allows the family to respond more openly. (The actual introductory phase was not sufficient for this family, especially for the father.)

M.: Yes.

Th.: Now can we know, who's the patient?

M.: Yes, I am.

Th.: Yes.

The mother presents herself as the "family problem" and thereby takes the pressure off the other members of the family, in particular her husband.

Th.: . . . the patient. . . .

M.: Yes, the illness is called Morbus Crohn.

The name gives the illness reality and legitimacy.

Th.: Yes.

M.: And it's now almost three years ago that it began.

Th.: Hm, hm. . . .

M.: Yes, and the intervals [between attacks] are getting shorter and shorter.

Th.: Hm, hm.

M.: And I've even had to be hospitalized with it twice already.

Th.: Hm.

M.: Seventy-three it was, or '74 *(looks at her husband)*, '73 was the first time, I was laid up six weeks in the hospital.

Th.: Hm, hm.

M.: And then after six weeks I had the gallbladder operation, to see if there was anything the matter with the intestine, because it hadn't really got any better, that. . . .

Th.: Yes.

M.: And then they decided it was the Morbus Crohn.

> *Mrs. Bolt describes the three-year course of the continually worsening illness.*

Th.: Yes, and how does everything look to you now?

> *By taking Mrs. Bolt's illness seriously, the therapist adapts himself to the family system. He recognizes the objective reality of the complaints and responds to Mrs. Bolt's subjective experience. He tries to make the family feel more secure by fulfilling their expectations of a medical interview.*

M.: Yes, it goes in phases. Sometimes I get a couple of good weeks and then it's bad again. It started again last week.

F.: Slimy movements, blood in the movements.

> *Mr. Bolt now strengthens his wife's description of her ailments and takes part in the discussion on his own initiative. His descriptions are indeed drastic; this may represent aggression towards his wife.*

Th.: Bloody movements, yes?

M.: Yes, and then. . . .

F.: Very tired, very tired.

Th.: Very tired?

F.: Yes, and then there's lack of blood as well, and . . .

M.: And then there's almost always these joint pains, it usually starts with that.

Th.: Ah, yes.

M.: And I've got those now . . . it'll be 14 days on Sunday that the joint pains started. And I stuck it out 'till Thursday and then it was so bad, no, it was Friday, I went to our doctor and he gave me another shot. The joints were OK for two days, and then he gave me two shots, here *(she points to the place)* near the spine.

> *The ailments have become worse in the last 14 days: a fresh crisis is obviously developing. This may be connected with the preliminary individual interview with Mrs. Bolt and the anticipated interview with the whole family. It is evidence of Mrs. Bolt's low ability to bear stress.*

Th.: Yes, hm.

M.: Yes, and it was two days, exactly two days good, and then the . . . and then I got the diarrhea again, and since then I've had both again.

Th.: Both?

M.: Yes.

Th.: . . . the joint pains and the diarrhea?

M.: Yes, usually they come together, it's only very seldom that it's one alone. It's mainly here on the right *(see shows the place and sighs)* and in the back *(moans)*. Perhaps all the joints affect each other, but before it wasn't as bad as it is now.

Th.: Ah, yes. Did you already have these joint pains before, or did both begin at about the same time three years ago?

M.: No, they are really . . . the joint pains began three years ago.

Th.: Ah yes.

M.: . . . the end of January and then the end, middle of March . . . end . . . and then the diarrhea began, and I didn't take enough notice of it then, perhaps. I guess I thought it would all go off, but then it got worse and worse, there was quite a lot of blood in the movements, and then in August, eh, I got a real high fever and then I ended up in the hospital.

Th.: Hm.

M.: It was then . . . about . . . last year, '75 in August, I got this gut bleeding that's from then till now. Then I also had. . . .

F.: *(Clears his throat)*

M.: . . . then this joint thing and diarrhea, and then all at once there was a lot of blood in the bowel movement, about three liters then.

Th.: So much blood, really?

M.: Yes, and that time I was in hospital 14 days, and then I came home, and then later on, it was another five weeks in hospital.

Th.: And before, more than three years ago, there was nothing like this going on?

M.: No *(shakes her head)*.

Th.: Hm, it began all of a sudden then?

M.: Yes, all at once with these joint pains. . . .

Th.: Ah . . ,

M.: . . . and . . . ah, wait a moment (*scratches her forehead*). Yes,
that was the first time, and then I got the shots.

> *The therapist gives the family and in particular Mrs. Bolt
> in her role of the designated patient the opportunity of talk-
> ing about her ailments. Such a procedure is necessary in fam-
> ilies with psychosomatic members. The therapist obtains some
> important initial information and can at the same time draw
> the father into the discussion.*

Events at the Start of the Illness

Th.: Yes, and it was at that time. . . .
M.: (*To her husband*) Yes, it was then when we'd just taken over
the business. Seventy-three, it began.
Th.: Sevently-three, when you took over the business, right?
(*Turns to her husband*).

> *The patient begins to think about the development of the
> illness. The family sees the development of the illness and
> the change in their way of living as parallel events; they
> observe no connection between them. The therapist does not
> offer a premature interpretation, but encourages the family
> to think about it themselves. There is a noticeable lowering
> of tension.*

M.: Yes, my parents-in-law and the youngest were having this cure . . .
Th.: Why were they taking this cure?*
F.: My father had asthma.
Th.: Your father had asthma?
F.: He died three years ago, war injuries.
Th.: Hm.
F.: And he took Annette with him and the mother, because of over-
strain, and they also had a cure prescribed at once, with bathing
rights.
Th.: The little one too?
F.: Yes, yes.

---

* The word "cure" (in German, *Kur*) refers here to a stay at some sanatorium or
spa, usually of several weeks' duration. Ordinarily, within German-speaking countries
such a cure is medically prescribed for a wide variety of (mainly chronic) ailments
and is paid for by the National Health Insurance.

M.: She had always had bronchitis.

F.: She always had something, whooping cough too . . . and then we sent her with them and they both went.

> *Both parents now themselves bring out in close succession a series of incidents associated with the start of the illness: the takeover of the business, the parents-in-law going on a cure, the daughter's bronchitis, the death of Mr. Bolt's father. For the first time it becomes clear that Mrs. Bolt is not the only member of the family who is physically ill.*

M.: She was always getting bronchial trouble.

Th.: Hm, hm. (*to Annette*) How are you now Annette?

A.: Oh, yes, fine.

Th.: You're well?

F.: Yes, the little one's OK now.

M.: Ah, yes, since we had her tonsils taken out, it's . . .

B.: (*Mumbles something, incomprehensible*)

M.: . . . better. Yes, then she had a bit of bronchitis again, but it went away again.

> *The illness is seen in the frame of the family development. The focus of the interview changes from Mrs. Bolt to the whole family. She is no longer the only one who is ill. The first example of the intergenerational perspective emerges in the similarity between the illness of grandfather and the granddaughter, but this goes no further. At this point in the interview, the family's purely organic concept of illness remains unchallenged ("war injuries," "tonsils taken out").*

Relationships and Conflicts

Th.: And Brigitte how are things with you?

B.: Fine.

Th.: Fine? You feel well?

F.: She is tougher, she . . .

Th.: You mean tougher than her? (*indicating Annette*)

F.: She doesn't get ill so easily.

Th.: Then we've got one strong one in the family (*indicates Brigitte, and then turn to Annette*) and here's someone who's susceptible, and (*to the mother*) she's not tough, right?

The therapist underlines the family "attribution," the split between the sensitive and the tough. He addresses the similarities between the members of the family (concealed coalitions), without referring to the mother's illness directly.

F.: No, no, no.

M.: Yes, I know I was before, but in these last three years . . .

F.: Very sensitive . . .

Th.: Very sensitive, right?

F.: Very sensitive, and that's the illness, I don't need anyone to tell me that. She thinks about tomorrow too much . . .

Th.: She thinks about tomorrow too much?

F.: Yes, she doesn't think about today, she thinks about tomorrow and the day after tomorrow: And when I think about it, I could really go crazy. That's nerves, isn't it?

Th.: Hm, eh could you explain that a bit more? How does she think about tomorrow and the day after tomorrow, for example?

F.: If we have a wedding on tomorrow, we have a lot of weddings in the big room, or some other sort of social event, maybe from a club and then perhaps all the other. . . . Ah (*groans loudly and imitates her impatiently*), I mustn't think about tomorrow, how are we going to get through the day? Sunday we'll have so many guests again, how are we going to get through the day? (*helpless*)

> *A basic complementary pattern becomes clear. The family is split into the "strong" and the "weak." Here we can recognize a paradox: the "weak" sensitive mother is the one who cares most about the success of the business. She does not, in fact, trust her "strong" husband with much responsibility. She feels that her husband does not give her enough support and so brings his "strength" into question. There is a disturbance in the related individuation, which is evident in deficient self-demarcation: At some points it is difficult to decide whether Mr. Bolt is quoting his wife or whether he is speaking for himself.*

M.: Yes, but to me, sometimes when I'm not too well . . .

F.: Yes, yes, but before . . . (*incomprehensible*)

Pause

F.: She never lets up, I'll tell you. I'm a business man, sometimes someone comes to me, and not just because he's thirsty (*quickly*), and I tell him, you should have called up half an hour ago, then it'd be already sitting on the table.

Th.: Hm.

F.: (*To his wife*) And if someone comes to her and wants a steak, he doesn't sit there for nothing . . . but she doesn't know how to take her time about it, everything has to be snip-snap, snap-snip (*clears his throat*) . . . she can't let up.

M.: That's not quite true, I do let up sometimes, but what if it just sometimes gets too much, I just lose my nerve that's all, I mean I would lose it, but I get all edgy (*sobs quietly*), and he doesn't get worked up, at least not so easily.

> *The therapist still follows the family's concept of organic illness, but now he goes a step further and presents the illness in relation to the wife's sensitivity and the family events and changes. The family can appreciate this connection without much anxiety and so are able to become more open. As a result the rigid division of roles becomes even clearer. The patient appears as the weak sensitive side of the family that is complemented by a robust, strong partner. The marital couple is locked in a state of negative mutuality.*

Unaccomplished Mourning

F.: Now, now, but just look at her (*points at his wife*). She's 38 years old today, 38.

M.: Thirty-nine! (*laughs*)

> *Mr. Bolt thinks his wife is younger than she really is. Wishful thinking or lack of intimacy?*

F.: Or 39 . . .

Th.: Thirty-nine-years-old today? Well, many happy returns! (*congratulates her and shakes hands over the table*)

M.: Thanks.

> *The therapist reacts with spontaneous friendliness to the sudden news that it is Mrs. Bolt's birthday. Instead of behaving in a neutral and restrained fashion, he enters into the reality of the family situation.*

F.: She can cry to order. Give the order, there come the tears. All because of her nerves, and then it starts.

> *Mr. Bolt repudiates in his wife what he fears in himself: the expression of feelings and the admission of weakness.*

M.: Oh, now . . .

Th.: Now why do you think you are crying just at this moment?

M.: (*Smiling*) Oh, I can't explain (*laughing and crying*).

Th.: Are you sure? Why do you think you are crying just now?

> *The therapist takes Mrs. Bolt's expression of feelings seriously and repeats his question, asking why she is crying. He is trying to help her understand her crying not just as a "nervous" symptom, but rather as something she should do openly so that she can accept the feelings and experiences that underlie the tears and express these in words.*

M.: I don't know if I'm really so sensitive, it happens automatically. (*Wipes the tears away*)

> *Mrs. Bolt subscribes to her husband's attributive interpretation. Both partners collude in repulsing painful and threatening feelings.*

Th.: Yes, were you always so sensitive, or has something been so stressful that you've become sensitive?

> *The therapist steers the family towards the idea that something has undergone a change.*

M.: I wasn't really so sensitive, but with this illness now I am a bit (*sobs*) . . .

Th.: Hm.

M.: (*Cries more bitterly*) . . . I'm very low nervously and mentally.

Th.: Hm.

M.: Because I see it's not getting any better.

Th.: Hm.

M.: It's just the reverse, always worse.

Th.: Hm.

(*Brigitte smiles at Annette and looks out of window.*)

> *The second "strong" member of the family joins the general emotional defense, not in words, but with glance and gesture.*

Th.: Yes, and it's not so easy, is it, if you've got no one in the restaurant . . .

F.: *(Interrupts the therapist)* Not at all easy.

Th.: . . . which you've got to build up and it's a struggle, and . . .

> *The therapist shows understanding for the situation of the entire family, including the father who up to this point has been not a copatient but rather a nonparticipating source of information.*

(Pause)

F.: She gets worked up easily, and it started—I can tell you exactly —it wasn't '73, it was '72. I was hospitalized then, serious appendix operation, I was *(incomprehensible)* only afraid to stay alive. Then I was home after four or five weeks, then my father he died—in August, and it was then it started with her, she went into the hospital.

> *Mr. Bolt, who is now taking a constructive part in the interview, suggests a further possible origin of the illness, in the course of which he comes unaided to speak about his own illness; up to this point the "weak" mother has appeared to be the only sick one in the marital pair.*

M.: Yes, in the hospital.

F.: And then on a cure and then in the hospital again, and then again a good friend of ours died. And that upset her again. Fourteen days later she was in the hospital again, and after he died, a man of 41 *(shows emotion)*, much too early to die. And those are the things that get her worked up, don't they, where she. . . . Others don't give a damn. They just think, well, he's dead and we shan't see him again. But she, she gets everything bottled up inside *(clutches his stomach)* and then it all comes out again *(points to his eyes and clears his throat)*.

> *Mr. Bolt is able to express some of his own fear and in his albeit somewhat crude and plastic way shows the beginning of a "psychological" understanding of his wife's illness. He sees, even if only mechanically and superficially, a connection between her illness and the dramatic events in the family.*

Th.: Yes, eh, is that how you found it when your husband had his
    appendix . . .
M.: Yes, before that I was OK.
Th.: . . . and then the death of his . . .
M. and F.: (Nod)
Th.: . . . father.
Both: Of father.
F.: Oh, there where she comes from, that was a . . .
M.: Hm.
F.: Three people in her parents' house died within six months.
M.: Yes.
F.: She comes from a . . . three within six weeks. She comes from a
    little place with 200 inhabitants, there maybe someone dies
    once a year, and then within six weeks her father, her mother,
    and then her aunt.
Th.: All in '72?

> *The therapist is affected by the number of tragic events in*
> *the family and supports the father in his attempt to contri-*
> *bute some explanation. Even at this point in the interview*
> *it is clear that within a short space of time both partners*
> *suffered severe losses with which they were unable to come*
> *to terms. It becomes more obvious that the family feels so*
> *threatened by the grief and memory of these losses that each*
> *member in his own way tries to protect himself from facing*
> *them. Instead of the partners being brought closer together*
> *in the general process of mourning, they have been alienated*
> *still further. Mrs. Bolt contributes to this alienation by with-*
> *drawing depressively into her physical symptoms, while Mr.*
> *Bolt blocks all feelings and arms himself with a demonstra-*
> *tive display of strength. This seems to be the basis of the com-*
> *plementary rigidity in the familial relationships that, for the*
> *time, has prevented the development of a positive mutuality.*
> *The family is in a state of malign clinch.*

F.: Oh, and whether it, I know . . .
M.: (At the same time) Yes, must have . . .
F.: . . . I'd know exactly.
B.: No, no Gran died in '73.

> *For the first time Brigitte takes part in the discussion spon-*

*taneously and tries—if only on a relatively concrete level—
to give some help in the attempt to reach clarification of the
development of the mother's illness. By correcting her mother
she is adopting a contrary position, but at the same time remains within the explanatory level the mother herself has
adopted.*

M.: No *(shakes her head).*

(All talk at once.)

F.: Oh yes, '73.

M.: No, in the year that Grandad died *(to Brigitte).*

F.: Yes, it was before that.

Th.: Yes, and then your father died, and your father died . . .

> *While the members of the family are taken up with the ex-
> ternal matter of dates, the therapist tries to steer towards the
> emotional content of the events.*

F.: *(Interrupts the therapist)* . . . and her mother and her aunt.

M.: *(Blows her nose)*

Th.: And also . . .

F.: A friend too.

Th.: Her mother and your father then too.

All: Yes.

Th.: Then the aunt too, is there anyone else . . . who lived together
with . . .

B.: Her sister.

(Short pause)

M.: Yes, it all happened within three months, or so, and then, well,
we wanted to go away. We take our vacation in the Black
Forest. And then on the day we planned to leave my mother
died, and then in that year his father died.

F.: Oh yes, that was . . .

> *By the way in which he has conducted the interview and by
> adapting to what the family themselves have offered, the
> therapist has succeeded in creating the first basis of trust,
> which has made it possible for the family to express some
> emotion in talking about heavily burdensome emotional ex-
> periences. Verbally too he abides by the open offer implied*

by the question "What was it that caused so much stress that you became so sensitive?" He gives no pointers, but allows the parents to present their own story in which they talk about their tragic experiences. All members of the family, including the children, are now deeply involved in the discussion.

Conflicts that Promote Illness

M.: And then the real illness began, and it was then, in March, that the whole story with the intestine began, and then my mother-in-law kept saying, it was. . . . I had my veins treated in that year.

Th.: Hm.

The first relational conflict becomes apparent at this point. Mrs. Bolt defends herself against her mother-in-law's misunderstanding. One can also ask whether she uses the mother-in-law to veil the connection between the illness and the deeper conflicts.

M.: I've had it since then, but that's not quite it, I had the hurting spot on my lower belly already when I was in Mannheim. The first time then I was in the Health Department with Mother, and then we went to Dr. X. and I had had the diarrhea already then, I'm sure of that.

Th.: Ah.

M.: *(Coughs)* And since then, I've sometimes been alright for about half a year, but now, recently, it seems to be every four or six weeks and the diarrhea—the movement is quite loose—almost like a paste, and now sometimes there's no blood with it, but in the last three days there's blood in it again.

This seems to indicate the development of another crisis. The ailments have gotten worse in the last three days. This is a warning and an appeal to the therapist not to ask too much of the family.

Th.: When things are better, is there anything perhaps that is less of a strain than usual?

The therapist reacts to the warning signal by emphasizing the positive: What is different, when things are going better?

He relieves Mrs. Bolt, but at the same time gives her the possibility of speaking about sources of stress.

M.: Oh yes, I feel well and I can work.

Th.: Hm.

M.: The worst of it is when there is work to do and I can't *(cries bitterly again)*.

Th.: Oh yes, I mean one can see that, and that it ends up in a vicious circle, doesn't it. You think you have to do everything and you find you can't and then comes the diarrhea, yes, and the more nervous you feel, the more diarrhea, and so on?

The therapist tries to develop a sympathetic understanding of Mrs. Bolt's problem by designating the situation as a vicious circle. At the same time, he gives an initial pointer to the development of the illness and shows how Mrs. Bolt's symptoms are secondarily stengthened. In supporting Mrs. Bolt, he comes a step away from a purely organic concept of the illness and indicates possibilities of working on the conflict connected with the illness.

M.: It really gets me down.

Th.: Hm.

M.: Yes, and then the loss of blood . . .

Th.: Hm.

M.: I get just incredibly tired. And I really can't do so much, and then I get so sensitive at times.

The therapist has actively guided Mrs. Bolt away from a superficial concept of the illness and prepared the way for the family to begin to be able to speak about their burden of memories and events and the meaning of the illness. At the same time, he develops a sympathetic understanding of Mrs. Bolt's painful situation so that she also will be able to participate in this step without oppressive feelings of fear and guilt.

The Conflict is Observable in the Interview

F.: Yeah, isn't it time you left off whining *(impatiently)*.

The marital couple attack each other openly. Mrs. Bolt's weapon is depressive recrimination, while Mr. Bolt is harsh and crude.

M.: Yes.

Th.: Yes, well, what do you mean?

F.: She ought to cut the tears, or the next thing we know she'll be in the hospital again.

> *The imminent discussion of the burden of experience and feelings enhances the tension between the partners. Both try by means of their habitual strife to restore the complementary homeostasis and overcome the difficulty. .Mr. Bolt in particular reacts defensively to the approaching grief, by harshly attacking his wife's conflict-loaded situation and tries to prevent her from giving free rein to her painful feelings.*

Coalitions and Assignment of Roles

M.: *(Laughs briefly)* Oh, *(peers searchingly around)* oh get my purse from over there *(A. gives it to her).*

Th.: I've got the impression you don't like tears.

> *Mr. Bolt feels under pressure now that the problem is openly discussed. The therapist understands this pressure and reacts positively to the partners' different positions. He thereby addresses their relationship directly without designating one of them as the guilty party.*

F.: No, no, no. You've got to be hard in this world, or you go under . . . *(M. wipes her nose and eyes.)*

Th.: You've got to be hard?

F.: *(Nods)* Sure, or else you go under.

Th.: You go under?

F.: *(Nods and indicates Brigitte)* She's not so fussy, but *(points to his wife and to Annette)* she's like her mother.

Th.: *(To Brigitte)* I see, so she's another harder type?

F.: Yes, yes, she won't go under.

Th.: No, she won't go under. And Annette?

F.: She's got to get tougher.

Th.: She's got to get tougher, right? *(pause)* Yes, now what happens when a tougher type hitches up with a sensitive type?

> *Now the various role assignments and coalitions in the family are clear: the father has to be strong ("so as not to go under") and the mother is weak. The children are shared within this*

system. The elder daughter is the father's ally and has to persist in her strong role at the price of the feminine and "weaker" side of her personality. In contrast, the younger daughter is bound to the mother and is seen as sensitive and weak. The precarious equilibrium of the family is in part the result and expression of this structure. One must accept that a therapeutic intervention aimed to achieve deep change in this family relationship could cause great anxiety.

Weaknesses and Strengths

F.: Yes, it wasn't always so, it's just crystallized over the years, right. Before, when she was still young, everything was OK, now it's —can't really say. We had a lot of work, and she just takes it too much to heart, the work; she takes the work far too much to heart.

> *Mr. Bolt introduces a longer time perspective. There seems to have been a phase when "everything was OK." Is Mr. Bolt conjuring up a myth that will allow him to maintain a distance from the burdensome present?*

Th.: Hm.

F.: *(Clears his throat)* I take a two-hour walk every day, even in the winter, and if I'm tired, I don't go and put my feet up, on the contrary. Maybe, it would do her good to walk a bit, doesn't matter if it's not fast, slowly'd be something.

Th.: *(To the wife)* Well . . .? Do you go for walks?

M.: No, I can't just now.

Th.: You can't? at all?

M.: With this joint thing, I can't walk at all *(sobs)* at the moment.

Th.: Hm, you can't walk. Yes, what's it like being married to a hard type?

> *The therapist tried to identify with the wife's point of view and establish his multipartiality.*

M.: Oh yes, up to now it's been fine.

Th.: Hm.

F.: You're looking at it like a psychologist. . . . I'm not such a . . .

Th.: *(Laughs)*

F.: . . . tough customer as you seem to think; I can give in sometimes, but, some of what you say is right . . . if we were all like her, we might as well shut up shop.

Th.: Hm.

F.: *(Groans)*

Th.: How's business, good enough, right?

F.: Yes *(nods)*.

Th.: Yes? There isn't any real need to worry about it, right?

The therapist emphasizes the positive aspect of the situation.

F.: No *(emphatic)*, none at all.

Th.: Hm.

F.: We've got beds for 25 guests as well *(scratches his neck)*.

> *The therapist so accentuates the differences between the partners that he provokes Mr. Bolt (almost in the sense of of a paradoxical intervention) to admit weaknesses, something which makes Mr. Bolt extremely anxious. This not only provides the therapist with a deeper insight into the family structure, but also prepares the ground for further steps designed to alter the system.*

Unconsummated Mourning

Th.: Yes, now, Mrs. Bolt, what did you experience at the time of all these bereavements, these deaths? What did you feel? Is that something you could put into words?

M.: Well, it's hard to say, but, of course, it was hard. *(Pause)* I didn't go home very much, but still, when I did go home, my parents were still there. And that was a good feeling. . . I mean, now, when I go home, I know, they aren't there any more. But, it was really hard at first. And then, you know, then the father-in-law, and he was in hospital some of the time, and, well, that really wasn't a good time for me. And it was kind of . . ., things were really a bit too much that year, and I never seemed to get really right again.

F.: *(Coughs)*

> *Having achieved a first impression of the relational gestalt and emotional forces in the family, the therapist steers the interview towards the most emotionally loaded theme: Mrs.*

Bolt's grief. With considerable emotion she speaks of her loneliness, in that she had no one with whom she could talk about her bereavement. (This has been Mrs. Bolt's longest and most consistent statement.)

M.: . . . I always hoped, that I would be (better) again, and didn't go to the doctor with the diarrhea, and. . . .

She withdraws again quickly into the "secure" area of illness.

Th.: Why didn't you go?

M.: Oh well, I just hoped that it would clear up again, I never thought it would be anything serious.

Th.: Hm.

M.: And then I had some shots. . . *(incomprehensible)*

F.: *(Blows his nose)*

Th.: Hm.

M.: . . . I had these shots almost every day for three months, and they affected the gut, and then the whole story began. Well, now when I get a shot for the joint pains, it goes straight through to the gut again.

Th.: Hm.

M.: And I'm not allowed to take any pain-killers 'cos that just affects the gut too much.

Th.: Hm. *(pause)* Yes, eh. . . . I've got the impression that these bereavements were very . . . and the other demands . . . that was really very hard for you, right?

The therapist refuses to be diverted and refers back to the burdensome situation again.

M.: Yes, in that year, it was real hard.

By developing a sympathetic understanding of Mrs. Bolt's position, the therapist makes it possible for her for the first time to express the pain that these bereavements caused her, and in this way he can initiate the work of mourning. At the same time, he gains further information about important events in the life history. Having previously supported Mr. Bolt he can now give his attention to Mrs. Bolt without Mr. Bolt feeling unfairly treated.

The Death of the Grandfather

Th.: Who was the most help to you in this situation? Or what helped you?

M.: Well, I helped myself most, really.

Th.: You helped yourself most?

> *Mrs. Bolt had not been able to turn to her husband in her grief. The alienation of the partners is particularly clear at this point.*

M.: I couldn't talk to anyone about it very much.

Th.: No? Did you try to talk to one of them about it sometimes?

M.: No, yes, the children were still little, and then we had . . . I mean, it was most hard for Annette when Grandad died, because she was always with the parents-in-law a lot and anyhow. . . . And she was Grandad's favorite grandchild and so, well the children couldn't really understand much about it then, right. Of course, they knew that he was gone, but children forget more quickly and. . . .

Th.: *(To Annette)* Do you still remember anything about it, Annette?

> *The therapist now draws Annette, the youngest and "sensitive" daughter into the discussion.*

A.: Yes

Th.: Did . . . how did you feel about it? Do you still know?

A.: Yes, then, yes, I still remember, I was there, Granny came down early and told us all that Granddad was dead.

Th.: Hm.

(The mother wipes her nose.)

A.: Yes, and then the evening before Grandad said, he said that . . . when I took him his dinner, he said, "in the morning when you come up I shall be dead," and he was.

Th.: Granddad said that?

F.: Yes, yes, she told us at once, as though he had known. She took up his meal in the evening, right.

Th.: And Grandad said. . .

A.: Yes.

Th.: . . . in the morning, if I am dead. . . .

A.: Yes.

Th.: . . . when you bring the breakfast.

A.: Yes.

F.: Next time you come, perhaps I won't be here anymore, that
was about it, right?

A.: Yes.

Th.: Well, well. And you were his favorite grandchild?

> *The therapist invites Annette to speak about what she re-*
> *members and so discovers an important family event, which*
> *may in fact represent a myth: a specific interpretation of*
> *reality to which all members of the family subscribe (cf.*
> *Stierlin, 1973). The true coalitions within the family come*
> *into focus with a multigenerational perspective. The grand-*
> *father tells neither his son nor his wife, but his favorite*
> *grandchild about his feeling of approaching death. Can we*
> *see this as evidence that father and son had difficulty in*
> *understanding one another?*
>
> *The work of mourning all these many deaths is too much*
> *for Mrs. Bolt. To protect herself from too deep a grief, she*
> *delegates Annette to bear part of the grief that she cannot*
> *own herself. Thus, a deficiency of related individuation*
> *within the family is evident. At the same time, the measure*
> *of alienation between the marital partners is cleared. Mrs.*
> *Bolt "couldn't talk to anyone about it." Do divisive aggres-*
> *sive feelings make it impossible for her to turn to her hus-*
> *band with trust and confidence?*

The Father's Grief

Th.: Yes? Hm. What kind of a man was Granddad?

F.: He was my type.

> *Does he see the grandfather as a "hard type"? Were both*
> *externally hard and internally soft, and did both find it*
> *hard to speak about their feelings? The therapist now ad-*
> *dresses himself actively to the vertical relational structures*
> *reaching over generations.*

Th.: He was your type, too?

F.: But, because of his asthma. . . .

Th.: Hm.

F.: And he had that. . .

Th.: We're talking about Granddad now?

F.: Yes, my father.

> *Indirectly through Mrs. Bolt's bereavements and Annette's report of the death of the grandfather, the interview reaches the bereavement the father himself has suffered.*

Th.: Your father, yes.

M.: That's what the professor in the hospital said, when I had to be rushed in in September . . . I am . . . this illness is like asthma.

Th.: Ah.

F.: Sensitive people, they're the ones who get asthma attacks, I just read that in a magazine, and now with modern medicine. . .

Th.: Yes, hm.

(The others move about uneasily in their seats.)

> *Mr. Bolt's fear of weakness becomes clearer and more comprehensible. He might be like his father, and like his father, he could die. In speaking about his father he allows his fear to approach closer.*

F.: Well, like them there, they've found out, in a split second or for some reason, and . . . *(incomprehensible)* And Professor L. he said, he meant, she could die like that, she could get that far.

Th.: Ah, Professor L., he spoke to you about it?

F.: Well, yes, and then with her.

Th.: And with you too, right?

F.: . . . there she was in the intensive ward, and he said to me, anything could happen. That could happen, even the worst. The end. Right.

Th.: Ah, ah.

F.: And he said then, it's like asthma, nervous, it's all to do with the nerves.

Th.: Yes.

F.: And getting all worked up, right, my father was always like that, and then he got asthma.

Th.: Ah.

F.: And then at the end he was very nervous, so that. . . he just seemed to wait for the next asthma attack, oh yes, he was never in good health again, right. . . .

Th.: Aha, what did he die of?

F.: From asthma.

Th.: He died from asthma?

F.: From asthma.

Th.: Ah.

F.: It was in the early morning, mother was lying beside him, and then she went over, and so, she had slept so badly, because he had hardly slept at all, and she . . . and then he went to sleep about half-past four. At half-past four they were still talking about the business.

Th.: Yes.

F.: And it . . . and at half-past six she just heard. . . . "I can't go on," he called out, "I can't go on," and he sat up, and then he was dead, that was it.

Th.: Ah.

F.: I ran over and tried heart massage, and up and down. It was over, there was nothing to be done.

Th.: Ah.

F.: That was it.

> The therapist sticks to the theme and refuses to be diverted: Mr. Bolt's fear of feelings and sensibility and his compensatory advocacy of strength are easier to understand. One begins to comprehend how by his demonstrative callousness he protects himself against the overdue work of mourning which could threaten both his self-image and his position in the family.

The Father's Legacies

Th.: How was it then that Granddad had asthma? He was sensitive too, right, and. . . .

F.: Oh no, that was from the war, that was his circulation.

Th.: No, no, I mean. . . .

F.: (Interrupts the therapist) That wasn't a family disease.

Th.: It wasn't a family illness?

F.: No, no.

> *Mr. Bolt rejects the possibility that this could have anything to do with a family illness and similarities between him and his father. The relationship between sensibility and the tendency to asthma which would then be implied would be too threatening for him.*

Th.: No, no, . . . Ah yes.

F.: But he was often in the hospital with his asthma, very, very often.

Th.: Ah.

F.: Oh yes, not a single year went by. In one year he would be in as much as 28 weeks, always at intervals—the doctor said then, every time you get over the bridge the asthma's gone.

Th.: Yes.

F.: He felt safe in there.

Th.: Yes.

F.: In the hospital, everything was under control, and at home he was always afraid that it would come on, and there'd be no one to help.

Th.: Yes.

F.: Twenty-eight weeks, and always at intervals of 14 days to three weeks, he would go into the hospital.

Th.: Ah.

F.: Always at home, but never in the hospital.

Th.: Yes, who looked after him at home.

F.: Yes, mother and me.

Th.: You too?

F.: After the war, I still remember exactly, we all had a hard time, I was 19, and he was freed early, in 45 he was let out of the American prisoner of war camp in Marburg, or wherever he was in the hospital.

Th.: Yes, hm.

F.: Every night he was gasping for air. And every night about three, half-past, I had to run for the nurse and she gave him a shot and then it was all O.K. again.

Th.: Ah.

F.: And then when he wanted to go for a cure, he didn't go for a cure very often, also because of the business, right, always only business, business, business.
Th.: What sort of a business was it then?
F.: A restaurant.
Th.: Also a restaurant.
F.: And then there was a farm as well.
Th.: Yes, hm.
F.: And when the cure was over, then he came home, and then it was OK again, and after a while it was back again. Then he had an operation. There are three doctors in Germany who operate for asthma.
Th.: Hm.

As he remembers his father, Mr. Bolt feels increasingly threatened and again reverts to the medical context. He was, however, close to expressing his anxieties and his feelings of grief.

F.: They make an incision here *(shows the position on the neck)* or somewhere, I don't know.
Th.: Hm.
F.: That's it, they make it up on the throat..
M.: *(Coughs)*
Th.: You said, he got it in the war, this asthma, how did it happen?
F.: Bronchial asthma.
Th.: Ah.
F.: Now can I—eh, oh yes from the war. How did it happen? Well, yes, perhaps it was so wet, or the way it was in the war, right.
Th.: Ah yes, yes.
F.: But I can . . . too. . . .
(Pause)

In this phase of the interview the therapist is intensively occupied with the father. As with his wife, it is only possible to establish contact with him through the illness. The emphatic way in which the therapist has "taken sides" has made it possible for Mr. Bolt to discuss overly burdensome experiences in connection with the illness of his father. The therapist has now obtained an insight into Mr. Bolt's double mission to care for his chronically sick father and also to see and represent his illness as the result of the war. This can perhaps go further to explaining why Mr. Bolt must appear strong and insensitive. He thereby fulfills the legacy which says that he must preserve his father's "honor" intact.

Reversal of Roles?

Th.: You yourself are always healthy, aren't you?

F.: Me?

Th.: Yes.

F.: I feel very healthy.

Th.: Ah.

F.: At most the appendix, and perhaps the usual childish things before, I don't know, and I broke my arm *(moves his left arm).*

Th.: You broke your arm?

F.: When I was 14, and since then it's been stiff.

Th.: Hm.

F.: And when I was three I had a lung and rib infection.

B.: *(Murmurs incomprehensibly)*

F.: Oh yes, I had a rib taken out then when I was three.

Th.: But now you look really fit.

(Pause)

F.: Till now, and if it only stays that way for 10 years more, we'll be lucky.

Th.: That doesn't sound quite so . . . *(laughs softly)*

F.: Well yes, I've got a big building project, and that'll mean a good 10-year stint, and then. . . .

> *One gets the impression that Mr. Bolt overreaches himself no less than his wife, and even more so in that by not showing any weakness, he can expect hardly any support or effort on her part.*

Th.: What sort of a building project is it?

F.: Ah, a big one.

Th.: A restaurant or what?

F.: Just nearby we've still got a big free area, and there we want to build a business inside underneath, an apartment in the first floor, five or six guest rooms on the second floor, and have the third floor as a penthouse.

Th.: That sure is a big project.

F.: Sure it's a big project alright *(nods)*.

Th.: How are you going to manage it with a sensitive wife?

> *Having informed himself about the actual living conditions, the therapist reverts to the couple's relationship. He addresses the basic problem: Mr. Bolt can expect no support from his wife in his overly ambitious project. To test possibilities for change in the system, the therapist offers the chance to question the wife's being labeled as sensitive. However, Mr. Bolt cannot accept this offer.*

F.: Yes, I hope she gets a bit tougher, now that the winter is over.

Th.: Hope she gets tough soon *(laughs quietly)*. That brings on the tears again, as soon as he says that.

M.: *(Smiles weakly and shakes her head)* No.

Th.: What do you think when he says that?

M.: Oh, I know him so well, I'm used to it.

Th.: Yes, but what do you feel like inside, when he said, like he just did, I hope she soon gets tough.

M.: Well, yes, I would wish the same myself.

Th.: Ah.

M.: *(Surreptitiously wipes some tears away with her little finger and puts the finger in her mouth, subdued sobs)*

Th.: Now why the tears again?

F.: Ah *(provoked, leaning forward)*, now look, it's, now I can . . . you . . . yes, say something, tell him why you're crying again.

M.: I can't help it, I don't know.

F.: The sledgehammer, would that help?

M.: *(Laughs, moves about on her seat, wipes the tears away)*

Th.: Sledgehammer? That's not one of our tools yet.

F.: *(Laughs loud, to his wife)* He hasn't shown you his tools yet, has he? You've still got a chance of getting your head in the vise, who knows?

Th.: It's gone that far, has it? You've had a go at her with the sledgehammer?

F.: . . . Yesterday I . . .

Th.: *(Laughs, turning to the mother)* Well, nothing seems to have dropped on your head so far, or has it?

M.: No, that would be the end.

> *The nearer Mr. Bolt comes to admitting his sensitivity and ceasing to play the strong tough role, the more aggressive he is towards his wife (sledgehammer). This demonstrates the paradoxical dialectics of strength and weakness. At this point Mr. Bolt is so threatened by his own weaknesses that he has to adopt an aggressively defensive attitude to weakness in his wife (projective identification). His aggression makes Mrs. Bolt cry and this in turn clearly demonstrates her power that comes from her "weakness." Her husband feels helpless in the face of her depressive outbursts. As "victim" she controls a long-armed guilt-releasing lever. The therapist's active intervention in steering the interview towards the true conflict situation revealed an important aspect of the situation that the partners had until now denied: the weakness and depressivity of the husband and the strength of the wife in her role of victim.*

Th.: That would be the end? *(pause)* Yes, what's to be done about it? What would you say, how would it. . . . Are any other members of your family living? *(turning to Mrs. Bolt)*

> *The therapist has discussed the family of Mr. Bolt and he now brings the discussion to Mrs. Bolt's family.*

The Hard Fate of Mrs. Bolt

M.: A brother.

Th.: Only one brother, and . . .

M.: Yes, he's at home, he's got our parents' business.

Th.: Yes, were your parents healthy or did they suffer from any illnesses?

> *The therapist uses questions about illness as a springboard; Mrs. Bolt finds such questions comparatively easy to answer.*

F.: *(Shakes his head)*

M.: Um, they were generally healthy, until they got old.

Th.: Yes, hm.

F.: Real Odenwald* types.

Th.: Real Odenwald types?

F.: Hm. Like she told you, they were four children in the family, together . . .

Th.: Hm.

F.: And the first was killed in an air raid, she, where she was in . . .

Th.: The first was killed in an air raid?

F.: In Freiburg. She was down there, what's it called, in the hospital.

Th.: Yes, now how was it, what happened to the brothers and sisters?

M.: I had two sisters, I'm the youngest.

Th.: You're the youngest, and then there were two older sisters and a brother as well. And the oldest sister was killed?

F. and M.: . . . in Freiburg.

Th.: In Freiburg?

F. and M.: Yes, yes.

F.: And the other, she was married and lived on a farm.

M.: *(Blows her nose)*

F.: Yeah, in every village there's a church and a churchyard, and she was walking through with the school children, and then she fell down on the path and hit herself, and 14 days later she got a headache, and two days after she was dead.

Th.: The other sister?

F.: The other sister *(nods)*. And then the husband, he married again, after a while. There were still the two children left; and a year later the husband died.

Th.: The husband died, too.

F.: And now the two boys they're more or less with the stepmother . . . well, they're over 20 now, and . . .

B.: Yes, they're married already.

F.: Over 20. The brother who's still at home, he was very badly wounded in the war.**

Th.: Very badly?

---

* The Odenwald is a hilly forested area East of Heidelberg and Frankfurt. It is supposed to give rise to rough, hardy types of men. Also, the Odenwald is supposed to be the legendary country of the Nibelungs. Odenwald means Odin's forest; Odin is a major Nordic God.

** 80 percent disabled.

F.: Yes.

Th.: What did he lose then?

F.: Shot through the legs, and arm shot up.

M.: (*At the same time*) The, the joint was smashed up, and the elbow was shot through, too. The one leg's 12 centimeters shorter than the other, and the arm 8.

Th.: Ah.

M.: His whole joint's missing here.

Th.: What does he do? I mean . . .

F.: The farming.

Th.: Ah, he works on the farm?

F.: Yes, yes.

M.: Oh yes, he was so badly injured. He used to have a job, and I was supposed to take over the business. But he's such an outdoor type, so he decided that he'd take over the farm.

Th.: Ah, you were supposed to take over the farm?

> In this phase of the interview, the therapist intervenes relatively little, rather he encourages both partners to talk about the past in their own way (though less with themselves than with himself). In the process an important mission that Mrs. Bolt was given by her parents becomes clear: she was supposed to take over the farm after her brother came home from the war badly wounded. One gets the impression that, although she couldn't admit it, she felt this was too much for her.

M.: Yes, that was the plan, actually.

F.: It suits him better like it is.

M.: (*Laughs*)

Th.: Yes.

M.: You can't really say that, you don't know.

Th.: Yes, now tell me, Mrs. Bolt, how did you bear it all? The two sisters dying so suddenly . . .

> The therapist attempts to feel his way into the past situation and encourages Mrs. Bolt as far as possible to reveal the pain that her memories arouse.

M.: Oh yes, that sure was a hard time (*cries*). I was only 14.

Th.: Yes.

M.: Yes, that was really hard then. And the two little children there.

Th.: Um.

M.: The big one was six and the little one was only nine months. Yes, it was hard.

Th.: Hm.

> *Mrs. Bolt's past and the many deaths and misfortunes of her family are discussed. The therapist feels his way into her past situation. It becomes clear that even as an adult she has not overcome the burden and grief of her past. Mrs. Bolt's missions and merit accounts show up in the light of the multi-generational perspective. Mrs. Bolt was the only sound member of the family. She therefore remained very closely bound to them and suffered strong feelings of "survival guilt." To assuage her guilt she had to stay strong and healthy—at the price of chronically overreaching herself and ignoring warning signals indicating exhaustion and legitimate regressive bodily needs.*

Alienation of the Partners

F.: *(Leans forward)* Yes, do you really think the whole thing goes back 20 or 30 years? You shouldn't trouble yourself about all that anymore.

Th.: Yes, do you know, that's just the problem. Although such things go so far back, we're always finding that they stay right down there underneath, right, *(hand on his abdomen)* and it really doesn't help at all if we say they happened so long ago. They just stay right there underneath, see?

> *The therapist tries to indicate connections that Mr. Bolt can accept without too great anxiety. For closely bound families time seems almost to stand still.*

F.: I get it, but who can help her or make her better? Only herself, nobody else can help.

> *Mr. Bolt, too, senses the loneliness and isolation in which the two partners live "together."*

Th.: Ah.

F.: You've got to be right there with it, yourself *(knocks his chest)*, you've got to know yourself.

Th.: Ah.

F.: And it's all, well, they're, you'd hardly believe *(indicates his wife)*. You've got to cope with the thing yourself *(leans back again in his seat)*.

Th.: Hm.

F.: All the doctors have said, she's got to know herself. I can do this or I'm allowed to do this, and not that.

M.: Yes, but it comes on so right out of the blue, like . . .

F.: *(Clears his throat)*

M.: . . . the illness, well, sometimes I think now I'm OK, and then I feel well, and I can work, and nothing's too much. And then, all of a sudden, *(suppressed crying)* there it is from one day to the next.

> *Mr. Bolt reacts to his wife's family history with a mixture of sympathy and fear. He has the chance to understand his wife better, but appears at the same time uneasy. The alienation between the partners is largely the product of their being so strongly bound up with their own families. Mr. Bolt confirms his helplessness in the face of his wife's suffering ("only herself, nobody else can help").*

Mutual Exploitation

Th.: What was the last time that it came on like that, from one day to the next?

> *The therapist comes back from the past to the present with its problems.*

F. and M.: *(At the same time)* It was . . .

Th.: Yes.

M.: Perhaps it was on Sunday with the inside trouble, last Sunday. Before, it was just the joints that were . . .

Th.: And it came on from one day to the next?

M.: Yes, it was then on Sunday again so. . . . I know that. . . . I got so tired and so, ah, I can't really say . . .

Th.: Something happened again on Sunday, didn't it?

M.: Oh yes, we had a lot of business at the weekend, and then on

Friday we had a golden wedding, and that's usually our day off,
and then well . . . somehow something's missing then when . . .

Th.: *You* had a golden wedding?

M.: No, no.

Th.: *(Laughs)*

M.: We had a golden wedding in the restaurant.

Th.: Yes.

M.: Yes, and that's why . . . I'm ill again . . . if it's too much. In the
week, you might say, in business, you look forward to the day
off. And then there was this golden wedding, they're neighbors.

Th.: Ah.

F.: She likes to put her feet up then on Fridays, when we've got
the day off. And that was an extra strain.

Th.: Ah.

F.: Saturday we had farmers' wives for the day and that was all go.
Coffee, breakfast, coffee in the afternoon, evening meal, and
overnight. It went more or less round the clock, no peace, and
because of that, now she's ill again.

M.: Oh yes, we had so much to do for the midday meal. Then, I
didn't have a second on Sunday . . .

F.: Yes.

M.: . . . to get a bit of peace, and that was then a bit too . . .

F.: Yes, and then in the afternoon the farmers' wives wanted coffee
again. That was just too much, I can see that. But you've just
got to say sometimes, "Now, I've had enough, now I'm going
to put my feet up," two, three hours.

M.: Yes, that's what I did on Sunday and then . . .

F.: *(Interrupts his wife, and both talk at once)* On Monday . . .

M.: On Monday, well I knew by then, this couldn't go on.

F.: No.

M.: And then the food was already ordered again.

Th.: Mrs. Bolt, why is it so hard just to say, like your husband says,
now I've done enough, now I'm going to lie down for a couple
of hours?

> *With this last question the therapist grasps an important part
> of the concealed relational structure. The "power of the
> weak" is revealed in Mrs. Bolt's unwillingness to trust her*

*husband to run the business alone. In this way she keeps him
in a constant state of dependence and herself gains a strong
feeling of importance. At the same time, it is clear that both
partners are only passing on to each other what they themselves suffered within their own families.*

The Strength of the Weak

M.: That's what I said on Sunday.

F.: *(Points with the index finger)* It's on Sunday.

M.: *(Simultaneously points at her husband)* And then he said, it's
enough now, it was too . . .

Th.: Why was it not possible?

F.: Yes . . .

M.: *(Simultaneously)* Yes, because they were already there again,
the next business had already started. We hadn't really finished
clearing up the kitchen from the midday meal.

Th.: *(Interrupts both)* Right, it really does seem to make sense what
your husband says, now you put your feet up sometimes and let
yourself . . . yes. . . . You need rest, you really need it, and . . .

M.: Oh yes, I do too, when I've got a bit of time, I always take a
nap after the midday meal, but from Thursday to Sunday it's
just simply impossible. There's just no possibility.

> *The therapist tries to intervene in the relationship with di-
> rect advice, but fails.*

F.: Oh yes, that's right *(ironically, nods agreeing)*.

M.: There wasn't a minute's peace, we were on the go from half-
past six in the morning till 12, or one at night . . .

Th.: Yes, would it be possible to take someone on who would . . .

M.: We're already only open from five in the afternoon, because
I can't cope with any more at the moment, healthwise, and I
normally take a nap every day, but that was . . . well, something
else every day.

Th.: Would it be quite impossible to get someone else in to help
when you get such a load like with a wedding?

> *Why does the family not take up the therapist's practical sug-
> gestions? Mr. and Mrs. Bolt have already explored the pos-
> sibilities themselves, without producing any change in the*

situation. It is clear that the mother is not going to let herself be so easily pried out of her role as victim. It is also clear that, from this position of a patient, she still indirectly controls the running of the business. To resolve the complementary rigidity of the malign stalemate into which the system has hardened requires further measures.

The Children as Delegates

F.: You see, she's not been able to get up normally one single day this week, only for breakfast, and then she's gone back to bed again, and then I've called her at five o'clock. But you mustn't think she goes to sleep when she's in bed.

M.: Ah, now . . .

F.: She's always brooding.

M.: *(Smiles and shakes her head)* Now . . .

Th.: She's always brooding.

F.: Yes.

Th.: What do you mean, she's always brooding?

F.: Oh, she's always thinking. What if it starts? What if I've got to go to hospital again? That's how I see it.

M.: No, you can't say that.

Th.: What do the children think about it?

> *The therapist turns now to the children. Are they caught up in their parents' conflict?*

F.: Yes, thank heaven, they don't know everything. She's *(indicates Annette)* so sensitive, right. She was with Granny, it's her Granny she loves best. Granny's just ill all the time now. Mammy was in the hospital, and I was there too, I was supposed to have 'flu. And then Granny, she went into the hospital too, with some woman's thing, and she had the usual sort of operation, and then she was soon at home again.

Th.: Ah.

F.: And she *(indicates Brigitte)*, she just clears off, right, but she's *(indicates Annette)* got no one to go to, right?

M.: *(Coughs)*

F.: Granny sick, Mommy sick, how's she supposed to react . . . *(claps his hands on his thighs)*.

M.: *(Blows her nose)*

Th.: Ah.

F.: Perhaps she thinks . . . *(to Annette)*, but she *(to Brigitte)*, she thinks, no, Mammy's sick and she clears off. She *(to Annette)* sits in school thinking, just turns it all over, right, that's how it is with her, but she *(turning to Brigitte)* she just clears off.

> *The children are caught in a delegational conflict. They are parentified and exploited. The tasks assigned them are appropriate neither to the capabilities nor to the needs of their ages. The distribution of roles, the strong father and the weak mother, is cemented with their help. The children bear the parents' burdens. Brigitte must deny weaker and softer sides of herself to retain her father's preference, while Annette (who is very infantile in a way that belies her age) has hardly any chance of achieving independent development.*

How Can the Mother Be Helped?

Th.: Yes, now girls, what do you think? You know your mother so well, much better than me, for example. What do you think, how can we help her?

B.: Well, practically she's the only one who can help herself, like he said, so that it all changes.

(Pause)

F.: Oh, the girls . . . *(gives Annette a light push)* come on, you should say something, right, she gets so easily upset.

Th.: Who gets so easily upset?

F.: The wife usually, which is normal with the children. Well, I just think then, to put it bluntly, go and take a running jump at yourself, and she can't, right, it's the illness *(indicates his wife)*. They don't always do what they're told, that's straight, and they don't behave so well, and they're not so clean and tidy, and then she gets upset. They've got their own room, but then there's no . . . and she gets so worked up.

> *Paradoxically, the therapist works against the exploitation of the children by demanding yet more from them. He helps*

them to make their parents into better parents. He is in-
volved in their deepest interests and prepares the way for age-
appropriate separation and personal development.

The Conflict between the Sisters

M.: Ah yes, that is . . .

Th.: Yes, would you explain why you get so upset then?

M.: Yes, for Christmas they had their room done over, newly papered
and carpeted and beautifully fitted out and all. And then they
promised me, good, when it was renovated and fresh and nice
again, then they'd keep it in order. And now it's all . . . so again
. . . not like it was, I mean to say . . .

Th.: Could you just . . .

M.: Yes, yes.

Th.: . . . just describe it to me, the mess.

M.: *(Simultaneously)* Well, it's not quite as bad as it was, but you
know, the way she comes and goes . . .

F.: *(Murmurs)* The disorder, yes.

Th.: But she gets so upset, disorder?

M.: Oh, Brigitte, she just climbs over it.

F.: *(Simultaneously)* She waits *(to his wife)* . . . I take a look, she
should really. One fine day the girl'll trip up and take a header
over the books and paper, then she'll come to it herself.

B.: There's nothing on the floor.

(Everyone laughs)

Th.: Is it really as bad as all that, Annette?

A.: Sometimes.

Th.: Sometimes? *(laughs)* What's it like at the moment, Annette?

A.: I don't know.

Th.: That, too?

M.: Yes, she's been getting like that too recently. Before she was
different. But recently she's just thrown the clothes and things
around any old how, when she's dressing. She goes sledging
once and . . .

F.: *(Yawns)*

Th.: How are things going in school? Could things be better there
too?

F.: She's *(turns to Brigitte)* poor in math, we could say . . . and she's *(to Annette)* below average in German. But apart from that we've got no complaint about school, right. At least nothing yet about her *(to Brigitte),* but she *(to Annette)* we heard again yesterday. But it's because of the business, she doesn't get to bed at a regular time, and she's sleepy in school, then . . .

> *By turning directly to the children, the therapist has revealed further functions that the children have for the parents: Brigitte allows her mother to express aggressive feelings that obviously relate to her husband (diversion to another object). In this way the conflict between the parents is kept within bearable limits and the emotional balance of the family is maintained. From the basis of parental delegation, the sisters live out the conflict that should, in fact, take place between the parents.*

The Result of Delegation

M.: Yes, they could go to bed separately, that doesn't have to depend on the business.

B.: *(Murmurs)*

F.: Oh yes, she won't go to bed alone.

Th.: How do you mean, she won't go to bed alone?

F.: No, she must have somebody there.

M.: Both go . . .

F.: *(Together)* I don't know, Mammy, the two of them can't be together, I know that, why . . .

B.: Oh yes, if she doesn't want to sleep in my room, you can't force her to.

(Father and daughter talk, but incomprehensible)

M.: The room is done up for both of them together, but . . .

B.: Oh, she can sleep in the room with me, that doesn't bother me, that is the . . .

F.: Yes.

A.: *(Quietly)* I don't want to go to bed with you.

B.: You don't have to.

Th.: Yes, now I'm not clear, why don't you want to be with your sister, Annette?

B.: Because she's scared. She flinches when I just walk past, and I haven't even done anything.

M.: You're always punching her, you can't even pass her normally.

B.: Yes, but if I . . . then she screams before I've even done anything, and I haven't even done anything.

Th.: Why do you always punch her then?

B.: 'Cause it's fun.

(*Brigitte and her father smile*)

F.: Because it's fun, she said.

M.: Fun to torment her, go on, admit the truth.

B.: Oh alright, it is fun to torment her. . . . I like tormenting people, I don't know why.

(*The father snorts.*)

Th.: You like tormenting people?

B.: Yes, I do it in school, too.

Th.: In school, too?

F.: (*Half yawns*) You shouldn't say that, child.

> *The father sanctions Brigitte's aggressive behavior, although he criticizes it openly.*

B.: Alright, not to everyone.

F.: (*Laughing*) Otherwise the professors'd get a bad impression of you, if you . . . in the school . . .

B.: (*Interrupts her father*) Oh yes, that's not the case with everyone.

Th.: (*Turning to the father*) I've just had a nasty thought; because if, like you say, she's like you, then perhaps you too enjoy tormenting people?

> *How the children are delegated and how they relieve their parents of a burden is now clear. They live out the parental conflict and, at the same time, provide a source of stimulus and concern which diverts the parents from their own conflict and both cements and veils their "emotional divorce." Unconsciously, through their covert recognition, the parents encourage Brigitte's aggressive behavior and contribute to Annette's inhibitions. These delegations have results for the children's relationship to their environment. How will the family react when the therapist draws a parallel between the behavior of the father and the daughter?*

Unequal Handling of the Sisters

F.: Oh, well.

B.: *(Stoutly)* Crap, that's crap—I don't really get the people upset, no, not really, just have a bit of fun.

F.: Right, that's more the idea.

Th.: But I'm still not quite clear why you like tormenting your sister, Brigitte?

B.: *(Emotionally)* Oh yes, she's, she's—they always think, well, she's so good, and, now, then, when she . . . then she starts it too sometimes . . . she torments me too sometimes, and if . . .

A.: Sometimes.

B.: *(Quickly)* And then when I do it back, yes, if I give her one back, then she screams for Mommy and then . . .

F.: *(Stretches, rubs his eyes, groans)*

B.: . . . and then *she* comes and bawls me out and she doesn't bother to find out whether I, I mean, that, that she can torment me just the same as I torment her.

M.: Yes, but, that's what you always say 99 percent of the time . . . you're the one who starts it.

B.: Oh yes, then if *(incomprehensible)* . . . and then it hurts and then she thinks I've started it.

M.: Oh yes.

B.: When it isn't true at all.

M.: Still, they just don't get on, that's the problem, it's real bad sometimes. . . .

Th.: Has it always been like that, that they don't get on?

M.: That . . . I guess so, because Annette was always the favorite with everyone, and then *she* was often jealous, and I guess, it's kind of crystallized with time, so that . . .

Th.: Does it look like that to you Brigitte, that Annette was always the favorite?

B.: Yes, with Granddad and Granny always.

Th.: Always, with Grandad and Granny, now just why was that?

B.: Well, yes.

F.: That's easy, that's easy to see with someone like that . . .

B.: That, that's it . . . with . . . it's just the same with my aunt. My two cousins, they're Granny's grandchildren too, and it's just the same for them, and when they say something, she's more or less the "little angel," and . . .

Th.: The little angel?

F.: (Laughs)

B.: Yes, that's what she says.

F.: Oh yes, she's really Granny's pet.

Th.: (Turning to Brigitte) And you're the holy terror?

B.: No, well, but, when something gets broken.

Th.: (Laughs)

B.: Or if something's missing or broken, then it's always me.

A.: Not true.

> *The parallels between the children and their parents emerge more clearly: the strong Brigitte is able to express her aggression, to build up an image of strength and capability, but at the same time risks being rejected by her environment. With little Annette it is just the reverse. The problem extends back through many generations; grandparents as well as the uncle and aunt are involved.*
>
> *The interview has opened a new perspective. The conflict may be seen on a vertical intergenerational plane. Feelings of injustice, envy, and jealousy burden the girls' relationship with one another and with their peers. Up until now it is particularly Brigitte who senses and expresses the injustices, and the therapist makes it possible for her to talk about these feelings.*
>
> *Brigitte cannot escape the exploitation and parentification without becoming caught up in a loyalty conflict with the parents.*
>
> *The therapist intervenes in this rigid system by giving the family members the chance to discuss openly the injustices and disadvantages they experience within the family. At the same time, he signifies to the parents that such open expression need hold no threat. This could be the first step in the "opening and balancing of accounts of guilt and merits."*

Blurring of Generational Boundaries

B.: It is.

M.: Yes, that's what usually happens, when you put your hands on something . . .

B.: *Well,* the last time you were looking for a fan or something, and I wasn't even there, and it was just before the meal, and then it was, "Brigitte's taken it."

M.: Well, I think you did, too.

B.: No, it wasn't me. It went down in the elevator to the cellar after the meal.

M.: Oh, did it.

A.: *(Murmurs)*

B.: And then there was a key missing, yes, and you had it.

M.: Yes, yes, because you're just the type, you can't keep anything in order. For example, in the mornings when you come and open the elevator, and then when I'm doing the room in the morning, I can look everywhere for the key—it's just not there.

B.: Oh yes, and who had the key last then—you've looked for the key and *you* just don't know where *you* put it down.

M.: Oh yes, that does happen, if I sometimes. . . .

B.: Yes, that's always happening.

M.: No, Mrs. S. must have left it on the table, I don't know . . .

B.: Right, then, see!

F.: *(Murmurs at the same time)* . . . with that thing. . . .

Th.: Is that another thing that gets you upset? And . . .

M.: Yes, when I keep on looking for something and it's not where it ought to be, I get upset, I just can't stand it. . . .

Th.: I see. . . .

M.: That's how it is with me, when I put a thing down, then that's where it should be, and then I can find it in the dark or. . . .

Th.: And when you get upset, what do you do then?

F.: She cries, then she cries.

M.: Yes, I guess I do.

A.: No *(Annette shakes her head).*

F.: Oh, tears.

B.: And then, then she says, she's going to give me a slap, but right up till now I've never had one.

F.: Yes, that's right.

M.: But you could still get one.

A.: Yes.

B.: Yes, I can see that coming *(sarcastically).*

A.: Yes, every day *(murmurs)*.

B.: *(Simultaneously)* . . . she says that five times a day.

Th.: Yes, that would be a big event, if you actually did get a slap, right?

F.: Yes, yes, it would be easier for her *(points to his wife)*, like this, it all goes down there *(lays his hands on his abdomen)*, she takes everything inside her. She ought to just give her one, she doesn't need to half kill her, just once, bim bam bam bim, then the whole thing would be over, finish.

> *Order in the household has very great significance for Mrs. Bolt ("she must be able to find things in the dark"). At the same time that this demonstrates her general capability, it also shows that she is almost compulsively bound to maintain the system in which she lives. The mother bears the main burden of bringing up the children, while the father's role is more peripheral. By taking up the subject of the slap, the therapist attempts to re-establish the intergenerational boundaries. Brigitte is thereby relieved and replaced in her age-appropriate role. He also offers Mrs. Bolt constructive possibilities of breaking the vicious circle of suppressed hostility, tears and illness.*

The Father Helps the Mother

Th.: That's what you do, right?

F.: Yes.

M.: Oh, you don't hit them either.

F.: Oh, I've got no reason, I wouldn't . . . enough time with her . . .

> *The parents do not pull together in bringing up the children. Instead of mutually strengthening each other's authority, Mr. Bolt disqualifies his wife in front of the children.*

Th.: You don't hit the children?

F. and M.: *(Speaking together inaudibly)*

F.: I don't have much to do with the girls, they don't upset me.

Th.: Do you think that he's only really tough on the outside, but basically he's very soft-hearted?

F.: I don't get worked up so easily on that account, really not.

M.: Yes, you just yell, and I can't do that, and you, if you get worked up, you just bawl the house down.

F.: Yes, and then it's over.

M.: Well, that's just not normal for everyone.

F.: Oh yes, and then it's gone, it's over, instead of swallowing the whole thing and letting it make you sick inside.

Th.: Hm, yes, that was not so badly put, right?

> *The therapist does not intervene in the couple's mutual denigration; rather he tries to induce the father to do something for his wife and to look for ways that would make it possible for her to be rid of her anger without "letting it make her sick inside." Brigitte would be disturbed and freed from her feelings of guilt related to her mother's illness.*

"Help" for the Mother?

F.: Ah *(groans aloud)*, I know, I just know how it is.

Th.: Oh *(pause)* Yes, Brigitte, what do you do then so that your mother can give you a slap?

> *The therapist relieves Brigitte still further by this paradoxical intervention. He values the child's concern for the mother positively. Despite this he uses the "symbolic prescription" of the slap to draw clear boundaries between the generations. Of course, this is in no sense an instigation to corporal punishment as a means of bringing up children.*

F.: *(Laughs aloud)*

B.: She said, she said . . .

Th.: *(Laughs)*

B.: She doesn't do it . . .

F.: *(Stands up and goes to the window)*

> *Mr. Bolt may feel himself under pressure from what is going on between mother and daughter. Is the system going to change? He expresses his feeling not in words, but indirectly through his actions.*

M.: Usually when I've got a reason to give you a slap, you're not there.

A.: *(Murmurs)*

Th.: Oh how's that? The little angel doesn't get any slaps, anyhow, right?

M.: Oh yes, she's had a few, but . . .

Th.: Oh, she's had a few?

B.: Yes, now and again, but very seldom.

Th.: *(Laughs)*

F.: *(Sits down again)*

B.: Only from Granny, she's not allowed to get away with everything there, she gave her a slap.

A.: *(Slides about on her seat and murmurs something)*

Th.: Yes, Mr. Bolt what are we going to do to help your wife so that she doesn't take everything so much inside her and make herself sick. So that instead she . . .

F.: Yes, I've been thinking about it, if she could only go to sleep for eight days . . . the doctor or the professor . . .

M.: *(Laughs)*

Th.: Go to sleep for eight days?

F.: Yes, there's a method or therapy, I don't know what you call it.

Th.: Should we put her to sleep or should we help her to slap somebody?

> How has Mr. Bolt come to make this astonishing "therapeutic suggestion?" Could it be that the idea of "putting his wife to sleep" is already a reaction to the implied changes in the family system? He seemed to be aware, and indeed advocated, that his wife would become "harder," but this suggestion seems to point in the opposite direction. Is the wish to "put Mrs. Bolt to sleep" an expression of his aggressive feelings towards her? In any event his suggestion is highly ambivalent.

The Children's Guilt and Loyalty Conflicts

M.: Oh.

F.: She's got to be able to do it herself, but that's just it . . . she can't, she just can't, she can't scream, she can't do it.

(Pause)

Th.: But at the moment she does in fact scream, right?

F.: She? At night, oh yes at night, she screams with pain the whole night long, ow! ow! ow!

M.: *(Laughs)*

F.: And in the mornings before she gets up, it takes at least half an hour before she puts a foot out.

M.: Oh, really. . . .

F.: *(Simultaneously)* Yes, from sheer pain, from sheer pain. Watch out, now we're off again, like a good psychologist, now she's at it again, they're just pouring out.

M.: *(Crying and shifting uneasily on her chair)* Oh you . . . man . . .

F.: *(Laughs)*

M.: Yes, but that's the pain in the joints.

Th.: Right that's the joint pains.

A.: *(Murmurs)*

Th.: What is it, Annette?

A.: Papa, should stop laughing.

Annette attempts to protect her mother from her father.

F.: *(Smiling)* You shouldn't torment Mommy, right?

Th.: *(Simultaneously)* Papa should stop laughing?

F.: Stop tormenting Mommy, that's it, isn't it?

A.: *(Turning to Brigitte)* . . . but sometimes it's your fault.

B.: Oh no . . . yes.

Th.: Whose fault is it sometimes?

B.: Yes, then they say, it's my fault, yes, that's what they always say, they're always telling me, it's my fault that Mommy's sick.

F.: *(Laughs)*

> *Annette attacks her father out of pity for her mother, who does not protect herself. Why does she extend her reproach to her sister? Is it a general rendering of accounts? Or does she want to divert the accusation from her father? These accusations of guilt and the obligations of loyalty bring us to the most important, and at the same time most difficult, points of the interview.*

B.: And Granny says it, they all say it, that it's my fault, that Mommy's sick.

> *Again the significance of the absent "third generation" becomes clear.*

F.: Oh yes, because you're the one who torments her the most and you don't do anything for her.

M.: *(Blows her nose)*

F.: You are . . . and some weeks . . . she does work, right, really . . .

Th.: Yes.

F.: On Sunday midday we had at least eight people in the kitchen for the midday meal, guaranteed, and also perhaps . . . *(incomprehensible)* She wasn't there, not for the whole midday period. And the next day she was behind the bar from five till nine and poured beer and wine. . . . I, when I came in it was, Papa you put your feet up, I want to work today and then she helped wait at table, and clear up and all the customers praised the wine and the orders, really fine, so there's nothing wrong with her, only . . .

Th.: Ah.

F.: When she doesn't want to, she doesn't do a thing. That's how she shows her anger. And I think then, leave her alone, it'll sort itself out.

Because Brigitte is being blamed, the father upholds her merits. He wants a fair accounting.

Concern with Accounts

M.: But you've got to control it a bit, in your case, too. Like this Sunday, it would have been a good idea if she'd have helped out.

F.: What am I supposed to do with the child. . . .

M.: *(Interrupts)* Well yes, you've . . . her *(incomprehensible)* . . . but I did have to help at the bar. . . .

F.: When there's five people in the kitchen, you can do without one of them.

M.: But what I. . . .

F.: We've got a good staff in the kitchen.

Th.: Yes.

F.: But that's it again, like I said before, the people want the food more or less waiting on the table. They could at least sit and wait a bit.

Th.: Yes.

M.: We've got so used to serving quickly.

F.: Right, right.

M.: . . . the people quickly. We work together in the kitchen, but when I'm not there. . . .

Th.: Yes.

M.: And with this cook, . . . he, he, he, he is, I have to be there all the time, and if I'm not there . . .

Th.: Yes.

M.: And on Sunday, he was alone at the bar and then he got nervous.

F.: Oh.

Th.: Eh.

M.: Oh, you can laugh.

F.: I said, I don't have anything to do with the food, I had my bar to see to and I served the wine, but serving the food, yes, hm, hm . . .

M.: Yes, yes, we have two waitresses for that, but they . . .

F.: The people they're sitting there and . . .

A.: *(Murmurs)*

Th.: Excuse me. Annette, why do you think it is your father's fault too?

A.: Sometimes he screams so.

Th.: Sometimes he screams so?

A.: Yes.

F.: What for? You should say that too. When, how, and why?

B.: She doesn't know.

A.: Yes, when Mommy's asleep, if she sometimes takes a nap, then you scream.

F.: I do?

A.: *(Murmurs incomprehensibly)*

F.: I scream, when she's still fixing food at half-past ten.

A.: Yes, yes.

(Simultaneously)

B.: Yes, that's true.

F.: Right, right, I ought to say, when I say that's enough for today and she just carries right on. OK, there are days when we can't just turn them all out.

Th.: Hm.

F.: On Mondays there's a men's group.

Th.: Yes.

F.: The men's gymnastic group. They come on Monday, they come at 10, 10:30, and some want to eat. But they're regulars. Then on Wednesdays there's the ladies from those men. They arrive at 10:30, but regular too. Well, we just have to be there.

Th.: Yes, hm.

F.: And on Tuesdays we can say, if possible, right, no more meals after 10.

M.: And on Thursdays there's the swimming . . .

F.: OK, OK, and Thursdays—OK that's an exception. Well, sometimes the parish council come, they have their meetings on Tuesdays, yes, you can't really turn them out. But when there's none of these exceptions and you can . . . turn them out. I still have to stay there till 12, 12:30. And if they get something to eat at one, then they sit even longer.

> *Is the mother really indispensable? Does she bend over too much to meet the guests' wishes? Her capability certainly wins her a degree of self-affirmation, but she nevertheless reproaches her husband and Brigitte with not helping her enough (and so being partly to blame for her overstrain and her illness). Her husband and daughter are on the defensive and retaliate with "you've yourself to blame if you work so much," which in turn, is an unjustifiable disparagement of the mother's actual contribution. The social reality of the family has particular significance at this point. Their mutual existence depends on a common effort. The problems discussed at this point will certainly be of great importance in the following phase of the therapy.*

Difficulties in Drawing up a Therapeutic Contract

Th.: Hm. You know we must, eh, begin to think about coming to an end.

> *The therapist sets a limit and introduces the closing phase of the interview.*

F.: Yes, yes, I would like that too.

Th.: And what shall we do now?

F.: Yes.

Th.: It seems to me, Mr. Bolt, you've had really good ideas: when you say your wife swallows all the irritations and the anger and that that's what makes her sick, right, or when you think she should let go more.

F.: But let up, too, really let up.

Th.: Let up, yes.

F.: No thinking.

Th.: Yes, now what should we do about this brooding and thinking?

F.: Yes, I don't know, that's perhaps more your line. Although I don't know, what sort of methods or means you use.

Th.: Hm.

A.: *(Stretches)*

Th.: Now, I had the impression as we were all talking, that, eh, things were really starting to come alive, I had the feeling. And to my mind that could really be the best thing, if everyone can say. . .

F.: Yes, we could really talk things out, only Annette she's still a bit shy.

Th.: She's still got to learn, right?

F.: Yes.

Th.: Mrs. Bolt, how did you find the discussion—particularly the last 15 minutes.

M.: Yes, what shall I say. It was quite normal, so that every. . .

Th.: Was quite normal?

M.: Yes, but whether it's really done any good *(incomprehensible)* I don't know.

Th.: What we actually have here, what we do here is, of course, family therapy. And basically that really isn't much different than what we've just been doing, right? We all sit down together and walk to each other. Because, it's our experience that many people really can't talk to one another about things.

> *There is a noticeable degree of anxious hesitation about continuing the family interviews. By acknowledging the family's openness and stressing the positive constructive side of the interview, the therapist tries to encourage the family to agree to extended treatment.*

Progress with the Therapeutic Contract

F.: Yes, yes.

Th.: And then we get blockages and misunderstandings and real loneliness. We've noticed that it helps to talk about it so that you can understand one another better. The question is, does this make sense to you? To have another interview?

F.: Well, I'll tell you, Friday is our day off.

Th.: Yes.

F.: Usually we watch TV—the rest of the week I never watch anything.

Th.: Hm.

F.: We usually watch till nine, and then, if the children have no school next day, we sit in the living room and they play and do a bit of gymnastics on the floor.

Th.: Hm.

F.: Something seems to be missing, I guess because of her tiredness and lack of blood, I guess it's the lack of blood that makes her tired all the time.

Th.: Well, yes and no. I think you hit the nail on the head; the mental aspects play a big part here, right, in the nervousness, and that, eh, somehow we've got to deal with the mental aspects, right, because operations and pills. . . 'cause. . . well. . .

F.: Ah, they're the end, you might as well close the book then.

Th.: Hm, close the book, you're right there, and that's why we've got to ask whether perhaps we should try to reach the mental aspects of the trouble, because I was very impressed by the way the two youngsters also took part, right, and something. . .

F.: Oh yes, this week we've all been sledging and I was outside every day, and they were so pleased that I came to watch them. All the kids had their fathers out there, and she could have come out, too. Well, I know she can't walk, but the fresh air would be good. Even if she can't walk, and then a slow walk, but she ought to get out. It's really no good, lie here, lie down there. I had to walk on my own, right.

At the end of the hour it becomes clear how much Mr. Bolt

longs for togetherness with his wife, even though he can only
express this wish indirectly as demands for mutual activity.

Th.: Yes, yes, now how are we going to do it Mr. Bolt? Do you
think it would make sense for you, from time to time. . . on
a day that's convenient to you. . . ·

F.: Oh, that'll do, the time.

Th.: That'll do?

F.: Ah, that is. . . .

Th.: How do you mean?

M.: Yes, now you mean we should have another talk like this one?

Th.: Well, that we should carry on the talk; we can think about it.
Maybe we should fix it for every two weeks or—so it's not too
much for you all—or sometimes. I think, it's become clear that
the mental aspect is very important here, right? And I don't
think it makes sense to wait so long that things get really bad
again and it comes to tablets and being hospitalized. The mental aspects, they're really the feelings, the things that go on
between you, right?

M.: Yes, but I keep on asking myself, the sickness is there, isn't
it? It's the organ that's involved. Can't that be got better?

Th.: Yes, it's surely there and it's been changed. On the other hand
it's become quite clear to me, that whether it starts being active
again, depends on the mental strain. Now, it seems to me that
you feel really over-strained, and in my judgment that's what
we've got to deal with, right?

M.: Hm.

Th.: That makes sense to me.

M.: Yes, yes, if you can get to the cause of it, but I must say I'm
not really with you there.

Th.: We've got to try and find it together. We must also I. . .

F.: And there's something else I want to say before we go, if it's
OK with you, if we fix another date. She doesn't have much
contact with other people. Y'know why. . . she's standing there
at the stove from five or 5:30 till 9:30. That's her part of it. . .
and she doesn't really see what's going on outside. And then
I say, oh come on, sit down with the guests a while, right? With

the overnight guests or the regulars, or families. Yes, and then she's too tired, and if she'd only come and talk to the people for half an hour, like we've just. . .

M.: I do sometimes.

F.: She'd have something else to think about then, but. . .

M.: If I once sit down, then I'm sitting down for an hour, hour-and-a-half, and my night's rest is more important to me sometimes than sitting. . .

F.: Like the talk.

M.: Oh no, I was sitting there last week, too, and I wanted to get to bed at 10:30 but then it was 12:30, and that's it that. . .

Th.: Well now, we're no magicians or conjurors, right? It would be an experiment for us, too. I don't believe there is any doctor who could say that he's got the whole answer. It's my feeling that with so much that's so alive and so much goodwill between you all . . . to show up . . . to get closer to the root of the matter, really to help, that we could get a long way. That's my feeling.

> *In the final phase the father proves himself a constructive advocate of therapeutic contract. The mother partly withdraws again into the organic concept of the illness, and this the therapist accepts. Mr. Bolt's strong rejection of the interview has changed in the course of the session to cautious expectancy.*

The Contract with the Whole Family

F.: Yes, only, how. . .

M.: I don't know.

F.: It's like this, they've got to go to school (*to Brigitte and Annette*) and then that's difficult.

Th.: Yes, we'll have to think it over well. . . I think, the important question is whether you think it makes any sense, and then if you do, we'll have to think how we can come to an arrangement about how often, and so on. Those would be the next steps.

M.: Oh no, I would say you ought to make the appointments, we can't do much. . . at the moment, of course. Do you want Fridays or some other day? *(to her husband)*

B.: Yes, do we want it to be in the morning again?

Th.: What, yes, it depends on how it goes.

F.: Yes.

Th.: . . . We ought to . . . I don't think I'd. . .

B.: *(Simultaneously)* That's it. . .

Th. 2: But we all work here together and . . . right, we could see you all when the children can manage it.

F.: It's no good at all for the children in the morning.

Th. 2: Yes, right, that's why we wanted. . .

Th.: Yes, then we must try to have it in the afternoon, and also so that you're not put out, that there's as little as possible conflict with your . . .

B.: Yes, how about between two and five.

F.: One hour.

Th.: One hour.

F.: Yes, yes, one hour.

B.: Between two and five.

Th. 2: Between two and five.

F.: Yes, yes.

Th. 2: Perhaps we should go downstairs now and look at the appointments, so that we. . .

F.: Yes, she has a stenography course *(indicates Brigitte)* and a piano lesson.

Th. 2: Thursdays between two and five.

B.: Oh, that's no good.

(All talk together.)

F.: Not so much talk, let's say now Mondays or Tuesdays.

Th. 2: Monday or Tuesday?

F.: Yes, let's fix it . . . then Monday or Tuesday.

B.: Every two weeks now . . .

F.: Coats on *(he gets up, they all stand up and shake hands)*.

M.: Annette, bring my purse.

Th.: Yes, don't forget anything, right?

Th. 2: Yes, we'll then . . .

M.: Yes, many thanks.

Th.: Yes, thank you very much for coming, it was not all that easy for you, was it? See you again soon.

> *The therapist draws up the agreement for the further interviews not with the parents alone, but also with the children: he makes the appointment for a time that suits all members of the family. In this way he both emphasizes the importance of all members of the family and tries to avoid one member being blamed for possible failures to keep the appointment. Finally the therapist thanks the family. In this way he, yet again, expressly acknowledges their achievement in this difficult situation.*

9

Case Discussion of the Bolt Family

Childhood

MRS. BOLT WAS BORN IN 1937 in the Odenwald. Her father and mother were respectively 40 and 42 years old. The difference in age between herself and her two sisters and brother ranged from 15 to 20 years. From the start, as the youngest child, she had the role of baby of the family. As far as possible within a strict, hardworking, thrifty farming family, she was spoilt by parents and siblings. Her mother was a deeply religious woman who went to church and to prayer meetings very regularly. She believed that the trials and suffering of mankind come from God. Conscientious care, but little warmth or cordiality, characterized her relationship to her children.

There was never any strife in the family, neither between the parents nor between any other members. The father was "kind and just, but strict." When she was 15 years old, he beat her for the first and last time on account of a small white lie: When she had been delivering milk, she had stayed too long with some of the village

172

youngsters, so that it was already dark before she got home. The father got worried and went to look for her. She got home ahead of him and then maintained that she had been with the other children at home.

Obedience and respect towards the parents, diligence, thrift and a deep bond to hearth and home were the foundation of her upbringing. As the youngest she was spared the grinding work of the farm: She should have a better deal, she should go out in the world, study and get on in life. But this was only on condition that she should always return to the family and share her experiences with her parents and siblings.

The Only Healthy Surviving Child

In the war the brother suffered severe wounds in the arms and legs and returned home an invalid. It seemed questionable whether he would be able to take over the parental farm.

In 1944 the eldest sister was killed in an air raid on Freiburg. From that time Mrs. Bolt remembers almost nothing except her mother's fatalistic resignation, but the impression that life became yet more friendless endured. Her second sister married onto a farm in a neighboring village. Mrs. Bolt looked after her children while the adults were working in the fields. At one time she herself took a small job to earn a bit of pocket money. Her parents opposed it; they maintained she did not need the money, but nevertheless let her go ahead. It was precisely then that her sister had what at first seemed to be a trivial accident, a slight fall. The sister did not take time off to recover as there was now no one to look after her children and she carried on working. Her condition worsened and she died 16 days later, totally unexpectedly, from a "swollen brain" (patient's term). Mrs. Bolt, then 13, felt deeply guilty. There was no possibility of mourning, of consolation or of discussion in the family. The mother immersed herself even more deeply in her religious beliefs. After a year, the brother-in-law remarried so that there would be someone to look after the children. A year later he died and the orphaned children remained with their stepmother.

A New Role

From this time on Mrs. Bolt's role in the family changed radically. She was now her parents' only surviving, healthy child and therefore felt herself deeply duty bound towards them. It was decided that she should later take over the farm. To prepare herself for this task she left the parental farm and independently found herself a position in a restaurant in the village of S. Tears still come to her eyes today when she narrates what she experienced there: 16 hours' work a day, low pay, and almost no free time. Although she was gentle and sensitive, unaccustomed to the effort required, and had to sleep in the kitchen, she also felt obliged not to disappoint the landlord. She finally fell ill with rheumatic fever and gave up the job after nine months; her tonsils were removed.

She took another job in a household where she was happy; there she felt the security of a daughter. Then her mother broke her back in an accident and was confined to bed for a year. This made it necessary for her to come home. A year later, when 17 years old, she took a job in a hotel in the Black Forest. Two years later ("I always was ambitious"), she moved to an agricultural school. It was not only the plan for her to take over the farm, but also her own wish to teach in an agricultural school, that led her to become the first girl from her home village to go on to a higher school.

Although she had hardly been at home since she was 14 or 15, inwardly she remained strongly bound up with her parents. For example, it was not until she was 18 that she went to the cinema without her parents.

Acquaintance and Marriage

It was on her 20th birthday that she met her first boyfriend (her present husband). They were taking the same course at the school. For some time they wrote to each other and he visited her occasionally. For her there was no question of a sexual relationship before the marriage. He became impatient and urged engagement and marriage. He was ready to move to her parents' farm, although it was also the intention that he should take over a farm and restaurant from his own parents.

It was only when Mrs. Bolt's brother, having made a late marriage in 1958, decided to run the parental business on his own that she became engaged and, having completed a course in hotel work, married at the age of 25. Against her parents' will she moved some hundreds of kilometers away to another farming and restaurant business.

The Marriage and Birth of the Children

From the beginning the young couple lived in his parental home, an old-fashioned farm and restaurant. Her parents-in-law and her mother-in-law's mother, the original owner, also still lived there. One brother of her husband, a businessman, lived in the neighborhood, but had no interest in the farm.

Her husband revealed himself in the marriage as an indulged child, still strongly bound to his mother. Both he and her mother-in-law demanded that Mrs. Bolt should care for him in the way that his mother had done.

There was also a strong tension between the two older women, who quarreled about the way the house should be run. The father-in-law played a subsidiary role. He was described as being sensitive and had been sick with asthma for years. Nevertheless, it was to him that Mrs. Bolt felt herself most attached. She tells how they held together and understood one another.

Two years after the marriage, the first daughter Brigitte was born. In 1965 Mrs. Bolt received a small gift of money from her father, which she used for modernizing the business. In line with her original plans, the main emphasis lay with the restaurant. From this point of time on, she gained influence in the house. She controlled the kitchen, looked after the guestrooms, and saw to the buying. Her husband took over the buying and selling of drinks and the work of the vineyard. The mother-in-law helped in the public rooms ("she likes talking to the people"); the father-in-law could do little because of his asthma. The 80-year-old great-grandmother was indecisive; sometimes she withdrew, then she started being active again and had a finger in every pie.

In the same year, the second daughter Annette was born by

Caesarean section. Mrs. Bolt left the hospital only three days after this operation, but on arriving home allowed herself no rest as the rebuilding and reorganization of the business were already well underway. Eleven days later she was in danger of her life with heavy bleeding which could only be stopped by a hysterectomy.

The Unstable Balance

There followed six years of hard work in which she felt herself overburdened, left in the lurch by her husband and rejected by her mother-in-law. The children did not get on together, the youngest, the "little angel," was from the beginning the favorite of the grandparents. The elder daughter became extremely jealous and tormented her little sister, which further provoked the old people's rejection. Annette had multiple fears of being alone and fell ill with bronchitis. Brigitte, on the other hand, helped in the restaurant from an early age, allied herself with her father, and was considered the more competent.

The family lived in an extremely unstable balance: there were strong tensions, little joy, little togetherness and much work. Mrs. Bolt had in this year suffered from time to time from gallbladder trouble and a constantly recurring inflammation of the gastric membranes.

In the years 1972 and 1973 there was a severe and crucial crisis in the family (described fully above), which resulted in Mrs. Bolt's present illness.

EVENTS IN THE FAMILY HISTORY

1936 Mr. Bolt born.

1937 Mrs. Bolt born, very much the youngest of her family.

1944 Mrs. Bolt's eldest sister killed in an air raid.

1945 Mrs. Bolt's brother severely wounded.

1950 Mrs. Bolt's second sister dies, leaving two children, ages six years and nine months. Mrs. Bolt blames herself deeply for not having given her sister enough help.

1951 Mrs. Bolt leaves home to work as a kitchen maid and was exploited.

1952 Mrs. Bolt ill with rheumatic fever; new job; in this job felt herself accepted as a child.

1953 Accident to Mrs. Bolt's mother. Mrs. Bolt returns to the family farm.

1955 New job for Mrs. Bolt.

1956 Mrs. Bolt starts at the agricultural school; is ambitious. She wants either to take over the family business or to become a teacher of agriculture.

1957 Mrs. Bolt meets her husband in the agricultural school. Her brother decides to take over the family business despite his disabilities.

1958 Engagement. Mrs. Bolt training in a hotel. Mr. Bolt urges marriage; her parents are against it.

1962 Marriage.

1964 Birth of Brigitte.

1966 Renovation and extension of the restaurant financed by Mrs. Bolt. Birth of Annette; uncontrollable bleeding necessitates a hysterectomy.

1972 Gallbladder and stomach trouble.
January: the business made over to the young couple by the parents.
April: Husband's life in danger from a severe inflammation of the appendix causing perforation.
August: Mrs. Bolt's father dies.
October: A friend of the family, aged 41, dies from a heart attack.

1973 January: Mrs. Bolt's mother dies. Mrs. Bolt suffers joint pains.
March: Mrs. Bolt's mother's sister dies; the diarrhea begins.
August: Mr. Bolt's father dies from a severe attack of asthma.
September: Mrs. Bolt is operated for removal of appendix

and gallbladder; inflammation of the small intestine diagnosed; treatment of varicose veins.

From this time, at intervals of three to four months, Mrs. Bolt has suffered severe attacks of blood-smeared diarrhea; hospitalized several times.

1975 August: Mrs. Bolt has heart trouble; serious internal bleeding, critical condition; hospitalized in the surgical clinic, inflammation of the large intestine diagnosed; inflammation of the kidneys.

September: The mother-in-law falls ill; a new building project is undertaken.

December: First appointment at the psychosomatic clinic.

1976 February: First interview with the family.

March: Relapse with hospitalization. The beginning of open dissension between the marital couple.

THE PRESENT SITUATION OF THE FAMILY

The Deep Division

In the family interview the Bolts showed themselves to be a deeply divided, "schismatic" family (Lidz et al., 1965) under severe tension in which the members were strongly alienated. The parents barely spoke to one another; they constantly sought to involve the interviewer as a middleman in their discussion.

At first Mrs. Bolt seemed anxious; she was the "patient" and worried that she was responsible for her own illness. It pained her that she was unable to accomplish all her many tasks (some of which she set herself). On the other hand, she complained bitterly that her husband did not understand her enough and that he showed too little consideration for her ill health. She tried to make allies among her guests and her doctors. Everyone confirmed her capability and her husband was constantly reproached by outsiders for being inconsiderate to his wife. He had a strong emotional bond with his own mother and countered these reproaches by demonstrating an unshakable "ideal of toughness." In his turn, he upbraided his wife

with being too sensitive and too weak—therefore, to blame for her own illness.

Even to a causal observer, the relationship between the partners involved an extreme division of roles which was openly expressed in their behavior. The wife spoke in a complaining, plaintive, depressive voice and presented herself as the weak, helpless victim of a brutal, egotistical husband. This role suited her husband who countered with emphatic comments about toughness, self-control, and "holding your own in life" which he spat out in a brusque voice. The relationship seemed to have rigidified into an extreme complementary "collusion" (malign clinch) between a weak, sensitive, incompetent, depressive woman on the one side and a strong, cold-blooded, pugnacious man on the other. The environment sustained and stabilized this complementarity of roles, providing sympathy or support alternately, first to one party and then to the other.

Dialectics of the Strong and the Weak

Closer consideration revealed, however, that Mrs. Bolt could not be so weak. From childhood on she was accustomed "never to complain, to accept what the Lord sends, to work hard, and not to spare herself." She was certainly not incompetent. It was through her own initiative and her dowry that the business was modernized and extended and was now doing so well. From her sickbed she kept the books, appointed new staff and settled disputes among them. She pressed to be let out of the clinic because her husband and his mother could not, in fact, run the business without her. She allowed these two only a very limited area of responsibility and hindered them from looking into important aspects of the business.

Indeed, her husband was not as strong as he first appeared, but was rather an insecure man, spoiled by his mother and tending to depression. He lay in bed late in the morning after drinking and talking at night with his cronies. He cheated the guests and the staff and seemed totally incapable of running the business on his own.

The power and strength of the "victim" (Mrs. Bolt) were obvious. But, because it would have caused Mrs. Bolt to feel profoundly guilty and Mr. Bolt to admit to weakness, they were at first unable to accept the implications of such an insight.

The Role of the Children

What roles did the children play in this context? An initial view suggested astonishing parallels. The two daughters were alienated; they hardly spoke to one another. Each of the pair seemed to be identified with one parent. Brigitte, the eldest, seemed almost precocious and definitely tomboyish with her short hair. She looked at least two years older than her age. She was "like her father"; she held her own and was aggressive, strong and competent. But she also tormented her mother and above all her younger sister, who began to cry if Brigitte so much as came near her. Annette, with her long blonde braids, was "the little angel" and loved by everyone, above all by the grandparents, who spoilt her unreasonably and favored her above her sister. She gave the impression of being shy and weak and was not particularly successful in school. She suffered from night fears and had chronic spastic bronchitis, a psychosomatic illness, and in this way too, resembled her mother.

Here, too, it was not hard to see the weakness of the apparently strong sister. Brigitte suffered because her little sister was loved far more than she. Her "badness" made her feel guilty. At the same time, however, she felt strongly the injustice that her mother and grandparents (indeed her whole environment) did her in withholding all sympathy and approval. Resigned, in fact almost embittered, she remained firmly in her role, entrenched in her apparent toughness. In return she received praise and recognition from her father, who particularly liked to boast about her "competence." Each child was extremely dependent on the support of one parent and in turn helped to sustain the parental conflict. The children suffered from strong feelings of guilt towards each other and towards the other parent, so that their lives were prematurely circumscribed by a massive "conflict of loyalties."

HYPOTHESIS REGARDING THE CENTRAL FAMILY DYNAMICS

Systems Rules

If we begin our analysis of the Bolt family on the basis of observed behavior, we see a deeply divided family. The parents attacked each

other openly and blamed each other, and each tried to displace the other. Mr. Bolt projected his own weaknesses and dependency onto his wife, who in turn, in her role of victim, put him under the pressure of strong guilt feelings. The environment was drawn in supportively.

Through this split in the parental relationship the children found themselves in a conflict of loyalties, because each parent enlisted one of the children on her or his side in an alliance against the other parent. The children's relationship to one another mirrors their parents' relationship. Annette, the "little angel" was identified with her mother's weak, feminine side and thereby disqualified. Brigitte followed her father's ideal of manly hardness at the price of her feminine identity and adopted a tense aggressive attitude to her environment. As long as Annette remained imprisoned in her fearful, confined dependency, Brigitte must be driven into her precocious, forced, stressful "pseudo-independence." The boundaries between the generations must be blurred and the children "exploited" (parentified) by their parents as referees and go-betweens, roles inappropriate to their ages. Nevertheless, this provided them with a great "moral strength" in relation to their parents and a strong feeling of their own importance.

The Family Prison

The entire family was in a state of taut cohesion, constantly in danger of losing its emotional equilibrium. There was an atmosphere that drove every outsider away because the feelings of emptiness, of hopeless confinement and of mutually aggressive watchfulness and devaluation were almost unbearable. There was no scope in the family for creative, imaginative play. Instead of providing its members with a sanctuary where their communications were met with openness and understanding, it was instead a human prison, in which the inhabitants spent their time forging plans of escape, dreaming of the good life outside, and mulling over touched up memories. They tried to make existence "behind bars" a little more bearable by forming cliques, by intrigue or simply by conformity.

The price was the renunciation of solidarity and trust and the complete lack of deep attachment.

The climate of such "family prisons" promotes the development of "psychosomatic personalities," as they are described in the literature (Nemiah and Sifneos, 1970, de M'Uzan, 1974). Characteristics of this form of illness are: attachment to the concrete; lack of imagination and feelings; undue conformity; a strong impression of helplessness and hopelessness; and a capacity for internalization of relationships (or "inner objects") that is both superficial (implies the need for the real presence of another person) and also deep (entails the longing for an idealized, closely attached relationship). Briefly, the disturbed individuation of the psychosomatic patient leaves her or him precariously swinging between the extremes of fusion and schizoid isolation and so makes her or him vulnerable to real or imagined loss or bereavement.

However, the comparison must remain metaphorical unless we can further define the forces that the prison "walls" confine and the "chains" that bind the members of such families together.

Relational Dynamics

Having started with the state of mutuality, our fifth perspective, we will now reveal further fundamental, though partly concealed, relational forces that are dynamically relevant to such a family. To do so we will use our four remaining perspectives: related individuation, the transactional modes of binding and expelling, delegation, and the debits and merits accounting. These different perspectives partly overlap one another and are closely related, in that they together build *one* common transactional pattern. Nevertheless, each can provide a view of a somewhat different level of the relationship.

Related Individuation. This concerns the degree to which the family is differentiated into relatively autonomous "inner-directed" members (with stably internalized inner objects) that are at the same time integrated in the family, and also the degree of integration of the entire family in the community.

Successful individuation is characterized by a "dialogic potential," namely the ability to maintain personal boundaries, to accept personal boundaries, to be flexibly adaptive, and yet still to remain in empathic contact with others.

All these functions seemed to be disturbed in the Bolt family. Indeed, we have the impression that this is the key to the disturbance in the family. Both parents had already suffered major disturbances of individuation in their families of origin.

Mrs. Bolt as the baby of her family was the recipient of the regressive caring-dependency needs of her emotionally impoverished family. The doting and projection she received from all sides were harmful in that they blocked and neglected the child's legitimate wishes for separation and autonomy. We know how much such apparent indulgence amounts to a deprivation. Heartless "smothering" in place of a circumspect but trusting motherliness is more harmful than beneficial.

Delegation. Very often such poorly individuated relationships lead to a crisis in adolescence. When Mrs. Bolt reached this critical phase, she had already lost her oldest sister and her brother had become a war-wounded invalid. Her first steps towards separation, as we heard, her taking a small job (against her parent's wishes), were encumbered with the death of the surviving sister. Mrs. Bolt felt extremely guilty, "because I was so egotistical and didn't help my sister." The crisis ended with feelings of obligation to the parents that were stronger than ever and the simultaneous separation of the young girl from the parental home. The delegational perspective makes it clear that from this point her role in the family changed. From now on, as the only surviving healthy child, she must replace the missing children for her parents, who, buried in their religious beliefs, were themselves unable to mourn their dead. For this reason she left the family and again experienced a gross exploitation, which she helplessly bore until the situation was finally ended by her first psychosomatic illness (rheumatism).

Binding. The success or failure of individuation is inevitably connected with the intensity and direction of the relational forces acting within the family (transactional modes of binding and expelling) and depends on the kind of missions that a child is given within his family. Finally, the process of individuation is also influenced by the ethical-existential obligations that arise from the distribution of debits and merits within the family.

In her role of "baby" Mrs. Bolt was regressively bound to her family (Id-binding). With each bereavement that her parents suffered in the subsequent period, fresh binding elements were added in which arousal of guilt played a major role (Super-Ego-binding). Mrs. Bolt felt the enormous meaning that she had for her parents.

Her central missions were connected with this binding: the mission to replace the lost children and to prepare herself to take over the family business. This forced her to leave the confines of the family without, however, giving up any of her strong loyalty to her parents.

Debits and Merits. On the debit side of her debits and merits account stands the regressive gratification she received from the entire family, her "survivor guilt" arising from her position as only surviving child and her (more or less unconsciously assumed) complicity in the death of the sister. Against these guilt-inducing debits stands her deep loyalty to her parents as her major merit.

Collusion within the Marriage

We need to view Mrs. Bolt's marriage against this background. The marriage took place only after her brother's decision, following his own late marriage, to take over the parental business. This had released her from her obligation to take it over herself. Her husband was, in his turn, closely bound to his own family and equally delegated to take over that business. The marriage was at first fairly stable: an extreme form of complementary collusion was set up between the partners. By indulging her husband, as his mother had done, and tolerating his staying closely bound-up with his own mother, she earned the freedom to maintain a close contact to her own parents. By her enormous efforts for their common existence she kept her husband permanently loaded with guilt (she was the exploited party) and at the same time kept him disenfranchised. Finally, the two children were divided between the two parents; by projective identification each of them was assigned one of the split-up family attributes: hard, independent activity or weak, dependent passivity.

Dynamics Presumably Triggering the Illness

The death of both Mrs. Bolt's parents and her father-in-law appeared to Mrs. Bolt as the central events in the years 1972 and 1973 when the illness began. At the same point, the young couple took over the responsibility for the business. The family was, so to speak, hit at its weakest points: 1) in its incapacity to come to terms with bereavement, and 2) in its incapacity for a flexibly adoptive autonomy. Both are elements of a deficient individuation and reflect the weakness of a family structure based on a lifelong actual dependence (rather than internalized relationship) on one's own parents.

One may ask why was it Mrs. Bolt who became ill and not her husband. It appears that Mrs. Bolt was more deeply affected both by the bereavements and by the lack of autonomy than her husband. Thus, her physical symptoms can be viewed as a defense against an emotional catastrophe, against feelings of being trapped, and against hopelessness and helplessness. These feelings she can only overcome by blocking *all* emotion, by cutting back to a psychological "vita minima." This, however, endangers the psychological organism's capacity for self-direction and regeneration. Important organs and/or systems come under too great a strain, develop disease and cease to function. Mr. Bolt understood this in a simplified form when he said "it makes her sick inside."

Why has a physical illness arisen and not, for example, neurotic symptoms? All participants seem to be more directly exposed and vulnerable to conflict and bereavement than neurotic individuals, who can (within limits) resort to the manipulation of phantasies and, hence, have more freedom to use mechanisms of repression. Being unable to use these mechanisms, the patient is thrown back on more primitive mechanisms of splitting, isolation and blocking of affect. Cognitive abilities, though, for example, the ability to test reality (a lack of which is prominent in psychotic symptomatology), remain unaffected. The disturbance is primarily on the affective-emotional level.

10

The Family Tests: Rorschach and TAT

IN THIS CHAPTER WE DESCRIBE the results of conjoint tests—the Rorschach and the Thematic Apperception Test (TAT) —performed by the Bolt family. This is introduced by a brief theoretical explanation.

THEORETICAL BACKGROUND

Assessment of Relationships versus Traditional Diagnosis

Relationship-orientated diagnostics is a relatively recent result of sociological and psychiatric research that is now beginning to be applied in clinical practice. The first sociological landmark was achieved in the early 1950s by Strodtbeck with his "Revealed Differences Techniques" (1951).

Psychiatrists working with schizophrenic patients then drew attention to the patients' families. Basic work was done by three American research groups (Bateson, 1972; Lidz, 1976 and Lidz et al. 1956; and Wynne, 1968) and the English group centered around Laing (1960, 1961, 1965). Gradually the focus of psychiatric interest moved from intrapsychic reconstructions to transactional models that attempt to depict the close, affective relationships between individuals. Whereas

186

traditional psychiatric diagnosis aims to label or classify the individual, interpersonal assessment attempts to comprehend the fluctuating interactions between two or more people (Singer, 1974).

The Practice of Transactional Diagnostics

In her review of transactional research, Hassan (1977) discusses the basic principles and paradigms of such transactional or relational diagnostics, in which the administration of various family tests are used.

Despite the family therapeutic "boom" and many valuable results, few clinicians have employed these tests. This may be due partly to the long-running controversy over the validity of projective tests. Whatever the reason, they have been in disrepute for many years and were, indeed, banned from the curricula of clinical psychology until the recent turn of opinion. Nevertheless, it remains as difficult as ever to derive any practically relevant statements from the test results.

A transactional assessment may be achieved through tests of individuals or of groups. When an individual test is used, the relational dynamics are assessed by the transactions between subject and investigator.

When several people are being tested together, two types of tests may be distinguished: dyadic tests and those involving more than two people. With dyads—for example, marital couples, siblings, or parent and child—the investigator usually leaves the room and remains as a silent observer (often behind a one-way screen). Group or family tests range from father-mother-child triads to three-generational groups involving the nuclear family and the grandparents.

The current literature gives some insights into the very varied applications of conjoint tests. But until now, to our knowledge, only Singer (1974) and Willi (1973) have explicitly worked out how the findings from such tests may be usefully applied for clinical assessment and therapy.

The following case presentation is based on Singer's current work and proceeds within a frame of reference developed mainly by Hassan (1974).

Principles of Conjoint Procedures

For the conjoint projective test, all members of the family are asked to participate in developing a fantasy suggested by one of them. In addition, together they must choose relevant perceptions and talk about them together. The test responses may be observed from two different perspectives centered either on the task or on the relationships. The task-orientated perspective is expressed in the verbal communication, that is, how the family communicate about their common goal, how they deal with differences of opinion, and whether they achieve consensus or not. The relational perspective focuses on levels of metacommunication, the emotional climate and role differentiations between the members of the family.

Conjoint tests expose, as it were, a cross section of the multiple relational strands running through the family. They alert the investigator to symptom-generating transactions, to resources for overcoming conflict, and to the degree of individual differentiation (related individuation) prevailing within the family. Therefore, information gained from conjoint tests supplies significant points for the long-term prognosis and planning of family therapy.

The categories we present below may serve as guidelines for the interpretation of conjoint tests. We used these categories in our summaries of the two conjoint tests, the Rorschach (see Table 1, p. 206) and the TAT (see Table 2, p. 207).

The microanalytical categories, *content* and *transactional flow,* refer respectively to the task and relational levels of the interview. Under content, the categories, *text* and *form* in the Rorschach and *action and focal conflict* in the TAT, emerge from the different characteristics of the various stimulus cards. The Rorschach inkblots and the TAT scenes generate different types of answers. In the Rorschach these answers relate primarily to "things" and in the TAT to relationships between people—yet this difference is not absolutely clear-cut.

The category *transactional flow* denotes the way in which the members of the family communicate with each other. For this report we chose an abbreviated form of Hassan's Scoring Manual

(1974) comprising only such items as had proved highly significant in an empirical investigation of parental couples.

The category of *decision making* refers in particular to the contribution individual members of a family make to a continual fluid dialogue. The ways in which the decisions are reached express ability to develop common frames of reference and to share thoughts and ideas, despite differences of opinion.

The category of *consensus* at the end of each card makes it possible to decide whether the family discussion has resulted in a definite common product or not. It provides a measure of the efficiency of problem solving (Reiss, 1971). The reader will find fuller descriptions and examples of these categories and the rules for their use in Hassan's Manual (1974).

The *authorship* category ("Who has the idea first?") is a relatively good criterium for assessing the impact of intrafamilial roles on various transactional processes. The differentiation of the subsystems "marital couple" and "parent-child" provides a starting point in role assessment. Further central factors in the familial role structure are the various role assignments (spokesman, silent member, strawman, scapegoat, etc.), the distribution of power (from leader to outsider) and reversal of roles (for example, parentification of children). It is, therefore, important to ask: Who takes the lead in answering ("opening move") and how? Who makes the summary? Who agrees (or disagrees) with whom? Who disparages whom or what? From the answers to such questions, inferences can be made about groupings, divisions, and alliances within the family.

The consensus which finally lends form to the exchange of opinion reflects the ability of the family members to reconcile their points of view and to conduct a meaningful common discussion. Questions that may be usefully asked about the consensus are: Did all members of the family concur in a specific solution? Were they able to recognize and cope with difference of opinion? What kinds of exchanges preceded the result?

The category of *affective attributions* includes all statements that influenced the emotional atmosphere.

Finally, in both tests the categories of *productivity* and *popularity*

express the degree of conformity with standard values and the existence of relative flexibility and multiplicity of standpoints.

The qualitative assessment of the whole family's productions with
respect to *content, transactional flow* and *affective attributions* provides a good estimate of the "family ego," that is, of the achievement
level of the family group as a whole, and of the degree of individuation of its individual members. Interruptions in the answering
process may be understood as symptoms of increased anxiety and
indications of "danger zones." Examples may be found in the Bolt
family transcript (below): Mrs. Bolt's fear at the beginning of the
Rorschach test (Card I) and later the lowering of the form level
after a difference of opinions (Card VIII); in the TAT Mr. Bolt's
remarks about "hallucinations" (Card 1); and his preoccupation
with death (Card 15). Such breaks or "minicrises" show up as
changed transactional structures and act as indices of the capacity
of the group to return to its original condition. Such transitory
phenomena should be distinguished from the family's long-evolved
coping style.

The categories of this system of interpretation are consistent with
the individual-orientated psychological frames of reference which
are generally used in analysis of individual projective tests. However, we intentionally excluded dimensions such as "motivational
conflict," "conflicts of needs," and "pathological drives (or instincts),"
because we wished to orientate ourselves on the observed data and
not to reconstruct inferred inner psychic events. We aimed to achieve
a comprehensive picture of the intrafamilial process that would per-
mit both a transactional diagnosis and therapeutic prognosis.

TRANSCRIPT OF THE CONJOINT RORSCHACH PROCEDURE WITH THE BOLT FAMILY

Th. = Therapist		F. = Father	(40 years)
I. = Investigator		B. = Brigitte	(12 years)
M. = Mother (39 years)		A. = Annette	(10 years)

I.: I would first like to read to you just what this test is about. The
idea is that you should solve some tasks together as a family.
It goes like this: each of you says what he or she thinks is

on the card. There are ten cards. Different people often see quite different things. Now, what we would like you to do is to try to agree with one another on one particular description. When you have finished with one card, put it here on the table and go on, on your own, to the next one. You have a maximum of five minutes for each card. You may begin now.

Card I

B.: *(Takes the first card)* What are we supposed to do?

F.: Can't really say *(wants to go to the next card)*

I.: Just a moment please.

M.: Bloodstains, but. . . .

I.: Yes, first you have to . . . This is the first card, right? When you have finished this card, then you go on to the next.

Th.: First each of you must say what it could be, and then you try to agree on one particular description. And then you go on to the next one. And please try to speak loud enough so that we . . .

F.: Oh, I get it.

Th.: . . . can hear you.

B.: A bat *(puts the card on one side)*

F.: Right.

M.: *(Very quietly)* Next.

Th.: Just a moment, have you agreed on one . . .

All.: Yes, yes.

Th.: Everyone agreed?

All.: Yes.

Card II

B.: *(Uncovers the second card)*

F.: What's this then? *(takes up the card and then gives it back to Brigitte)*

M.: *(Speaks hesitantly)* Perhaps it could be a butterfly. Look this way up. *(takes the card and turns it round)*

F.: Yes, that's what I would have said.

B.: Does it matter if you turn it round?

F.: No.

B.: Somewhere you have to . . .

M. and F.: *(Together)* Yes.

B.: . . . or, how are you supposed to hold it?

I.: How you like.

F.: How you want to.

I.: Shall I repeat?

F.: No, we've understood, we've understood.

I.: Yes.

B.: Yes, a butterfly, butterfly. *(the others nod in agreement)*

A.: Yes.

Card III

F.: Let's go. *(He indicates to Brigitte that she should go on; Brigitte grasps the third card and turns it all ways around.)* Jesus, it gets better all the time! I don't know what I'm supposed . . .

Th.: I didn't quite understand what you said.

F.: I'm asking myself, what I'm doing here. Such stuff, right. Anyhow that's what I think about it, and you can write it all down for all I care. *(angry)*

M.: *(Looks at the third card)* It's difficult to say. *(Annette takes the card from her mother and looks at it.)*

B.: A crab. *(turns the card)* A crab's claw. *(Annette tries to take the card out of her hand and look at it herself, Brigitte turns the card further.)* Like this it's a crab, get it? This way round it's a crab.

F.: That way it's a crab. *(Annette takes the card in her hand, but Brigitte takes it away again.)*

B.: *(Brigitte to Annette)* Leave go!

F.: *(Murmurs)* Oh, let her have a go!

Th.: I didn't quite catch that.

F.: She thinks it's a crab. *(takes the card in his hand)*

M.: That's right.

A.: No.

I.: You say no? Could you explain that a bit perhaps?

F.: *(Takes the card and shows it to the mother and to Annette)* It is. I can't explain it anymore.

M.: *(Takes the card in her hand)* It could be a highway, look there, with a tree in the background, but I can't say precisely either.

Pause

F.: *(Rubs his nose with his finger and murmurs)* Oh, go on, it's a crab or something.

I.: *(To Annette)* What do you think?

A.: Oh.

F.: That's kind of a tough question for her, isn't it?

I.: Now you said "no" Annette, didn't you? Can you explain that?

B.: She said "no" to the crab.

A.: *(Takes the card and looks at it)* Oh, what Mammy said, a highway. *(moves her hand towards her mother)*

F.: Now just look here!

M.: Yes, yes . . . *(murmurs)* That's what I think too.

Th.: But what are you all going to agree on? A crab or a highway?

F.: Now look here, that's an animal not a highway! Where's the highway then?

M.: *(Shows the father on the card)* Well yes, at least here in the background, *(pause)* a couple of flowers. . . .

F.: *(Interrupts his wife and murmurs)* Oh, flowers, something else as well . . .

Card IV

B.: *(Takes the fourth card and turns it around)* An animal.

Th.: Sorry I didn't quite catch that.

B. and A.: *(Together)* An animal.

M.: It certainly could . . .

A.: *(Points to the drawing)* Look there at the bottom, an animal.

F.: It could be a mouth, jaws, look here jaws. Jaws, here . . . *(shows how on the card)*.

B.: *(Skeptically)* Jaws, he thinks.

A.: *(To her mother)* What do you see?

Pause

F.: It could be a dog. *(pause)* You could certainly turn it round.

B.: Yes, a dog then, right?

A.: Yes.

M.: *(Nods)* Mm.

Card V

B.: *(Takes the fifth card)* It could be the skin of an animal.

M.: Yes, it could be an animal skin.

F.: Animal skin . . . *(murmurs)* Let's move!

B.: An animal skin. *(The father turns the card round impatiently and Brigitte uncovers the sixth card.)*

Card VI

F.: Oh, this one's a moth.

B.: Yes, a moth.

F.: Ugh! *(turns the card round quickly and wants to go on)*

B.: Oh, come on, wait for Mommy! *(uncovers the card again)*

F.: Oh, not all . . . *(waves it away)*

B.: This is a moth? *(shows the fifth card questioningly to each in turn and then puts it aside; uncovers the sixth card and turns it around)* That could be another skin.

A.: Yes.

F.: Sure, it's a skin.

B.: Skin, an animal skin. *(puts the card aside)*

I.: *(To the mother)* You agree with that?

M.: Yes, sure.

F.: Yes *(nods)* sure.

Card VII

(Brigitte uncovers the seventh card and turns it. Long pause. The father takes the card in his hand and turns it.)

M.: *(Takes the card from the father and turns it around)* It could be an armchair, or something else, or that . . .

F.: *(Murmurs)* Ugh, ooha, ugh! *(points on the card)*

Th.: I beg your pardon I didn't quite catch that, Mr. Bolt.

F.: Ugh! *(gesticulates wildly)* As far as I'm concerned that's a spirit. There, that thing there.

I.: Sure, you know, like I said, different people see quite different things.

F.: Well sure, you're right there, but. . . . Well, I see.

I.: And when you see something different, perhaps you could talk about it a bit, couldn't you?

F.: Well, yes, then I . . . *(waves it away)*

I.: Just a moment! Have we all . . .

B.: An armchair, an armchair.

F.: *(Murmurs)* An armchair or something, I don't know.

Card VIII

(All look at the eighth card.)

F.: Those are rats, right?

B. and A.: *(Together)* Yes, yes.

B.: *(Shows on the card)* Yes, there are two animals.

A.: Yes, there's two of them. *(shows on the card)*

I.: Rats?

B.: Yes, there's two animals.

F.: Yes, or mice, what difference does it make, or wild pigs, right, could be too.

M.: That's a bit like a butterfly. *(shows on the card)*

B.: Yes, but it could be butterflies.

(Annette puts the card aside, and Brigitte uncovers the ninth card.)

Card IX

F.: *(Murmurs)* Oh my, isn't this quite something.

I.: Pardon me.

F.: These pictures are getting really great, sure thing! *(acts uninvolved, leans back in his chair)*

A.: *(Looking at the picture with Brigitte)* That could be two heads.

B.: Yes, two heads, there and there.

A.: Yes, *(shows Brigitte)*.

F.: *(Coughs)* Those are two heads! Here and here. *(shows on the card)*

B.: There are two heads.

A.: Yes.

I.: *(To Annette)* Excuse me, what did you say?

A.: Yes, two heads, there *(shows where)*.

I.: Mm, and what do you think? *(to the father)*

B.: Right, it's two heads?

F.: I don't rightly know anymore. *(takes the picture in his hand and looks at it)* I've no idea. What stuff. Stop, I've no idea, what should I say!

(Pause)

I.: Excuse me?

F.: No idea.

B.: It's two heads. Look up here.

F.: Where are they supposed to be then?

M.: Where?

B.: Look, up there, there! *(Annette shows her mother exactly)*

(Pause)

M.: *(Very softly)* Pfuh, it's hard to say.

F.: Hm? *(blows his nose)*

M.: Hard to say . . .

B.: *(Interrupts her mother)* There are two heads, up here. *(shows the card around once more and then looks at the circle around her)* Finished?

F.: Yes, thanks.

B.: *(Covers the ninth card and then takes up the tenth)* Oooh!

Card X

I.: You could turn it around if you want.

B.: It looks so like a body, that way round. I'd say that that up there is the backbone.

F.: Yes, yes.

B.: It looks like a backbone and that there outside the body here *(shows on the card)*.

A.: No, where?

I.: You can see something different, right?

A.: I don't know.

M.: Yes, that's an animal skeleton, or . . .

F.: Yes, yes.

B.: Yes, right, part of a body.

I.: *(Turning to Annette)* Can you see what the other two see or can you see something else? Go ahead, say it.

A.: Yes, then, that's like a spider, like this. *(shows on the card)*

I.: Hm, what else?

B.: *(To Annette)* Keep your place.

F.: *(To Annette)* Sit up properly or that chair's going to fall over! *(takes the card and turns it by two corners)* That's the way it should be, to my mind.

B.: It's a body, right?

F.: A body. *(wants to put the card away)*

I.: *(To Annette)* And you, you think it's a spider?

A.: Yes.

F.: Spider, she says it's a spider.

B.: Right then a body and a spider.

I.: *(To Annette)* Only a spider, what else?

A.: No, yes, and that here, a body too.

I.: Thanks very much.

Transcript of the Conjoint TAT with the Bolt Family

I.: Different families see it quite differently, right?

F.: *(Takes all the Rorschach cards and stands them upright)* See! What's that supposed to do for me? What am I supposed to do there? What's the point? Has that got anything to do with medicine? What on earth's the good of it?

I.: Well then, all families when they look at something together . . .

F.: *(Interrupts the investigator)* OK, OK.

I.: . . . together . . .

F.: *(Interrupts the investigator again)* But those are so, you can look, but I've not the faintest idea what that's . . . *(points to the cards)* what's it called . . . what's that supposed . . .

I.: *(Interrupts the father)* You think . . .

F.: . . . what is that?

I.: You've really no idea?

F.: *(Puts the cards irritably and noisily on the table)* No I haven't! It's my belief I'm perfectly healthy. I've never needed a doctor *(the therapist comes into the room with the TAT cards)* and what should I do with this thing now, that can't be any use to me?

I.: But all the members of a family, eh . . .

F.: *(Interrupts the investigator)* Yes, that's what I thought—a talk with a doctor or the professor, like you said, about whether you've got family worries or worries about the children or difficulties, right? That's what I imagined, but this here, what's that supposed to be! *(questioning gesture)*

I.: You can't see any connection?

F.: No, I can't! I can't see how there can be any connection with illness.

Th.: Suppose the doctor in the clinic takes an X-ray, or blood test, or makes an ECG, you understand. . . .

F.: *(Interrupts the therapist)* Yes, yes.

Th.: . . . well, at first, it's hard to see what that's. . . . Well, you could say then, too, I've got this pain here or there, and now all at once they're doing something with these rays. Nevertheless, the doctor needs it for his investigation, to make his diagnosis. In just the same way, these investigations are aimed to find out something more about you than we can do in an interview alone.

F.: I get it, I get it. She's the patient, isn't she? But I don't know what the children and I are supposed to think about it, though. But like I just said, for myself, I don't know that I can stick out such a course of quackery. I don't know what it's all about.

Th.: Still, you were willing to come this morning . . .

F.: *(Interrupts the therapist)* Yes, how much longer does it go on?

Th.: . . . till eleven o'clock . . . and then there's still the talk to get through.

F.: And a break for a smoke every once in a while. *(smiles, all laugh)*

I.: Sure!

Th.: I've got just four more cards here. Perhaps I should give the instructions.

I.: Please go ahead.

Th.: The pictures you will see on these cards are more of actual things, figures, or people. What you have to do is also a bit different. It's not so much to say what it could be, to describe it, rather we would like you to make up a story for each of these cards. It's really a test of imagination, to make up the most exciting story in which something happens.

F.: *(Gestures at Brigitte and murmurs)* Brigitte, she's good at things like that.

Th.: Perhaps you could begin like this, first you say what could be happening in the picture at the moment—what the people are thinking, feeling, and what they are doing at that instant. Then you could think about what led up to the circumstances in the picture, and how the story began and ended. Right? The story should also have an end. There are about five minutes for each card this time too. But, you should try to arrive at one common story. . . .

F.: *(Interrupts the therapist)* Yes.

Th.: . . . that everyone can contribute to. You can take the cards one after another as you did last time.

F.: *(To Brigitte)* Put it down.

> *Card 1: A boy looking at a violin which is lying on a table in front of him (see Murray, 1943).*

B.: *(Uncovers the first card)* Well, I think the boy doesn't want to play the violin anymore.

F.: *(Thinking deeply)* Has he been looking at it long?

B.: Yeah, or he didn't want to.

M.: *(Looks at the card)* Mmmmm.

F.: He doesn't get anything out of it.

(Pause)

B.: He's thinking about something to do with the violin which he's supposed to play. Whether he's going to play it or not.

F.: Yes, or whether he's just going to clear off. *(To the mother)* Yes, go on, say something, you say something. They want to interview you too.

M.: That's what I think too.

F.: You think too! Go on—you must have some idea yourself.

(Pause)

B.: And perhaps he's afraid to tell somebody that he doesn't want to now.

I.: Yes, *(to the mother)* your husband's right. *(to Brigitte)* Hold on a moment!

B.: *(To her mother, demandingly)* Yes, you say something.

M.: Yes, and then he's played enough and he's tired and doesn't want to anymore.

F.: *(Murmurs)* He's having hallucinations.

I.: Sorry?

F.: *(Smiling)* Hallucinations. Like from watching TV.

B.: *(Shakes her head at her father)* Man!

M.: Annette how about you?

A.: Or he's practiced something but he can't do it, and then he's scared, then he's sad because he can't do it.

F.: Yes, because he can't understand, like *(pause)*. . . . What a disaster. Or is there something else to say.

B.: That he's real scared because he can't do it in front of his violin teacher or the teacher, where he learns it.

(Pause)

F.: *(Murmurs)* How does it go on then? *(pause)* His parents get no joy out of him *(to Brigitte)* like you.

Th.: Excuse me, I didn't quite understand.

F.: That he's no joy to his parents. . . .

M.: *(Interrupts the father)* He knows . . .

F.: . . . that they've bought the violin for him . . .

M.: *(Interrupts the father)* . . . but he knows, perhaps, that it's not right for him.

B.: Perhaps he liked the idea of playing it before, and now he knows he doesn't like it after all.

(Pause)

B.: Is that it? *(wants to put the card aside)*

M.: Hm.

Th.: How does the story end?

B.: Well, before he did, before he did enjoy it . . . perhaps he'd really looked forward to getting a violin and now after all he's found out that he doesn't like . . .

F.: *(Interrupts Brigitte)* It's too difficult . . .

B.: Yes *(pause)*. That's it, right?

Card 2: A country scene: A young woman with books under her arm stands in the foreground. In the background, a man is working in some fields and an older woman looks on (see Murray, 1943).

F.: Can we go on? *(Brigitte turns the second picture over; the father takes the picture in his hand and murmurs)* That looks like some sort of Bible picture, doesn't it? *(gives the picture to Brigitte)*

B.: That looks like women, religious, she's got a hymn book or a Bible in her hand. *(pause)*

M.: *(Looks at the picture)* You're right.

(Short pause)

F.: The man's in the field. *(pause)*

B.: Or it could be that that's the wife, this one here, and that one's the daughter who's just coming home from school. And that's the father, who's working in the field. . . . *(pause)*

F.: This one's the mother, and that's the daughter on the left.

M.: *(Looks at the picture and interrupts the father)* No, that's the farm. . . .

F.: *(Interrupts his wife)* No, just listen a minute. . . .

M.: . . . or she's coming from school.

B.: She's just come out of school, and that's why she doesn't want to help her father. *(pause)*

I.: *(To Annette)* And what do you think?

A.: *(Very softly)* I don't know.

I.: Go ahead say it.

A.: No, I don't know.

F.: It's too difficult for her. *(pause)* Go on you could say something: that's the mother, the father. . . .

B.: *(Interrupts the father and at the same time points to the card)* The child and . . . and here's the daughter.

F.: And this here's the field, and there behind's the farm.

B.: Right, it really does look as if perhaps she ought to be helping.

F.: And that's the forest, there.

B.: And, the girl's got to help him now. Perhaps, she was looking forward to being able to read or something.

M.: Yes, or perhaps she wants to go quite another way, perhaps she wants to study and the parents, they're quite set against her having a career.

B.: Right, then she doesn't want to stay and work on the farm. . . .

A.: (Interrupts Brigitte) Yes.

F.: Right.

B.: . . . she wants to study.

F.: And then she leaves the farm, and that's the end (clears his throat) That's quitting the land.

B.: Right, then she leaves the farm because she wants to study and doesn't want to work on the land. (Brigitte turns the third card and shows it to everyone.)

(Pause)

Card 8: An adolescent boy looks straight out of the picture. A gun is visible to one side. In the background is a blurred dreamlike picture of a surgical operation (see Murray, 1943).

I.: Well?

B.: I think he's dreaming what's in the picture behind him.

F.: That he's going to have his stomach cut open. (pause) Ah yes.

A.: He's dreaming it.

F.: Operation.

B.: Yes, that, that's what he could have dreamt, that there.

F.: That's a dream.

B.: Right.

F.: You see how the pictures show that he's going to be operated.

B.: That he's going to be operated there and he's scared about it, so he had this nightmare.

F.: Yes.

M.: Mm, mmm, that's a gun there on the side.

B.: Oh, so it is!

I.: Pardon me?

M.: That's a gun there at the side, isn't it.

F.: I don't know what that is there.

B.: And then in the end the operation works out OK. Before it, he was real scared that the operation wouldn't go so well in the end.

I.: Annette?

F.: *(To Annette)* Well, what can you see in the picture?

B.: *(To Annette)* Go on, you've got to say something too!

A.: Oh he's dreaming that he's going to have an operation and he's scared.

(Pause)

B.: Right, then the operation really is OK in the end.

F.: But you can't see that in the picture.

B.: OK, but we're supposed to make up an ending, aren't we?

M.: Yes, that sure is a nightmare, because I can see the gun at the front and then the operating room and *(short pause, the father looks impatiently at his watch)*, and then in the end. . . .

B.: I think that's it.

Th.: Finished?

All.: Yes!

> *Card 15: A haggard man with folded hands stands between gravestones (see Murray, 1943).*

Th.: Then we'll just do one last . . .

F.: *(Murmurs to himself)* I guess they'll just put off the interview with the Professor then *(looks at the card)* Looks like death. *(smiles)*

(Short pause)

B.: Well, it's in a burying ground.

M. and A.: Hm.

F.: Yes. *(short pause)* There's a man sitting in the burying ground.

B.: That's a woman.

F.: Stuff.

I.: What did you say? *(pause)*

B.: *(Interrupts the others)* Yes, then it's a burying ground, and she's sitting . . . perhaps her husband has died or something like that, it must be.

A.: *(Looks at the picture)* No.

F.: That's not a person. That's death in the burying ground, not a person, a normal person.

B.: Here at the back, that's kind of odd . . . right not a normal person.

(Pause)

Th.: Has something happened? What's the end of the story?

B.: It's hard to say, but to my mind *(pause)* you can see almost nothing but graves under. . . .

F.: *(Interrupts Brigitte)* It's hard to say.

B.: . . . you really can't draw much of a conclusion from it and even simply. . . .

(Pause)

F.: They're all the same in the burying ground, it's all the same whether they're rich or poor.

(Pause)

B.: *(To her mother)* Say something, come on say something!

M.: Well I can see there that someone's died and . . . *(pause)*

B.: Well, we can't really find any conclusion about the way it ends.

F.: *(Whispers)* Right, I'm knocking off!

B.: *(To her mother)* Have you got anything more to say?

M.: *(Shakes her head)*

B.: No more.

Report on the Consensus Rorschach and TAT
of the Bolt Family

The conjoint test with the Bolt family was performed with a practical aim in view, and therefore the test situation differed from the usual one in three important points:

First, the designated patient was the mother, while in most family research projects the index patients are children.

Second, as stated in the protocol, the investigator remained in the room during the test procedure. His few structuring comments may have affected the spontaneous family transactions. On the other hand, the family's reaction to attempts made during the test to change certain forms of communication (for example, efforts to induce silent members of the family to take part) were an indication of their receptivity to therapeutic intervention.

Third, the family was assessed as a whole, although it has often proved valuable to supplement the consensus procedure with individual test data on the children and the marital partners. It appears that group transactions may both obscure and emphasize specific features of an individual's style (Singer, 1968; Wynne, 1968). Every procedure reveals different aspects and problems and obscures others.

In the following report we assume that the family may be seen as a unit within which the verbal and nonverbal behavior of each member is meaningful and regulative in its effect.

The interpretation of the test results is divided into the following sections:

1) Overview of the interview process;
2) Characterizations within the family;
3) Summarizing remarks.

Overview of the Interview Process

After an initial "warming-up phase," all the members of the family concentrated on the task and tried together to reach adequate solutions. Despite Mr. Bolt's objections and negative comments, the other members of the family continued to apply themselves. Mr. Bolt's disruptive efforts did not, therefore, prejudice the family's final result.

It is worthwhile to reconstruct the answering process for each of the tests. The first card of the Rorschach test disturbed the family noticeably. They seemed to find it hard to interpret the picture; the test instructions were not correctly followed; and the family appeared uncoordinated. Everyone seemed somehow "put out." This is apparent in the mother's concrete, but unspecific answer of "blood stains"; in the father's constant tendency to contradict her; in Brigitte's question about the way she should hold the card; and in Annette's expressionless face (turned towards the video camera). The investigator's structuring comments led Brigitte and her mother to help the others find a common focus of attention by offering and explaining a potentially acceptable interpretation. Mrs. Bolt's rapid adjustment to the situation contrasted with her husband's persistent obstructive tendency which gave the impression that he "only wanted to get through somehow or other." Annette, who at first followed

Table 1
Rorschach Technique
Microanalysis of Family Productions

Card No.	Productivity	Text	Popular	Accuracy	Differentiation	Integration	Authorship	Agreement	Disagreement	Continuation	Disqualification	Disconnection	Dismissal	Uncertain	Consensus (end each card)	Affective Attributions
I	2	Bloodstains	+	↔	↑	↓	M.									
		Bat	−	↑	↔	↔	B.	F.							+	
II	1	Butterfly	+	↑			M.	A. F. B.							+	
III	2	Crab	+	↑			B.	M. F.	A.						−	F.: Jesus, it gets better all the time!
		Highways, trees and flowers	−	↑	↑	↔	M.	A.	F.							
IV	2	Animals	−	↑	↓	↓	B.	A. M.		F.						
		Dog's face	−	↑	↑	↔	F.	B. M. A.							+	
V	1	Animal skin	+	↑	↔	↔	B.	M. F.							+	
VI	2	Moth	+	↑	↔	↔	F.	B.								
		Animal skin	+	↑	↓	↓	B.	A. M. F.							+	
VII	2	Spirit	−	↔	↓	↓	F.								−	F.: As far as I'm concerned that's a spirit
		Arm chair	−	↑	↔	↔	M.	B.		F.						
VIII	3	Rats (mice)	−	↔	↔	↔	F.	B. A.		B.						
		2 animals	−	↑	↑	↔	B.	A.			F.					
		Butterfly	+	↑	↔	↔	M.	B.							+	
IX	2	2 heads	−	↔	↔	↓	A.	B.			F.	M.			−	F.: Oh my; isn't this quite something!
		Body	−	↔	↑	↑	B.	F.	A.			A.				
X	2	Animal skeleton	+	↑	↑	↑	M.	A.							+	
		Spider	+	↑	↑	↑	A.				B.					

LEGEND: + = yes; − = no; ± = indefinite; ↑ = high; ↓ = low; ↔ = medium

the interview in silence, began to take part later, on the investigator's express instigation.

Gradually each member of the family found his or her accustomed mode of participation and the interpretation of the cards was finally successfully accomplished.

Immediately after the Rorschach Test, Mr. Bolt's pugnacity resurged so that the beginning of the TAT was delayed. He involved the investigator in a discussion of the relevance of psychological tests and only unwillingly agreed to compromise and look at the four TAT cards.

Table 2
Thematic Apperception Test (TAT)
Microanalysis of Family Productions

Card No.	Productivity	Popular	CONTENT Plot	CONTENT Focal Conflict	Authorship:	Decision Making — Continuity Agreement	Disagreement	Contribution	Decision Making — Discontinuity Disqualification	Disconnection	Dismissal	Uncertain	Consensus (end each card)	AFFECTIVE ATTRIBUTIONS
1	1	+	Boy does not want to play the violin	own wishes vs. obligations to one's parents	B.	F. M.		A.					+	B. unwilling vs. afraid / F. bored, (hallucinations) / M. tired / A. afraid, sad
2	2	+	Biblical scene: one woman with a bible in her hands	descriptive	F. B.	M.							+	none
			young woman living in the country fantasizes leaving home	own wishes and needs vs. obligation or loyalty to one's parents	B.				F. M.			A.	+	B. unwillingness to help vs. duty to do so / M. matter of fact discussion / F. quitting the land
8	1	+	a young man dreams about being operated on	anticipatory anxiety vs. favorable outcome	B. F.	A.		M.				F.	+	B. afraid / A. afraid / M. nightmare / F. none
15	1	+	burying ground scene	anxieties evoked by death related imagery	B. F.	M.	B. A. F.				F.		+	B. F. weird / M. A. none

Although the TAT structures the feasible answers more than the Rorschach, it shows up even more clearly the relational patterns already revealed in the Rorschach. Brigitte was the first to speak about each card, while the other members of the family, including the mother, amplified her suggestions. This consolidated Brigitte as leader and intermediary whose role it was to promote cooperation and mutual respect between the members—apparently a constant group pattern. In the Rorschach, the parents frequently disagreed, but without explaining their differences of opinions. There was more agreement over the TAT themes. The individual members of the family ascribed different emotional states to the people in the TAT pictures, which, despite their sticking to relatively narrow categories, may be understood as attempts at self-differentiation. On Card 8 Mrs. Bolt saw physical injury as the central point of the story and paid particular attention to the gun in the background, which the others had failed to notice. Finally, the family's inability to find an end to the last TAT story indicates both a certain degree of "self-revelation" and also perhaps their fear of the end of the interview or of the separation which could be a starting point for therapy.

Characterizations within the Family

The following aspects are discussed independently: 1) the general family style; 2) the parents; and 3) the children.

The General Family Style. Closer study of the test protocol strengthens the impression that the orientation to reality and strong conformity of the Bolt family was based on a highly restricted style. The way in which the individual members of the family observed and defined objects, and relationships between people and their own feelings was thoroughly conventional. Their hurried and often conspiratorial mode of communication showed a need to avoid intensive discussion and argument. Each answer sequence ended with a short exchange of words. Although members discussed the ideas clearly and decisively, lively and potentially enriching associations were absent. Against this background the role structure of the family with its attributions and divisions became clear. The apparently predominant dyad of Brigitte and her father contrasted with the apparently less influential dyad of Annette and her mother. No important role changes were apparent during the tests.

The Parents. Even though both appeared restricted, Mr. and Mrs. Bolt differed widely in their cognitive-communicative styles. Having recovered from her initial shock, Mrs. Bolt was able to concentrate on the test, and could adequately work out and describe the cards. Mr. Bolt was, in contrast, depressed and rebellious, muttered to himself, got involved with irrelevancies, and from time to time used a somewhat bizarre language. These two methods of ordering and structuring experience made it impossible to recognize any common point of reference and practically excluded any dialogue between the married couple.

Faced with Mr. Bolt's obstinacy, Mrs. Bolt could only fight or withdraw. She withdrew, but nevertheless took the opportunity to have an indirect influence on the family. In their daily transactions her reproachful, aggressive silence must have continually reinforced her husband's explosive reactions, and vice versa. In the context of this "choked" marital interaction, Mr. Bolt made an ally of his daughter Brigitte, involving her as a referee in a three-cornered relationship. Annette was left to herself and only occasionally covertly recruited to Mrs. Bolt's side.

What effect each parent had on the development of the children can be deduced from the individual contributions to the tests. Mr. Bolt seemed to be an authoritarian, labile man who was quick to anger. He disturbed the course of the test by his loud interruptions. His contributions consisted mainly of instructions to others, superficial, dramatic outbursts and negative remarks. Having reacted to the various cards with perplexity, he then proceeded to disparage the achievements demanded. From the start he tried to conceal a feeling of inadequacy ("I express myself badly") by repeatedly attacking the test setting. From his long-winded dialogue before the test began, it was clear that he strove to distance himself from his wife's illness. In addition, Mr. Bolt's style was characterized by the tendency to define his perceptions in a strictly stereotyped fashion. However, he had one particularly likable trait: from time to time he cracked a joke and, by making everyone laugh, relaxed the atmosphere, for example, in his appealing request for a break for a smoke. Whenever his sense of humor was involved, it was possible to imagine that he would have liked to neutralize the excessive emotion which he showed towards his wife's problems and obligations.

Mrs. Bolt spoke softly and was submissive and somehow colorless in comparison with her lively husband; however, she proved to be constructive. After the initial short fluster caused by her interpretation of the first card ("bloodstains"), she collected herself and carried out the instructions for the tests in a controlled, matter-of-fact way appropriate to the task. Her interpretations were sensible and easy to follow. She made alternative suggestions to most of the Rorschach cards which often contradicted her husband's ideas. Mrs. Bolt's pauses and opportunist hesitation in arriving at a final answer created a certain tension that heightened her listeners' interest. Her contributions, which the others often solicited, were always given just when they would have a significant effect on the discussion. The observed behavior suggested that she held her own in the family by means of covert and indirect tactics.

The parents as individuals offered their children two different models of how people think and get along with one another. Mrs. Bolt's clear language and mode of thinking showed that she was firmly anchored in objective reality. The supplementary details and alternative suggestions that she added to the common effort expressed her mental flexibility. She was undoubtedly more resilient in her thinking than her husband, who mostly stuck to an interpretation once it had been chosen. Her behavior was a vivid example of the effective power of a reserved manner. Mr. Bolt, on the other hand, lost himself in a torrent of words that swarmed with bizarre and farfetched ideas and connections. He had a low "tolerance of ambiguity and complexity." While he gained a good deal of attention from his loud sergeant major voice, it was his wife who quietly had the determining influence on the family's decisive process. He was more a "paper tiger" than the strong man he imagined himself to be.

The productivity and mutual influence of the parents were in inverse relation to the frequency of their verbal contributions. Mrs. Bolt had the most ideas (though only slightly more than Brigitte) in the Rorschach whereas in the TAT she had been rather silent. The different influences of husband and wife seem to relate to their power strategies, "to the control of attention and persons" (Mishler and Waxler, 1968). While Mr. Bolt's lengthy statements revolved around his own problems, Mrs. Bolt, attuned to the others' modes of thinking, was repeatedly able to find the most opportune moment for her remarks, which then invariably tipped the discussion in some decisive direction. A successful start to therapy depends on exact understanding of such strategies.

The Children. Brigitte, the eldest daughter, functioned as the family spokesman. Because most communications were directed to her—everyone spoke to her and sometimes through her—she played an important role in the maintenance of the family cohesion. During the tests it was she who usually held the cards and gathered the suggested interpretations into a unified and sensible answer. Whenever her parents disagreed, she intervened as a conciliatory agent. She combined some of the good characteristics of both parents. Whenever she took up her father's offer to lead the discussion, she became like him, loud and aggressive, but she then led the discussion in a considered and rational way that reflected her mother. Brigitte seemed to be a precocious and perhaps overly independent teenager. The defensive aspect of such a stance appeared in her impatience and disapproval of weakness or doubt in others, particularly in her younger sister Annette.

Annette was as alert as her sister, but was, however, always thrust back into her role of compliant observer. She sought refuge with her mother by whom she sat (sometimes almost on her lap) and copied her mother's behavior. She was usually timid and unsure, and her occasional attempts to express independent ideas were immediately blocked by Brigitte and her father, who both diverted attention from Annette's ideas to her behavior, which they reprimanded severely. Under this cross fire—the order from both parents to take part in the discussion and the criticism of her behavior—Annette opted for safety first. She let on that she had no opinion and could not understand anything that she saw or heard. This was reminiscent of her mother's covert tactics and suggested that she concealed a strong will for self-affirmation behind her reserved manner.

Annette was overprotected and infantilized by both parents, which severely crippled her personal initiative. (Her mother says, for example, "The tests are too hard for her.") As soon as Annette began to act with any self-reliance, she was made a scapegoat. This is a dangerous constellation. Made to feel guilty for making autonomous decisions or acting with self-reliance, her motivation to learn must be weakened, and she will be misguided into an assumed helplessness. Children who grow up in such constellations are very often later rejected as "dropouts" or "weaklings."

The sisters were complementary in their roles. Brigitte embodied the Id-ideal of the family. She accomplished the tasks assigned to her with competence and, at the same time, helped the family out of its difficulties. Annette, on the contrary, was kept in a subordinate role of helplessness and dependency. The parents' insecurity when faced with the test situation accentuated this polarization.

Finally, the two sisters and Mrs. Bolt competed for the father's attention. Brigitte easily outrivaled Annette and claimed as much of her father's notice as her mother, who was further incited by this behavior.

The TAT scene on Card 2 indicated the problems that the family must face as soon as Brigitte really stood on her own feet: a young woman with books under her arm stands in the foreground; in the background a man is working in the fields and an older woman looks on. Brigitte and her mother were of the opinion that the young woman wants to go away, while Mr. Bolt saw this departure as "quitting" the land—a form of "betrayal."

Summarizing Remarks

The competitive distance and deficient communication between the married couple originated partly in their different experiences and modes of communication. Therapeutic attempts to get them to talk about their problems could, therefore, result in their becoming yet more distant. One might expect Mrs. Bolt to accept the therapy and ally herself with the therapist, while at the same time indirectly sabotaging the common explorative effort by her "intelligent reservation" (a form of subterfuge). Mr. Bolt, on the contrary, would probably at first deride the therapy as "quackery" and then take refuge in projective maneuvers, for example, in recrimination directed at his wife or the therapist.

A cotherapeutic team with male and female therapists would probably be the best for this family in which two strong women confront a man who continually demands acknowledgment of his "boss" position and who is easily swayed by his emotional reactions. If cotherapy were refused, a male therapist would be preferable. By acting both as a "muffler" and an example with which Mr. Bolt could identify, the therapist would be able to help Mr. Bolt accept the feelings that have for so long disturbed him.

At the center of the family problematics was the question: Who controls whom and how? It could be that the husband's apparent intractability expressed his struggle to avoid entering into any mutual obligation with his wife and to protect himself from her covert manipulation. By appearing indifferent to the family's problems he maintained his integrity and individuality. His wife had then to produce yet more symptoms to compel his involvement.

The test report shows that we can gain much important information by observing the behavior of a family as they solve standard problems together. The patterns that appear in the behavioral modes of the individual members of the family emphasize the structure rather than the content of the familial interaction. Concealed, yet inferrable dimensions of individual experience are intentionally excluded.

11

The Therapeutic Prospect

THIS CHAPTER SUMMARIZES AND INTEGRATES the information from the various sources—individual interview, first interview with the family and the family tests. In doing so we concentrate on those questions that must be asked at the beginning of every therapy:

1. What are the main conflicts in this family?
2. What forces maintained this conflict?
3. How could these conflicts be resolved?

WHAT WERE THE MAIN CONFLICTS IN THE BOLT FAMILY?

At the time of the interview the main conflict lay between Mr. and Mrs. Bolt. Both were trapped in a situation in which they were divided by petty quarrels and cold alienation, where neither had anything to say to the other. There seemed to be no way out of this apparently hopeless situation. Feelings of being caught and of hopelessness pervaded the family climate.

Mrs. Bolt reproached her husband with lack of understanding and not caring. She felt he exploited her and did not acknowledge all she had done for the family.

For his part Mr. Bolt criticized his wife's weaknesses, which he called "sensibility." She ought to be "tougher" and, in his opinion, was herself to blame for her illness, because she "took everything too much to heart."

These extreme rigid positions imposed restrictions on both partners. As the "sick and weak" member of the family, Mrs. Bolt could receive no acknowledgment of her actual competence, above all in the business. As the Rorschach test showed, she could only assert her influence in a surreptitious and indirect way. Her husband, on the contrary, as the "strong and capable" one, was often close to his limits, as, for example, when he had to run the business on his own while his wife was in the hospital, a situation which Mrs. Bolt registered with quiet satisfaction. ("Just let him see how he can get along without me.") Furthermore, in his position of tough independence Mr. Bolt's strong desires for care and indulgence were frustrated. Each of the partners found the other hostile, disappointing and lacking in solidarity.

Naturally these conflicts affected the children. They were recruited as allies and found themselves in conflicts involving their loyalty feelings to both parents. They repeated their parents' extreme division of roles. Brigitte, the eldest, was a precocious, aggressive girl whose premature independence overtaxed her. While those around her acknowledged her competence, they nevertheless ignored her unsatisfied wish for dependency and need for contact, which were expressed in her reaction, "I think it's fun to torment people." She was in danger of becoming a scapegoat and outsider.

Annette, the "little angel," on the contrary was very appealing, though at the price that nobody relied on her for anything—this emerged in the test situation. She remained infantile and dependent —she had, for example, to be freed from the institution's toilet— and had already adopted many of her mother's indirect strategies. This was revealed mainly in her conflicts with her sister. She herself suffered from psychosomatic complaints (chronic spastic bronchitis) and fear symptoms. The sisters, like the parents, were hostile and tormented and fought one another.

The affective climate of the family was infected with a hardly bearable hostility, mutual disappointment and jealousy, and finally with a hopelessness and helplessness that only the most strenuous defense could keep at bay. This is conveyed to the outsider as a crippling mental suffering.

The disturbance in the Bolt family is accompanied by a deep depressivity, a threat which they all clearly sense and which isolates them from each other so that they are unable to confront the danger together.

WHAT FORCES MAINTAINED THESE CONFLICTS?

How did this family arrive at this position? Why could they not free themselves through their own efforts?

To answer this question we must return again to the triggering situation in 1972/73. It was then that the family lost its already precarious equilibrium and found itself in a crisis which lasted until the time of the interview. What happened?

Mr. and Mrs. Bolt had just taken over sole responsibility for the business from the parents, when, within the space of a few months, they were hit by no less than five deaths. Both Mrs. Bolt's parents died, her godmother, Mr. Bolt's father and a younger family friend.

How did they come to terms with these bereavements? At this point, basic differences emerge. Mr. Bolt, who himself had been critically ill shortly before, denied the bereavement: "There's nothing to be done . . . what's dead is dead . . . life has to go on . . . there's no point in weeping." Obviously this attitude was easier for him than for his wife, since he still had his mother, who even then remained the person to whom he was most attached. Mrs. Bolt was aware of this. He was just as incapable of the real work of mourning, of coming to terms with bereavement, as his wife.

Mrs. Bolt's misdirected grief took another course. She became involved in a process of "persistent pathological mourning" (Lindemann, 1944) that lasted up till the time of interview. The bereavements remained as painfully alive for her "as on the first day." She was able to feel hardly anything but grief; she had lost all interest in what was happening around her, and was enervated and taciturn. When she "pulled herself together," she was noticeably rigid and controlled, but this brittle mask easily broke down in tears. ("The tears come to order," her husband said.) She was undoubtedly the hardest hit by the bereavements.

What effect did this inability to mourn have on the family? In our view, both Mrs. Bolt's physical illness and the family conflict described above were its result. Both parents (and probably the children also) tried in different ways to control the feelings of bereavement, grief and abandonment that continually compelled awareness. Each stood alone in the fight against grief, since the members of the family were so alienated that, even in this situation where they had such need of each other, they remained mutually hostile.

How was it that the Bolt family's mourning took this wrong turn? Other families have suffered such massive bereavement and have found different, constructive ways of coming to terms with it without producing illness. (However, one should not overlook the significance of pathological mourning as the starting point of massive conflict.)

As our earlier interpretation of the case showed (cf., Chapter 9), both Mr. Bolt and his wife came from poorly individuated and massively bound-up families. Neither had achieved inner separation from the parents or succeeded in internalizing a living picture of the parents. They, therefore, remained more dependent than other people on real contact with the—to them—important living members of their families of origin.

The partners were more alike than appeared at first. Both had strong dependency needs, were not able to form as deep relationships with others as with their parents, and were therefore extremely threatened by their parents' death. While the parents still lived, this similarity permitted a tolerably stable relationship, but with the parents' death it plunged him into a deep crisis.

How Could These Conflicts Be Resolved?

Is a process of later maturation at all possible when the disturbances originated so long ago? What are the first therapeutic steps that must be taken?*

---

* At the time of the first interview our team generally followed the concept of "healing through existential confrontation" (see above). In view of the malign stalemate between the partners, one would now consider whether a system-changing "paradoxical" operation in the initial phase would afford the subsequent therapeutic work on the conflicts better chances of success.

The first step is to create a trusting relationship with all members of the family. Sometimes this is possible even in the first interview (cf., Chapter 8).

How could one enlarge this basis of trust? In our experience the most effective method is a "multidirected partiality"—i.e., the therapist's sympathetic understanding of *all* participants, an understanding and fairness towards even the (relatively) scapegoated members of the family (namely Mr. Bolt and Brigitte).

With families such as the Bolts who are so handicapped in coping with grief, it seems particularly important that the therapist to some extent replace the lost objects, at least at the beginning of the treatment. In the transference process, therefore, she or he takes on maternal as well as paternal qualities. This transference is, however, only the beginning and a part of the therapeutic process. Using and strengthening the positive relationship as a base, the therapist must now try to bring the partners together again, primarily by showing each the positive sides of the other. In this and subsequent phases the therapist must strive to free the buried positive resources of the family.

The Bolts, for example, possessed an unexploited fund of true sensibility and empathy in their father, a ready helpfulness in their children, and experience and commonsense in their mother. By helping this family to realize this potential, the therapist could help them to achieve a higher degree of self-evaluation and to experience and recognize their community.

Only after these first steps can the therapist try to approach the actual process of mourning; otherwise, the family would experience this process as a move backward. Suffering and pain are renewed, burdensome feelings which until now have been fended off return to the awareness. Now, however, these feelings no longer need to be suppressed in the old, destructive way, because the family has achieved another basis for dealing with them. The threat of painful feelings diminishes as the members of the family learn to talk about them and to comfort and support one another. The whole process consists of constant reciprocal actions. As the family catches up with the overdue work of mourning, the whole family system changes.

At the same time, it is only change in the system that makes the true mourning possible.

In this process the degree of "related individuation" is especially significant. The therapist supports the individual members of the family in their efforts to set up their own boundaries and their tolerance of those of others. This is the only way to prevent their falling into the old isolated and isolating positions. The therapist promotes a relational and communicational style based on dialogue and, thus, fosters a positive mutuality within the family. In the process, the individual members learn to listen to what the others say, to tune themselves to the others' wavelengths, and to cope with controversy. They learn to express and to acknowledge differences of opinion between the others and in themselves. With progressive differentiation, the "external" bonds based on indulgence, infantilization and guilt are transformed into mature "inner" bonds. The members learn that one may stay internally bound although physically separated. Such a lesson seemed particularly necessary for the Bolt family, since the separation of the developing children would be the hardest task before them.

In addition, the therapeutic process reveals the multiple missions which the parents themselves pursue and which they, in part, hand on to their children. Excessive demands, conflicts of loyalty and missions, delegations or collusions that interfere with age-appropriate needs, all must be analysed, and the burden redistributed.

Finally, the mutual accounts of debts and merits are reopened and rebalanced. For this purpose one must ask: Who does or did what for whom in the family? Was it positive or negative? The "debtors" must be given the chance to pay their accounts. Mrs. Bolt, for example, had to learn to give her husband the chance to honor the enormous contribution she had made to building up the family fortune, and, if possible, to repay it by some contribution of his own in another sphere. The therapist can promote this process through specific interventions, for example, through prescriptions or by orientation towards real or symbolic reparations.

As we have reiterated, in the last analysis the therapist depends in all interventions on his or her own intuition, empathy and experience to provide the family with real help in the complex process

of structural change. Together with the practical experience of dealing with families, intuition and empathy are the most important
instruments and indispensable qualifications of the therapist's art.

Epilogue

THE THERAPEUTIC AIMS AND TASKS described above
—rapprochement between the parents, work of mourning, disclosure
of pathological delegation and balancing of accounts—fit into the
model "healing through encounter," which guided our therapeutic
work at the time of the first interview and, in many respects, remains
central for us. However, since then it has become clear that we could
have used other models (cf., Chapter 4). Therefore, we decided to
discuss briefly the strategy we used at that time in the light of our
present ideas and also, to report on the therapy that followed.

The Bolt family came to us for a further five sessions over a period of three months from the first interview. The 12-year-old Brigitte then informed us that the family would not be able to attend
the next interview as there was too much work in the restaurant.
The parents would make contact again when they had more time.
After four months the therapist telephoned and spoke to the father,
who was pleased at our renewed interest and immediately agreed to
a fresh interview. Only the parents turned up; the children did not
want to come. We heard that the mother was physically much better.
She was having regular treatment from a naturopath whom she saw
three or four times a week. There she was given an injection and
always had a short interview.

The relationship between the parents had changed. The mother no longer put up with things so easily. New staff had been taken on to give her some relief. Mr. Bolt seemed much more depressed and unsure than in the earlier sessions. There was no trace of his initial toughness. We could find out little about the children. ("They're fine, perfectly normal.") He saw no reason for continuing the family interviews.

What had happened? Was the treatment successful because Mrs. Bolt's physical illness (colitis ulcerosa) was for the time in remission? Today we are skeptical about this success.

In the family interview we had concentrated primarily on the mother as the "patient." Her grief, her delegation as bearer of care and concern and her feeling of being unfairly treated by her husband and mother-in-law were central themes. Yet on the relationship level this meant that the parents' roles had been exchanged but the basic pattern remained. The husband had become the weaker, depressive, suffering partner, while Mrs. Bolt used her new found feeling of strength and superiority to attack her husband openly. Now she avenged herself for previously suffered injustice. Just as before, the conflict was not resolved in a constructive dialogue, and the children remained imprisoned in the loyalty conflict between the parents. The remission of the colitis ulcerosa had removed the basis for continued treatment. In other words, we had achieved a degree of symptomatic healing without changing the underlying pathologic family system.

Hence we must now ask whether an approach based on the model of "healing through systemic change" would have been a better means of improving the entire family's situation. If we had used this model, it would have been necessary to conduct all the sessions, including the first, somewhat differently. Instead of promoting an "existential encounter" aiming at confrontation, and final reconciliation, and concerning itself with basic family issues (bereavement, grief, unfairness, etc.) and the disclosure and interpretation of concealed family conflicts, we would have had to confine ourselves to gathering information about the central relationships within the family and their history. Such an approach would have revealed many aspects of the Bolt family. In particular, it would have focused on the way in which, by complying with certain covert family rules, they maintained a precarious equilibrium between the strong and the weak. As long as the mother and Annette, the youngest daughter, were weak, sensitive and physically ill, the father and Brigitte, the elder daughter, could and had to remain strong, insensitive and healthy. We would have been able to predict that whenever a "weak" member becomes "strong," another can and must become weak in order to maintain the balance. Accordingly, a crisis in the form of physical illness must always threaten if too many become simultaneously either weak or strong. We would have been able to recognize this relational pattern by looking back over several generations. Mrs. Bolt's change of roles after her brother's injuries or her mother's illness are examples, as well as the change after the death of the father-in-law. It would also have been seen that the children were already obeying the same rules.

With the above pattern in view, we could possibly have devised a paradoxical intervention along the following lines: we could have warned Mr. Bolt that by helping his wife to "health and strength" he himself risked becoming weak. At the same time, we could have predicted to Mrs. Bolt that, if we helped her to become healthy, more responsibility and burden would fall on her shoulders. Faced by these prospects, we could have told the family that we hesitated to introduce treatment for Mrs. Bolt and preferred instead to wait. This meant, we would have had to schedule the interviews at longer intervals and to view every symptomatic improvement, every sign of growing strength and awakening health in the mother (or Annette), as grounds for concern. It is our present view, based on subsequent experiences with many similar cases, that an intervention of this sort, carefully geared to the members' intellectual and experiential level and referring back to, as well as using, their own words as much as possible, would have offered a good chance to open up this difficult, rigidified family system. After the system had "opened up," it would have been easier to initiate and promote change through, for example, the individual and shared experience of grieving.

Bibliography

*Ackerman, N. W. (1958) *The Psychodynamics of Family Life*. New York: Basic Books.

Bandler, R. and Grinder, J. (1975) *The Structure of Magic*. Vol. 1. Palo Alto, Calif.: Science and Behavior Books.

*Bateson, G. (1972) *Steps to an Ecology of Mind*. New York: Ballantine Books.

Berger, M. M. (Ed.) (1978) *Beyond the Double Bind*. New York: Brunner/Mazel.

Bloch, D. (Ed.) (1973) *Techniques of Family Psychotherapy: A Primer*. New York: Grune & Stratton.

Boszormenyi-Nagy, I. (1965) A theory of relationships: Experience and transaction. In I. Boszormenyi-Nagy and J. L. Framo (Eds.), *Intensive Family Therapy*. New York: Harper & Row.

Boszormenyi-Nagy, I. (1972) Loyalty implications of the transference model in psychotherapy. *Archives of General Psychiatry*, 27: 374-380.

Boszormenyi-Nagy, I. (1975) Dialektische Betrachtung der Intergenerationen-Familientherapies. *Ehe*, 3 & 4: 117-131.

*Boszormenyi-Nagy, I. and Spark, G. (1973) *Invisible Loyalties*. New York: Harper & Row.

Bowen, M. (1960) A family concept of schizophrenia. In D. D. Jackson (Ed.) *Etiology of Schizophrenia*. New York: Basic Books, 346-372.

Bruch, H. (1962) Falsification of bodily needs and body concepts in schizophrenia. *Archives of General Psychiatry*, 126: 85-90.

Bruch, H. (1978) *The Golden Cage*. Cambridge: Harvard University Press.

Ferreira, A. J. (1963) Family myth and homeostasis. *Archives of General Psychiatry*, 9: 457-462.

Franklin, P. and Prosky, Ph. (1973) A standard initial interview. In D. A. Bloch (Ed.), *Techniques of Family Psychotherapy: A Primer*. New York: Grune & Stratton.

Glick, I. D. and Kessler, D. R. (1974) *Marital and Family Therapy*. New York: Grune & Stratton.

Grinder, J. and Bandler, R. (1976) *The Structure of Magic*. Vol. 2. Palo Alto: Science and Behavior Books.

*Haley, J. (1963) *Strategies of Psychotherapy*. New York: Grune & Stratton.

Haley, J. (Ed.) (1971) *Changing Families*. New York: Grune & Stratton.

Haley, J. (1976) *Problem-Solving Therapy*. San Francisco: Jossey-Bass.

Haley, J. and Hoffman, L. (1968) *Techniques of Family Therapy*. New York: Basic Books.

Hassan, S. A. (1974) Across-tasks communication patterns between parental couples having disturbed and non-disturbed offspring. Unpublished dissertation.

Hassan, S. A. (1977) Familie und Storungen Jugendlicher. *Familiendynamik*, 2: 69-100.

Jackson, D. D. and Yalom, I. (1966) Family research on the problem of ulcerative colitis. *Archives of General Psychiatry*, 15: 410-418.

Karpel, M. (1976) Individuation: from fusion to dialogue. *Family Process*, 15: 65-82.

Kaufmann, L. (1972) *Familie, Kommunikation und Psychose*. Bern: Huber.

*Kaufmann, L. (1975a) Familientherapie. In Ch. Müller (Ed.) *Psychiatrie der Gegenwart*, Vol. 3, 2nd edition.

Kaufmann, L. (1975b) Considértions sur la thérapie des schizophrènes. *Evolutionary Psychiatry*, 40: 363-378.

Laing, R. D. (1960) *The Divided Self*. London: Tavistock.

Laing, R. D. (1961) *The Self and Others: Further Studies in Sanity and Madness*. London: Tavistock.

Laing, R. D. (1965) Mystification, confusion, and conflict. In I. Boszormenyi-Nagy (Ed.), *Intensive Family Therapy*. New York: Harper & Row, 343-364.

Laing, R. D. (1971) *The Politics of the Family*. New York: Pantheon.

Langsley, D. G. and Kaplan, D. M. (1968) *The Treatment of Families in Crisis*. New York: Grune & Stratton.

Lidz, T. (1963) *The Family and Human Adaptation*. New York: International University Press.

Lidz, T. (1968) *The Person: His Development throughout the Life Cycle*. New York: Basic Books.

Lidz, T. (1973) *The Origin and Treatment of Schizophrenic Disorders*. New York: Basic Books.

Lidz, T. (1976) Theorie der Schizophrenie. *Familiendynamik*, 1: 90-112.

Lidz, T., Cornelison, A. R., Fleck, S., and Terry, D. (1956) Schism and skew in the families of schizophrenics. *American Journal of Psychiatry*, 114: 241-248.

Lidz, T., Fleck, S., and Cornelison, A. R. (1965) *Schizophrenia and the Family*. New York: International Universities Press.

Lindemann, E. (1944) Symptomatology and management of acute grief. *American Journal of Psychiatry*, 101: 141-148.

Minuchin, S. (1974a) *Families and Family Therapy*. Cambridge: Harvard University Press.

Minuchin, S. (1974b) Structural family therapy. In S. Arieti et al. (Eds.), *American Handbook of Psychiatry*. Vol. 2. New York: Basic Books, 178-192.

Minuchin, S. et al. (1967) *Families of the Slums*. New York: Basic Books.

Minuchin, S. et al. (1975) A conceptual model of psychosomatic illness in children: Family organization and family therapy. *Archives of General Psychiatry*, 32: 1031-1038.

Minuchin, S. et al. (1978) *Psychosomatic Families: Anorexia Nervosa in Context*. Cambridge: Harvard University Press.

Mishler, E. G. and Waxler, N. W. (1968) *Interaction in Families: An Experimental Study of Family Processes and Schizophrenia*. New York: Wiley and Sons.

Murray, H. A. (1943) *Thematic Apperception Test*. Cambridge: Harvard University Press.

M'Uzan, M. de (1974) Psychodynamic mechanisms in psychosomatic symptom formation. *Psychotherapy and Psychosomatics*, 23: 103-110.

*Napier, A. Y. and Whitaker, C. A. (1978) *The Family Crucible*. New York: Harper & Row.

Nemiah, J. C. and Sifneos, P. E. (1970) Psychosomatic illness: A problem in communication. *Psychotherapy and Psychosomatics*, 18: 154-160.

Overbeck, A. and Overbeck, G. (1978) Das Asthma bronchiale im Zusammenhang familiendynamischer Vorgänge. *Psyche*, 32: 929-955.

*Paul, N. and Paul, B. B. (1975) *A Marital Puzzle*. New York: Norton.

Peck, B. B. (1975) *A Family Therapy Notebook*. Roslyn Heights, N. Y.: Libra Publishers.

Reilly, D. M. (1975) Family factors in the etiology and treatment of youthful drug abuse. *Family Therapy*. 2: 149-171.

Reiss, D. (1971) Varieties of consensual experience: I. A theory for relating family interaction to individual thinking. *Family Process*, 10: 1-128.

Richter, H. E. (1963) *Eltern, Kind, Neurose*. Reinbek: Rowohlt.

*Richter, H. E. (1974) *The Family as Patient*. London: Souvenir Press.

Richter, H. E., Strotzka, H., and Willi, J. (Eds.) (1976) *Familie und seelische Krankheit*. Reinbek. Rowohlt.

Sager, C. J. and Kaplan, H. S. (Eds.) (1972) *Progress in Group and Family Therapy*. New York: Brunner/Mazel.

Selvini-Palazzoli, M. (1974) *Self-Starvation*. London: Chaucer.

*Selvini-Palazzoli, M., Boscolo, L., Cecchin, G., and Prata, G. (1978a) *Paradox and Counterparadox*. New York, Aronson.

Selvini-Palazzoli, M. and Prata, G. (1978b) Pourquoi un long intervalle entre les séances? Praxis et théorie dans notre traitement de la famille du schizophrène. Vortrag 6. *International Symposium on the Psychotherapy of Schizophrenia*. Lausanne, Sept. 28-30, 1978.

Shneidman, E. S. (Ed.) (1967) *Essays in Self Destruction*. New York: Aronson.

Shneidman, E. S. (1969) Suicide, lethality, and the psychological autopsy. In E. Shneidman and M. Ortega (Eds.), *Aspects of Depression*. International Psychiatry Clinics. Bd. 6, No. 2. Boston: Little & Brown, 225-250.

Singer, M. T. (1968) The consensus Rorschach and family transaction. *Journal of Projective Techniques*, 32: 348-351.

Singer, M. T. (1974) Impact versus diagnosis: A new approach to assessment techniques in family research and therapy. Unpublished manuscript presented at the N. W. Ackerman Memorial Conference, Venezuela, Feb. 12, 1974.

Singer, M. T. and Wynne, L. C. (1965a) Thought disorder and family relations of schizophrenics. III. Methodology using projective techniques. *Archives of General Psychiatry*, 12: 187-200.

Singer, M. T. and Wynne, L. C. (1965b) Thought disorder and family relations of schizophrenics. IV. Results and implications. *Archives of General Psychiatry*, 12: 201-212.

Sluzki, C. E. (1978) Marital therapy from a systems theory perspective. In T. J. Paolino and B. S. McCrady (Eds.) *Marriage and Marital Therapy*. New York: Brunner/Mazel, 367-394.

Steinglass, P. (1978) The conceptualization of marriage from a systems theory perspective. In T. J. Paolino and B. S. McCrady (Eds.), *Marriage and Marital Therapy*, New York: Brunner/Mazel, 299-365.

Stierlin, H. (1959) The adaption to the "stronger" person's reality. *Psychiatry*, 22: 143-152.

Stierlin, H. (1969) *Conflict and Reconciliation*. New York: Science House.

Stierlin, H. (1970) The functions of inner objects. *International Journal of Psychoanalysis,* 51: 321-329.

Stierlin, H. (1971) *Das Tun des einen ist das Tun des anderen.* Frankfurt: Suhrkamp.

Stierlin, H. (1972a) Family dynamics and separation patterns of potential schizophrenics. In *Proceedings of the Fourth International Symposium on Psychotherapy of Schizophrenia.* Amsterdam: Excerpta Medica, 156-166.

Stierlin, H. (1972b) A family perspective on adolescent runaways. *Archives of General Psychiatry,* 29: 56-62.

Stierlin, H. (1973) Group fantasies and family myths—some theoretical and practical aspects. *Family Process,* 12: 111-125.

Stierlin, H. (1974) *Separating Parents and Adolescents.* New York: Quadrangle.

*Stierlin, H. (1975a) *Von der Psychoanalyse zur Familientherapie.* Stuttgart: Klett.

Stierlin, H. (1975b) Schizophrenic core disturbances. In J. G. Gunderson and L. R. Mosher (Eds.) *Psychotherapy of Schizophrenia.* New York: Aronson, 317-322.

Stierlin, H. (1976a) Einzel- versum Familientherapie schizophrener Patienten. Ein Ausblick. *Familiendynamik,* 1: 112-123.

Stierlin, H. (1976b) Rolle und Auftrag. *Familiendynamik,* 1: 36-59.

Stierlin, H. (1977a) *Adolf Hitler: A Family Perspective.* New York: Psychohistory Press.

Stierlin, H. (1977b) Übertragung und Gegenübertragung im Lichte der Familientherapie. *Familiendynamik,* 1: 182-197.

Stierlin, H. (1978a) *Delegation und Familie.* Frankfurt: Suhrkamp.

Stierlin, H. (1978b) *Psychoanalysis and Family Therapy.* New York: Aronson.

Stierlin, H. (1978c) Psychomatic disorder and levels of differentiation-integration: An approach to family psychosomatics. *Psychiatria Fennica,* 189-199.

Stierlin, H. (1979) Status der Gegenseitigkeit: Die fünfte Perspektive des Heidelberger familiendynamischen Konzepts. *Familiendynamik,* 4: 106-116.

Stierlin, H. Wirsching, M., and Knauss, W. (1977) Family dynamics and psychosomatic disorders in adolescence. *Psychotherapy and Psychosomatics,* 28: 243-251.

Strodtbeck, F. L. (1951) Husband-wife interaction over revealed differences. *American Social Review,* 16: 468-473.

Trüb, H. (1971) *Heilung durch Begegnung.* Stuttgart: Klett.

*Watzlawick, P., Beavin, J. H., and Jackson, D. D. (1967) *Pragmatics of Human Communication.* New York: Norton.

*Watzlawick, P., Weakland, J. H., and Fish, R. (1974) *Change: Principles of Problem Formation & Problem Resolution.* New York: Norton.

Weeks, G. and L'Abate, L. (1978) A bibliography of paradoxical methods in psychotherapy of family systems. *Family Process,* 17: 95-98.

Willi, J. (1973) *Der gemeinsame Rorschachversuch.* Bern: Huber.

*Willi, J. (1975) *Die Zweierbeziehung.* Reinbek: Rowohlt.

*Willi, J. (1978) *Die Therapie der Zweierbeziehung.* Reinbek: Rowohlt.

Wirsching, M. (1979) Familientherapie bei psychosomatischen Krankheiten. In P. Hahn (Ed.), *Psychologie des 20 Jahrhunderts. Bd. 8: Psychosomatische Medizin.* Zurich: Kindler.

Wynne, L. C. (1968) The study of intrafamilial alignments and splits in exploratory family therapy. In N. W. Ackerman, F. L. Beatman and S. N. Sherman (Eds.), *Exploring the Base for Family Therapy.* New York: Family Service Association, 95-115.

Wynne, L. C. (1969) The family as a strategic focus in cross-cultural psychiatric studies. In W. Caudill and T. -Y. Lin (Eds.) *Mental Health Research in Asia and the Pacific.* Honolulu: East-West Center Press.

Wynne, L. C. and Singer, M. T. (1963) Thought disorder and family relations of
    schizophrenics. II. A classification of forms of thinking. *Archives of General
    Psychiatry*, 9: 199-206.
Wynne, L. C., Singer, M. T., Bartko, J., and Toohey, M. L. (1977) Schizophrenics and
    their families: Recent research on parental communication. In J. M. Tanner (Ed.),
    Developments in Psychiatric Research. London: Hodder & Houghton, pp. 254-286.

---

* These titles are recommended as introductory texts.

Name Index

Ackerman, N. W., 225n, 228n

Bandler, R., 41, 225n
Bartko, J., 229n
Bateson, G., 12-13, 28-29, 98, 186
Beavin, J. H., 228n
Bentman, F. L., 228n
Berger, M. M., 225n
Bloch, D., x, 225n
Boscolo, L., 227n
Boszormenyi-Nagy,. I, x, 8, 19, 26-27, 39-40, 225n
Bowen, M., 19, 29, 95, 225n
Bruch, H., 21, 33, 225n

Caudill, W., 228n
Cecchin, G., 227n
Cornelison, A. R., 226n

Einstein, A., 12
Engewald, M., xi

Ferreira, A. J., 43, 225n
Fleck, S., 226n
Framo, J. L., 225n
Franklin, P., 225n
Freud, S., 41

Glick, I. D., 225n

Grinder, J., 20, 225n

Haley, J., 7, 13, 28-29, 41, 81, 226n
Hassan, S. A., 105, 187-189, 226n
Hegel, G. W. F., 5, 13-14
Hoffman, L., 7

Jackson, D. D., 13, 105, 226n, 228n

Kaplan, D. M., 226n
Karpel, M., 19, 226n
Kaufmann, L., 95, 226n
Kessler, D. R., 225n
Kraus, W., 228n
Kuhn, T., 6

L'Abate, L., 31, 228n
Laing, R. D., 21, 95, 186, 226n
Langsley, D. G., 226n
Lidz, T., x, 93, 95, 186, 226n
Lin, T. -Y., 228n
Lindemann, E., 216, 226n

McCrady, B. S., 227n
Minuchin, S., 31-33, 41, 53, 55, 105, 178, 226n
Mishler, E. G., 210, 226n
Murray, H. A., 203, 226n
M'Uzan, M. de, 182, 227n

231

Napier, A. Y., 52, 54, 227n
Nemiah, J. C., 182, 227n

Ortega, M., 227n
Overbeck, A., 106, 227n.
Overbeck, G., 106, 227n

Paolino, T. J., 227n
Paul, B. B., 227n
Paul, N., x, 32, 53-54, 227n
Peck, B. B., 227n
Prata, G., 227n
Prosky, Ph., 225n

Reilly, D. M., 102, 227n
Reiss, D., 19, 95, 189, 227n
Richter, H. E., x, 227n
Rucker-Embden, I., ix-xi
Rudgesch-Ballas, I., x

Sager, C. J., 227n
Selvini-Palazzoli, M., x, 11, 28-29, 31, 33, 52-53, 81, 96, 227n
Shaw, B., 5
Sherman, S. N., 228n
Shneidman, E. S., 102, 227n
Sifneos, P. E., 182, 227
Singer, M. T., x, 19, 95, 186-187, 205, 227n, 229n
Sluzki, C. E., 53, 227n

Spark, G., 225n
Sperling, E., x
Steinglass, P., 53, 227n
Stierlin, H., ix-xi, 9, 12-13, 17-18, 20, 23, 27, 30, 41, 43, 52, 80, 94-95, 97-98, 100, 105-106, 227n-228n
Strodtbeck, F. L., 186, 228n
Strotzka, H., 227n
Sullivan, H. S., 6

Terry, D., 226n
Tooney, M. L., 229
Trüb, H., 52, 228n

Watzlawick, P., 13, 28, 81, 228n
Waxler, N. W., 210, 226n
Weakland, J. H., 228n
Weber, M., 51
Weeks, G., 228n
Werdt, J., x
Wetzel, M., ix-xi
Whitaker, C. A., 52, 54, 227n
Willi, J., x, 187, 227n-228n
Wirsching, M., ix-xi, 105, 228n
Wolf, I., xi
Wynne, L. C., x, 19, 94-95, 186, 205, 227n-229n

Yalom, I., 226n

Subject Index

Adolescent, 33, 54; *see also* Female adolescent, Male adolescent
  and drug abuse, 100-101
  and family therapy, 49, 61, 63-64, 77, 80, 94, 97-98
  and individuation, 183
  and parent relation, 22, 80, 97-98
  underachieving, 8-10
Affect; *see specific affects*
  and defense, 19, 185
  and id-binding, 21-22
  and mourning, 115-116
  and perception, 18
Aggression, 180-181, 209, 211
  and delinquency, 98
  hidden, 98
  and suicide, 103
Alcoholism, 101, 104
Allergy, hereditary disposition of, 110
Ambivalence, 18, 31, 33, 45, 49, 60, 91
Anaclitic transference reaction, 22
Anger, 63, 74
Anorexia nervosa, 11, 29, 31-33
Anxiety, 35, 46, 63, 69, 73, 82, 89, 190
Appendicitis, 114-115
Asthma, 110, 115-118
Audiovisual material and family therapy, 57-58, 65, 68-69
Autism, 18

Autonomy, 17, 20, 23, 184 185, 211; *see also* Individuation, Separation

Behavior therapy, 9
Binding, 20-22, 24-25, 34, 49, 54, 78-79, 84, 90, 92, 100-101, 106, 182-184
Blocking, 185
"Break-away guilt," 10, 21, 106
Bronchitis, 176, 180, 215
Butazolidin, 114

Caesarean, 114, 175-176
Cancer, 110
Cause and effect relation, 6
Child abuse, x, 99-100
Child psychiatry, 45
Child (ren)
  and family, 10, 19-20, 50-51
  and family therapy, 57, 59-63, 67-72, 75-76, 82, 204-207, 210-212, 219, 221, 222
  handicapped, 104
  hyperkinetic, 63, 76
  and marital discord, 62-63
  obese, 21
  -parent relation, 20-21, 23-26, 41-45, 61-63, 68, 71, 73, 75-77, 79-80, 85-93, 105-106, 173-175, 180, 183-184, 189, 208-212, 215, 222-223

Circular model of family, 6, 61
Clinch relationship, 29-31, 33-34, 41, 52-
   53, 81, 85, 89, 102, 106, 178-179,
   217n
Clinical example of:
   alcoholism, 101
   children in family therapy, 75-76
   drug abuse, 101
   family therapy, interview situation, 62,
      74, 85-90
   marital conflict, 63
   psychosomatic illness, 114-171
      family dynamics of, 172-185
      psychological testing, 118-204
Colitis, 114, 222
"Collective cognitive chaos," 19, 95
Communication
   in family therapy, 41, 51, 74, 80, 85, 88,
      95, 204-205, 208-210, 212-213, 219,
      222
   and individuation, 16-17, 19, 21, 105,
      181, 188
Communications theory, 6
Communication therapy, 9
Compensation, 36
Competition, 28-29
Complementarity
   in ecosystems, 5
   and negative mutuality, 29
"Consensus sensitivity," 19, 95
Conflict and Reconciliation, (Stierlin), 13,
   17
Cotherapy, 39
   indications for, 45-46
   problems of in family therapy, 45
Counterphobia, 22
Countertransference, 7, 41-43, 54
Court referral and family therapy, 64, 91-
   92, 97
Cybernetics, 6, 12-13

Das Tun des einen ist das Tun des
   anderen, (Sticrlin), 13
Death
   of parent, 217
   preoccupation with, 190
Defense, and affect, 19, 36, 41, 45, 93, 97,
   108
Defense mechanisms, 185; see specific defense mechanisms
Delegation, 20, 23-26, 34, 49, 79-80, 84, 92,
   101, 106, 182-183, 219, 221-222

Delinquency and family therapy, x, 9, 36,
   97-99
Denial, 108
Depression, 101, 104, 116, 178-179, 216,
   222
Diabetes, 110
Diagnosis
   and family therapy, 48-49
   traditional versus relational, 186-187
Dialectic approach, and understanding
   interpersonal relations, 13-15, 61
Diarrhea, 114, 116, 178
Divorce and family therapy, 91-93
"Double-bind" concept, 12
Drawing tests, interpretations of, 76
Drive, instinctual, 190
Drug abuse and family therapy, 100-102,
   104
Dyadic testing, 187
Dyslexia, 87

Ecosystems
   complimentariness and, 5
   interdependence of, 5
Ego-binding, 21, 106
Ego ideal, 25
Egotism, 13
Electroencephalogram, (EEG), 85
Empathy, x, 17-18, 35-36, 39, 42, 45, 52,
   96, 100, 219-220
Ethical dimensions of family therapy, 15-
   16, 19, 21
Evolution and individuation, 16-17
Existential reality, 27
Expelling, 20-22, 24-25, 34, 49, 78-79, 84,
   92, 100-101, 182-184

Familiendynamik, x
Family; see also Child (ren), Family dynamics, Family therapy, Father,
   Grandparent, Mother, Parent
   circular model of, 6, 61
   in clinch relation, 29-31, 33-34, 41, 52-
      53, 81, 85, 89, 102, 106, 178-179, 217n
   and communication, 41, 51, 74, 80, 85,
      88, 95, 204-205, 208-210, 212-213,
      219, 222
   and divorce, 91-93
   and individual, 5-6, 14
   and intrafamilial conflict, 8, 15, 19, 189-
      190, 212-217
   and loyalty, 26-27, 33-34, 79-80, 84, 92,

96, 99, 101, 106, 180-181, 184, 219
and metacommunications, 188
and multigenerational legacy, 26-28, 34,
    39, 80, 84, 100-101, 103, 182, 223
Family clans, 26-27
Family dynamics; see also Binding, Dele-
    gation, Expelling, Family therapy,
    Legacy, Loyalty
and clinch relation, 29-31, 33-34, 41,
    52-53, 81, 85, 89, 102, 106, 178-179,
    217n
and communication patterns, 41, 51, 74,
    80, 85, 88, 95, 204-205, 208-210, 212-
    213, 219, 222
and family history, 172-178
and individuation, 7, 33, 84, 93, 182,
    187, 190, 217
and individuality, 6, 14, 19
and malign stalemate, 28-32, 34, 41, 81,
    96, 106, 217n
and multigenerational legacy, 26-28, 34,
    39, 80, 84, 100-101, 103, 182, 223
mutuality, state of, 13-14, 27-33, 36, 81,
    84-85, 182, 219
and related individuation, 17-19, 21-22,
    33-34, 78-79, 82-83, 92, 96, 99, 100,
    102, 105-106, 182, 188, 215, 219
and transactional patterns, 20-23, 33-34,
    78-79, 84, 106, 186-187
vertical versus horizontal structures, 14-
    15, 28, 92
Family myths, 27, 43-44, 84
Family Process, x
Family psychotherapy, 8
Family rules, 43
Family secrets, 43, 52, 63-64
Family therapist; see also Family therapy,
    First interview, Therapeutic inter-
    vention, Therapeutic situation
active role of, 40-41, 49-50, 55, 75, 218-
    219
age as consideration, 71-72
and empathy, 35-37, 39-40, 42, 45-46, 52,
    96, 219-220
establishing trust, ix, 41, 44, 50, 59, 65,
    109, 218
and first interview, 9-10, 23, 25, 28, 35,
    39, 43, 46, 57, 66-91, 107-108, 114-
    171, 214
and first telephone contact, 59-61, 70
initiating contact, 58-61, 66, 73-74
and interpretation, 55, 76-77, 107-108,
    190, 222

and intuition, 36, 219-220
and multidirectional partiality, 39-40,
    42, 68, 71-72, 80, 92, 100, 218
as participant observer, 37-39, 76-77
sex of, as consideration, 71-72
as "the stronger person's reality," 30-32,
    52-53
therapeutic stance of, 38-39, 96
Family therapy, ix, 22; see also, Family
    dynamics, Family therapist, First
    interview, Therapeutic intervention,
    Therapeutic situation
activating systemic change, 52-54, 81,
    96-97, 222
and active restructuring, 53-55, 82
and child abuse, 99-100
and children, 57, 59-63, 67-72, 75-76, 82,
    204-207, 210-212, 219, 221, 222
and collecting data, 65, 69, 85, 188-204
and communication problems, 41, 51,
    74, 80, 85, 88, 95, 204-205, 208-210,
    212-213, 219, 222
and cotherapy, 45-47, 212
and crisis, 93-94
delegation model of, 25-26
and delinquent adolescent, 97-98
and diagnosis, 48-49
and drug abuse, 100-102
elements of concept, 12-14, 186-187
ethical dimensions of, 8, 15-16, 19, 21
and family history, 172-178
and family members
    arriving late, 66-67
    present, 10-11, 61-64, 67, 70, 86
    and separation or divorce, 91-93
and fees, 64, 83
and first interview, 9-10, 23, 25, 28, 35,
    39, 43, 46, 57, 66-91, 107-108, 114-
    171, 214
    initial phase of, 66-78, 84, 86-87
    middle phase of, 84, 87-89
    final phase of, 81-83, 85, 89-90
and first telephone contact, 59-61
and frequency of sessions, 53-54
goals of, 71, 73, 82, 85, 89
and handicapped child, 104
and "healing through encounter," 52-
    55, 82, 97, 221
and "healing through existential con-
    frontation," 217n, 222
and index patient, 8-9, 25, 43-45, 72-73,
    85-90, 93-97, 204
and individual treatment, 9, 36, 64, 97

and interpretation of family style, 55, 76-77, 107-108, 190, 208-213, 220
and intrafamilial transactions, 8, 15, 19, 41-43, 67, 189-190, 212-217
linear causal model of, 6
and malign stalemate, 28-32, 34, 41, 81, 96, 106, 217n
motivation for, 49-51, 81, 85
multigenerational aspects of, 26-28, 34, 39, 80, 84, 100-101, 103, 182, 223
as paradigm, 6, 60
and paradoxical treatment, 31, 85, 96, 217n, 223
and projective testing, 74, 85, 188-214
and prognosis, 188, 214-220
and psychoanalysis, 7-9, 15, 35-36, 52-54
and psychosomatic illness in family member, 105-110, 114-223
and psychotic family member, 94-97
and referral, 64, 83, 85, 96-97, 106, 108
and Rorschach, 188-213
and schizophrenic family member, 93-97, 105-106, 186
and suicide potential, 102-104
and TAT, 188-213
and team work, meaning of, 46-49, 51
and therapeutic contract, 50-51, 82-83, 94, 102-103
time limits set, 82, 90
training for, ix, 57-58, 69
and transactional diagnosis, 186-187, 190
and transfamilial transaction, 41-43
Father
-child relation, 180, 208, 211-212, 223
and family therapy, 19, 60-61, 72, 76, 80, 87, 205, 208-213, 218, 222-223
Fantasy
and idealization, 42
manipulation, 185
Feedback systems, 12-13
Female adolescent, 11, 31-33, 54, 211
First interview, 9-10, 23, 25, 28, 35, 39, 43, 46, 57, 66-91, 107-108, 114-171, 124
cognitive stability in, 37
and diagnosis, 48-49
directions for further therapy, 51-55, 82
family members present, 61-64, 67
final phase of, 81-83, 85, 89-90
initial phase of,
    entering treatment room, 67-68
    evaluating, 83-90
    and greetings, 66, 68-69, 77
and mood, 67
opening questions, 69-72
seating family, 68
initial contact, 58-61, 66
middle phase of, 84, 87-89
    defining mutuality, 81, 84
    and delegation, 79-80, 84
    and interventions, 81
    recognizing related individuation, 78-79, 84
and motivation, 49-51, 81
waiting time for, 65
Frigidity, 36, 93
Fusion
and isolation, 19, 182
and related individuation, 105-106

Gallbladder operation, 114, 116, 177-178
Geriatric psychiatry, 11
Gestalt, 28, 77
Gestalt therapy, 9, 19-20
"Ghetto" family, 100-101
Grandparent(s) and family, 52, 61, 80, 82, 97, 115-116, 175, 180, 187
Grief, 108, 216-218, 223
Group therapy, 9, 40, 57, 65
Guilt, 10, 13, 22, 25, 29, 39, 63, 87, 89, 97, 116, 173, 179, 183-184, 211; see also "Breakaway guilt"
massive, 24, 103
and shame, 39, 43, 49, 99, 104, 108

Hallucinations, 18, 190
Handicapped children, 104
Hassan's Scoring Manual, 188-189
Helplessness, sense of, 103, 182, 185, 214-216
Heroin, 100-101
Hopelessness, sense of, 102, 104, 182, 185, 214-216
Hyperkinesis, 63, 76
Hysterectomy, 114, 176-177

Id-binding, 21-22, 79, 106, 184
Idealization, 42, 182
Identification, 8, 184
Id-ideal of family, 211
Impotence, 36, 93
Index patient, 8-9, 25, 43-45, 72-73, 85-90, 93-97, 204
Individuality
concept of, 6, 14
sense of, 19

Individuation, 7, 33, 84, 93, 182, 187, 190, 217; *see* Related individuation
and communication, 16-17
and self-differentiation, 17
and separation, 31, 54, 79, 182-185
Infant in family interview, 62
Inhibition, 77, 92-93
Instincts, 190
Integration, 51n
Intelligence Quotient (IQ), 85
Interdependence and individuation, 17
Internalization, 182-183, 185, 217
Interpersonal relation
and competition, 28-29
and concept of causality, 6-7
and projective testing, 188-213
psychiatric diagnosis of, 186-187
and related individuation, 17-23, 95, 186-187
transactional assessment of, 187
Interpretation, 55, 76-77, 107-108, 190, 222
"Intersubjective fusion," 19
Intervention; *see* Therapeutic intervention
Interview: *see* Family therapy, First interview
Intrapsychic conflict, 8, 15, 24, 27, 36, 95, 186
Intuition, 36, 219-220
Isolation, 16, 18-19, 27, 182, 185

Jealousy, 176, 215

LSD, 100
Legacy conflicts, 26-27, 33-34, 79-80, 84, 92, 96, 99, 101, 106, 180-181, 184, 219
Linear causality model of family therapy, 6
Loyalty conflicts in family, 26-27, 33-34, 79-80, 84, 92, 96, 99, 101, 106, 180-181, 184, 219

Male adolescent, 80
Malign stalemate in family, 28-32, 34, 41, 81, 96, 106, 217n
Marijuana, 100
Marital relations, 10, 14, 115-116, 175-176; *see* Family dynamics
and family therapy, 46, 54, 62-64, 88-89, 106, 189, 204, 212, 214-216, 219, 222
and malign clinch, 178-179
and related individuation, 19-20, 84

sex disturbances in, 61, 64
and state of mutuality, 28
Marital therapist, 30
Marriage
and birth of children, 175-177
and engagement, 174-175, 184
Masochism, 29
Merging, 18-19
Metapsychology and psychoanalysis, 16
Morbus Crohn, 114
Mother
and battered child, 99
-child relation, 23, 69-70, 76, 79, 85-90, 208, 215
-daughter relation, 24, 101, 172-174, 180, 183, 211-212, 215, 223
and family therapy, 60-61, 205, 208-213, 218, 222-223
and schizophrenic offspring, 30
-son relation, 78-79, 85
Motivation
and autonomy, 211
in family therapy, 49-51, 81, 85
Mourning, 8, 25, 32, 49, 53-54, 80, 95, 101, 102, 104, 106, 108, 113, 182-185, 216-218, 221-222
Multigenerational perspective of family, 26-28, 34, 39, 80, 84, 100-101, 103, 223
Mutuality
positive versus negative, 13-14, 27, 36, 219
state of, 28-33, 81, 84-85, 182
Mystification, 29, 79, 95-96, 106

Narcissistic gratification, 23
Negative transference, 40
Neurosis, 93, 185
Nonverbal behavior, 77, 205

Obesity, 21
Observation and theory, 12
Obsessive compulsive neurosis, 93
One-Way Screen in family therapy, 57-58, 68-69, 81, 187

"Palo Alto group," 13
Paradoxic intervention, 31, 85, 96, 217n
Paranoid states, 18
Parent (s)
and adolescent, 22, 33
-child relation, 20-21, 23-26, 41-42, 45, 61-63, 68, 71, 73, 75-77, 79-80, 85,

91-93, 105-106, 173-175, 180, 183-184, 189, 208-212
and child abuse, 99-100
and delinquent child, 97-98
family background of, 52, 61, 80, 82, 85, 88-89, 97, 103, 216
suicidal, 103
Passivity, 21, 184
Peer groups, 14, 101, 106
Perception and affect, 18
Physical illness, multifactorial model of, 110
Play therapy, 64, 85, 87
Preschool children, 61
Primal scream therapy, 9
Problem solving and projective testing, 189
Projection, 43, 105, 183-184
Projective testing
affective attributions and, 189-190
and family therapy, 74, 85, 188-213
interpretation, 205-220
and test situation, 204-205
and role assessment, 189
and Rorschach, x, 113, 117, 188-213
task oriented perspective of, 188
and Thematic Apperception Test (TAT), x, 113, 117-213
Psychiatric diagnosis and interpersonal relations, 186-187
Psychoanalysis, 42, 65
developmental, 16
dynamic, 16, 27
economic, 16
and family therapy, 7-9, 15, 35-36, 52-54
genetic, 16
Psychoanalytic theory, 16
Psychodynamic theory, 16, 27
Psychosocial stress, 110
Psychosomatic illness
in family
communication characteristics, 105
dynamics of, 180-185
and family history, 172-178
and importance of illness, 106-107
and related individuation, 105-106
and family therapy, x-xi, 93, 114-171, 222-223
and Rorschach, 186-213
and Thematic Apperception Test, 186-213
"Psychosomatic personalities," 182
Psychotherapy, 6-7, 45

Psychotic disturbance and family therapy, x, 8, 93-97, 185

Rage, 100, 103
Reality testing, 185, 208, 210
Reconstruction, 186
Regression, 100-101, 183-184
massive, 21-22, 106
and sexuality, 17
Related individuation, 17-19, 21-22, 33-34, 78-79, 82-83, 92, 96, 99, 100, 102, 105-106, 182, 186, 188, 215, 219
Relationship-oriented diagnosis, 186-187
Repetition compulsion, 101
Repression, 185
Research
on affective relationships, 186-187
on battered children, 99
on family, 6
and family therapy, 57-58, 66, 69
and schizophrenic family members, 94
Resistance, 43, 45, 60-61, 85
"Revealed Differences Techniques," (Strodtbeck), 186
Rheumatic arthritis, 93, 114, 183
Rheumatic fever, 174, 177
Role differentiation in family, 188-189, 208
Rorschach testing and family therapy, x, 113, 117, 188-213

Sadomasochism, 30
Sceno-box, 57
Schizophrenic disturbance, 11, 93
and family, 29, 93-96, 105-106, 186
and family therapy, 95-97
and institutionalization, 96
and medication, 96
and mother, 30
and related individuation, 18, 95-96
Scientific revolution, 6
Self-demarcation, 17-18, 79
Self-differentiation, 17-18, 208
Self-evaluation, 218
Self-victimization, 98
Separating Parents and Adolescents, (Stierlin), 23
Sex therapy, 9
Sexual intercourse, 17
Sexuality, disorders of, 29-30, 61, 64, 93
Shame and guilt, 25, 43, 50, 97, 99, 104, 108

Sibling
  death of, 25, 80, 95, 101, 106, 173, 184
  newborn, 61
Sibling rivalry, 8, 14, 62, 176, 180, 215
Social class
  and economic problems within family, 104
  and family therapy, 41
Social worker and family therapy, 64-65
Somatic disorders, 104, 110
Splitting, 185
Structural theory, x
Suicidal potential, x, 43
  and depression, 101
  factors involved, 102-103
Superego-binding, 21, 33, 184
"Survivor guilt," 173, 184
Symbiotic fusion, 18, 79, 84-85, 87, 90
Synanon model and drug abuse treatment, 101

Thematic Apperception Test (TAT), and family therapy, x, 113, 117-213
Theory and observation, 12
Therapeutic contract in family therapy, 48, 50-51, 82-83, 95
Therapeutic intervention, 8-9, 12, 30-33, 41, 46, 81, 83, 90, 100, 204, 219-220
  and chronic psychosis, 93
  and delegation in family, 16, 23-26, 79
  and multigenerational legacy in family, 16, 27-28, 80

and related individuation, 16-20
and state of mutuality, 16, 28-33
and transactional modes of binding and expelling, 21-23, 79
Therapeutic situation
  surroundings in, 56-57
  and videotaping, 32, 53, 57-58, 68-69
Therapist; see Family therapist
Toddler, 61
Tonsillectomy, 114, 174
Topographic theory, 16
Training and family therapy, ix, 57-58, 69
Transference, 7, 41-43, 218
Transactional modes, 20-23, 33-34, 78-79, 84, 106, 186-187
Trauma, 26

Ulcers, gastric, 114
"Undifferentiated family ego mass," 19, 95

Varicose veins, 114, 178
Videotape as therapeutic tool, 32, 53, 57-58, 68-69

Welfare department and family therapy referral, 97
Withdrawal, 19, 23, 49, 57, 72, 104, 209

Youth agencies, 64, 85